Writing an Icon

Writing an Icon

Celebrity Culture and the
Invention of Anaïs Nin

Anita Jarczok

SWALLOW PRESS · ATHENS, OHIO

Swallow Press
An imprint of Ohio University Press, Athens, Ohio 45701
ohioswallow.com

© 2017 by Ohio University Press
All rights reserved

To obtain permission to quote, reprint, or otherwise reproduce or distribute material from Swallow Press / Ohio University Press publications, please contact our rights and permissions department at (740) 593-1154 or (740) 593-4536 (fax).

Printed in the United States of America
Swallow Press / Ohio University Press books are printed on acid-free paper ♾ ™

27 26 25 24 23 22 21 20 19 18 17   5 4 3 2 1

Library of Congress Cataloging-in-Publication Data
Names: Jarczok, Anita, author.
Title: Writing an icon : celebrity culture and the invention of Anaïs Nin / Anita Jarczok.
Description: Athens, Ohio : Swallow Press, [2017] | Includes bibliographical references and index.
Identifiers: LCCN 2016051564| ISBN 9780804011754 (hardback) | ISBN 9780804011761 (pb) | ISBN 9780804040754 (pdf)
Subjects: LCSH: Nin, Anaïs, 1903–1977. | Authors, American—20th century—Biography. | Literature and society—United States—History—20th
   century. | Celebrities—United States—20th century. | BISAC: SOCIAL SCIENCE / Women's Studies. | LITERARY CRITICISM / Women Authors.
Classification: LCC PS3527.I865 Z726 2017 | DDC 818/.5209 [B] —dc23
LC record available at https://lccn.loc.gov/2016051564

Parts of chapter 3 originally appeared in "Anaïs Nin, Feminism and Celebrity Authorship—Negotiating Image and Identity in the Interviews," in *Stardom: Discussions of Fame and Celebrity Culture*, ed. Katarzyna Bronk (Oxford: Inter-Disciplinary Press, 2012), 13–21, and "Anaïs Nin, Feminism and Celebrity Authorship—Negotiating Image and Identity in the Interviews," in *Search for the Real: Authenticity and the Construction of Celebrity*, ed. Andrew Sepie (Oxford: Inter-Disciplinary Press, 2014), 83–98.

Parts of chapters 3 and 4 appeared in earlier form in "Eroticizing Nin, Eroticizing Women: Philip Kaufman's *Henry & June*," *A Café in Space: The Anaïs Nin Literary Journal* 8 (2011): 57–77 and "Anaïs Nin and the Business of Reviewing and Management of Her Public Persona, 1966–1977," *A Café in Space: The Anaïs Nin Literary Journal* 9 (2012): 82–101.

Contents

Acknowledgments — vii

INTRODUCTION
Anaïs Nin and Her Diary — 1

ONE
Literary Celebrity, the Modernist Marketplace, and Marketing the Diary — 13

TWO
Public Promotion of the Private Self
Anaïs Nin's Self-Constructions in the Diary — 47

THREE
Public Relations of the Self
Anaïs Nin, Feminism, and Celebrity Authorship — 88

FOUR
Success, Scandal, Sex, and the Search for the "Real" Anaïs Nin — 140

CONCLUSION
Anaïs Nin in the Twenty-First Century — 205

Notes — 213
Bibliography — 241
Index — 257

Acknowledgments

First, I wish to acknowledge and thank Dr. Sinead McDermott and Dr. Patricia Moran for reading the earliest manuscript version of this book and for all their advice and guidance. My research was made possible by a Women's Studies scholarship from the University of Limerick and funding from the Irish Research Council for Humanities and Social Sciences. Without this financial assistance, I would not have been able to complete my studies. I also would like to thank all the people who directly or indirectly contributed to the writing of this book: Dr. Carmen Kuhling, Professor Brenda Silver, and the anonymous reviewers of the manuscript for their invaluable suggestions and critique; Paul Herron for providing materials on Anaïs Nin; the librarians at the Anaïs Nin Collection at the University of California, Los Angeles, for their helpful assistance with my archival research; Anna Jaskier for devoting her time to double-checking the accuracy of the quotations; Angela Przelomski for her comments on the introduction; and Gillian Berchowitz, Nancy Basmajian, and Ricky Huard along with all the other staff of the Ohio University Press for their encouragement and help throughout the writing and publishing process. I am grateful to Tree Wright for letting me use excerpts from Nin's original journals and letters.Finally, I am indebted to my family and friends, especially those who provided their constant support regardless of the many kilometers separating us. Special thanks to my parents my brother, and to my friends Aleksandra and Darragh Browne, Lisa Breford, Anna Jaskier, Julien Lynagh, and Katarzyna Papkoj.

Introduction
Anaïs Nin and Her Diary

A few weeks after Madonna published *Sex*—a provocative book containing highly erotic, verging on pornographic, imagery and language—a short article entitled "Pages: No Monopoly for Madonna" appeared in the *Los Angeles Times*. "Harcourt Brace Jovanovich would like to remind the world that Madonna does *not* hold the patent on sexual confessions," it announced in the opening sentence. The article further suggested that it was not Madonna but Anaïs Nin, a long-dead diarist and author of erotic stories, who paved the way for sexually explicit revelations. An occasion to mention Nin's name arose because Harcourt Brace Jovanovich, a major American publisher, printed the very same year, in 1992, another installment of Nin's unexpurgated diary. Entitled *Incest,* more shocking than Madonna's *Sex,* Nin's diary revealed, as the *Times* article duly reported, that Nin "was simultaneously sleeping with her psychoanalyst, her cousin Eduardo, her husband *and* her father." Madonna's controversial erotic fantasies faded, the article seemed to imply, when contrasted with the outrageous stories from Nin's life. But juxtaposing Nin with the famous pop star served another purpose than just ranking these two female artists on the controversy scale: it was also a way of promoting the forgotten cultural icon with the help of a celebrity who was then at the top.[1]

Nin and Madonna have a lot in common, but above all, both are controversial personalities whose image underwent many transformations. *Sex* was a major turning point in Madonna's career. Prior to its publication, Madonna had a following among many feminists, who regarded her as "a symbol of unrepressed female creativity and power—sexy, seductive, serious, and strong."[2] With the release of *Sex*, however, the pop icon lost her radical edge, because her book was seen as paying homage to a patriarchal pornographic culture. The publication of Nin's unexpurgated diaries, which revealed a new face of the author, similarly disappointed certain groups of readers.

Nin emerged on the American literary scene in 1966 with the publication of the first installment of her multivolume *Diary of Anaïs Nin* (reprinted in the United Kingdom as *The Journals of Anaïs Nin*) and almost instantly became a cultural symbol, a role model, and a celebrity revered by many of her contemporaries. Nin was invited to give lectures and interviews; she was filmed, photographed, and recorded. Young women in particular identified with the personal and professional struggles depicted in the volumes of her *Diary*. Considered a pathfinder, Nin was celebrated for her candid confessions, insights into female psychology, and distinctive writing style. Nin's popularity reached new levels shortly after her death in 1977. The posthumous release of her erotic stories, praised for the exploration of sexuality from a female perspective, made her a best-selling author.

But a decade later, her stature as a representative of women and a reliable narrator of her life story diminished. The unexpurgated diaries and biographies published in the 1980s and 1990s disclosed many painful and discreditable details about Nin's life, including the fact that she had an incestuous relationship with her father and that she had lied in her previously published *Diaries*. Much of the attention Nin received at that point was quite negative, especially in feminist circles. Once esteemed for her efforts to achieve artistic and personal emancipation, Nin was thereafter regarded as a devious manipulator, a liar, and a master of self-promotion. She became a controversial figure whose life attracted more attention than her works.

Since Nin came to the limelight in 1966, a variety of stories on her have appeared. Some of them were produced by

Nin in her *Diary,* which during her lifetime became a major medium through which she developed her persona—a version of herself manufactured for the public. Nin, like Madonna, was in charge of how she wanted to present herself to her audience, and she carefully crafted her image. But Nin's self-portraits came down to us saturated with the culture and times she lived in. For instance, Nin's concept of femininity was shaped by the way she was brought up, the books she read, the experiences she went through, the acquaintances she made, the narratives she encountered—in a word, by the ideas about femininity that circulated at that time.

But Nin did not have a monopoly on the construction of her public personality, and stories about her were also disseminated in biographies, films, plays, critical studies, and memoirs on her. None of these sources captured the real Nin, although a few might have promised to do so. Every text constructed a different Nin and a different account of her life, and just as it is impossible to fix the meaning of any text, so too is it impossible to determine who the real Anaïs Nin was. However, what is important is which story is chosen for attention, and how it is told. Critics, scholars, reviewers, fiction writers, biographers, playwrights, filmmakers, and fans who attempted to portray Nin did not write in a cultural vacuum. Like Nin, they were affected by the times and places they inhabited. They therefore supplied their own version of Nin rather than capturing a real person, and their portraits of Nin convey to us not only their attitude toward the author but also cultural phenomena that helped foster this attitude.

Since the beginning of the twenty-first century, Nin has been largely absent from academic curricula, scholarly debates, and popular culture. That said, scholars do comment on Nin's works, but they do so either in the journal *A Café in Space: The Anaïs Nin Literary Journal* or in monographs devoted to Nin. Rarely does one find articles on Nin in mainstream academic periodicals. Nin also inhabits popular culture, but she hardly ever makes it to the headlines the way she did in previous decades. But paradoxically, this absence of Nin today, which stands in stark contrast to her very prominent presence in the 1960s and 1970s and then in the 1990s, makes Nin an interesting case study.

When we consider the expanding literature on celebrity culture and Nin's popularity in American culture in the 1960s and 1970s, the fact that there has not been a single study devoted entirely to Nin as a celebrity, a public figure, or a cultural phenomenon is astonishing.[3] Viewing Nin as a celebrity is a great way to learn more not only about Nin herself but also about American culture. Tracing the trajectory of Nin's celebrity, the reception of her writings, and the changing constructions of her public persona facilitates the examination of the rise and fall of cultural icons. Whereas in the 1960s and the 1970s Nin was considered an important writer and a voice of the generation, in the 1990s she was reduced to a "major minor writer."[4] The changing portraits of Nin enable an analysis to be made of the interplay between Nin and the culture that first brought her to prominence and then pushed her off the pedestal. By looking at which version of Nin prevailed or was privileged at a given time, the dominant cultural movements, together with the ways in which they produced the Nin that met their own needs, can be identified and examined.

The specificity of Nin as a case study also yields stimulating insights into celebrity culture studies and autobiography studies. Bringing these two disciplines together can enhance our understanding of the complexity of public personalities. The specific trajectory of Nin's celebrity status facilitates an examination of the fallen icon. Nin's example demonstrates that falling out of grace is closely connected with both changes in image and cultural shifts. The fact that different portraits of Nin were emphasized/constructed at various times reflects changing American culture and highlights the importance of market factors in the creation of her persona. Nin's example also illuminates, and has the potential to advance, some important issues in autobiography criticism. It brings to light the dynamic relationship between the stories we tell about ourselves, our identity, and our cultures. The multilevel construction of the Nin persona serves as a good illustration of how the self is fashioned through narratives, not only obvious ones such as diaries but virtually all stories that invite us to give an account of ourselves and our lives (such as lectures and interviews). It also points to the malleability of identity, which changes with every story told.

The analysis of the complex process of the construction of Anaïs Nin's public persona (or rather, personae) by herself and by a variety of media in the United States requires consideration of the following questions: How have Nin's name and persona been used? What has she come to signify? What sort of statements has she been brought to support? What products has she advertised? What debates has she triggered? What was her own contribution to her image making? And last but not least, In what ways have these constructions corresponded with cultural phenomena? Throughout this book Nin is approached as a construct or a set of representations, rather than as a historical individual. It is necessary, however, to investigate how Nin the person intervened in her career and in her image production, because her involvement was a driving force behind the creation, distribution, and promotion of her public personality. Although I do not try to identify the authentic Nin—that is, I am not preoccupied with determining who Anaïs Nin really was or which of the versions of her that have been circulating in the media is accurate—the section that follows contains a brief biography of Nin for the benefit of those readers who might not be familiar with her life and achievements.

WHO IS ANAÏS NIN?

Anaïs Nin is commonly considered an American writer despite the fact that her birthplace was France.[5] Born in Neuilly, near Paris, on 21 February 1903, she was the first of the three children of Joaquín Nin y Castellanos and Rosa Culmell y Vaurigaud. She was followed by two brothers: Thorvald and Joaquín. For the first eleven years of Anaïs's life, the family moved around in Europe—France, Germany, Belgium, Spain—as her father was determined to make a success of his career as a pianist. Joaquin senior abandoned the family in 1913, and a year later, Anaïs's mother took her three children to the United States. Aboard the ship to New York, Anaïs Nin started her lifelong pursuit—her diary. At first her intention was to record everything for her father, but her diary quickly became her confidante and daily habit. The first volumes of her diary were written in French; she switched to English in 1920.

Nin dropped out of school early. At the age of sixteen, she managed to convince her mother that she did not benefit from formal schooling and that she was capable of educating herself. Soon afterward she started working as an artists' model at the New York Art Workers' Club for Women. In 1921, she met Hugh Parker Guiler, a banker of Scottish origin, whom she married on 3 March 1923. The newlyweds moved to Paris in December 1924 and remained there until the outbreak of World War II. In 1931, Nin met Henry Miller and his wife, June, and a year later she published her first book, *D. H. Lawrence: An Unprofessional Study,* which, as Philip Jason notes, "appeared in a limited edition and received limited attention."[6]

The other two works released in France in the 1930s, *House of Incest* and *The Winter of Artifice,* fared no better. *House of Incest* was self-published in 1936 by Siana Edition: a printing press established by Nin, Henry Miller, and their mutual friend and fellow author Michael Fraenkel. Despite "all the enthusiasm and promotional zeal, the first edition of *House* had a tiny print run that did not get far beyond Nin's immediate circle."[7] *The Winter of Artifice*—a collection of short novelettes—printed by the Obelisk Press came out in the summer of 1939, just a few months before Nin moved to the United States because of the commencing war. Circumstances were not conducive to the promotion of the book, and its release did not boost Nin's literary career either.

In the early 1930s, Nin attended her first psychoanalytic sessions with Dr. René Allendy, whom she left later for Dr. Otto Rank. She maintained sexual relationships with both therapists. Around the same time, she also reunited with her father, and this reunion went beyond a usual father-daughter relationship, as it developed into a sexual affair. In 1934, she underwent her first abortion, which she later described in her *Diary* as a stillbirth. Nin engaged in many sexual liaisons during her Parisian years, her last major lover in Paris being Gonzalo Moré, a married communist who followed Nin to New York.

After spending fifteen years in France, Nin and Guiler moved back to America in 1939. Nin swapped the bohemian Parisian society of Miller for the artistic circles of New York writers, painters, photographers, and filmmakers such as, to enumerate a few, Maya Deren (a choreographer, dancer, and experimental filmmaker), Robert Duncan (a poet), Dorothy Norman (a photographer and editor of the journal *Twice a Year*), and the writer Gore Vidal. In the United States she continued her therapy, first with Martha Jaeger, then with Dr. Clement Staff, and finally with Inge Bogner. She also continued to have numerous love affairs. Nin's biographer, Deirdre Bair, observes that while her "lovers in the 1930s represented what she called 'years of erotic madness' with adult men . . . the period 1945–1947 represented erotic madness of a different kind, usually with mere boys half her age."[8]

Nin engaged energetically in the enhancement of her literary career from the very beginning of her stay in New York. She established important acquaintances and did her best to see her works, both diary and fiction, in print. In the 1940s, she started writing erotic stories for a private collector, and these were released after her death in two volumes: *Delta of Venus: Erotica* (1977) and *Little Birds* (1979). She also began submitting shorter pieces and articles to alternative magazines such as *Twice a Year*, the *Phoenix*, and *Furioso*. Bair comments, "Anaïs, realizing that the path to commercial publication was uncertain, intended to build up a solid list of publications in various little magazines as a way to bolster her planned assault on commercial American publishers."[9]

Nin intended to reprint *The Winter of Artifice* in the United States, but when neither she nor her literary agents managed to interest publishing houses in her work, she bought a printing press in 1942 and named it Gemor Press after her lover, Gonzalo Moré, with whom she ran it. However, the publication of *Winter of Artifice* (1942) not only failed to boost her literary career but also brought financial losses.[10] Her next book, the collection of short stories *Under a Glass Bell* (1944), which was published by Gemor Press, sold three hundred copies in the first three weeks and received several reviews, one from the prominent critic Edmund Wilson, writing then for the *New Yorker,* who commented that the volume contained "really beautiful little pieces."[11] However, neither these two collections nor her novel *This Hunger* (1945), which was also self-published, brought her any considerable degree of popularity. Even when her novels started to be printed by commercial publishers—beginning with E. P. Dutton's release of *Ladders to Fire* in 1946—they received mainly unfavorable evaluations, and none of them brought Nin the recognition she craved (although it is worth mentioning that one of her novels, *A Spy in the House of Love,* sold over 100,000 copies in the late 1950s, thus becoming her first commercial success).[12]

The year 1947 was significant for Nin personally, as she met two men who played a crucial role for the rest of her life: the writer and actor James Leo Herlihy, the author of *Midnight Cowboy* (1965), who became her devoted friend and supporter; and Rupert Pole, sixteen years her junior, who became her lifelong partner. Beginning in 1947, Anaïs Nin led a bicoastal life, shared between Los Angeles and New York and between Rupert Pole and Hugh Guiler, respectively. Nin married Pole in 1955, thus committing bigamy, because she had never divorced her first husband, Hugh Guiler.

In 1957, Nin met the young literary agent Gunther Stuhlmann, who would thereafter represent her interests. Stuhlmann—whom Nin introduced rather briefly in her diary as "an intelligent man who loves literature, does translations, worked in films"[13]—turned out to be a very loyal and dedicated representative who took good care of Nin's literary business, even after her death. In 1961, however, impatient at the lack of publishing opportunities, Nin took the initiative into her own hands and got in touch with an independent publisher, Alan Swallow, and offered to collaborate with him. Swallow agreed and set out to reissue her short stories and novelettes. He also released the collection of her five novels in a single volume entitled *Cities of the Interior*. These reeditions did little to boost Nin's status. Not until the joint release of the first volume of Nin's *Diary* by Swallow Press and Harcourt, Brace and World in 1966 did she became popular with the general public. The publication of the first volume of her *Diary* turned her instantly from an author followed by a small coterie into a celebrity writer.

When Nin became a public figure with her own income and when her name started to appear in the records of the Internal Revenue Service, she had to annul her marriage to Rupert Pole. Nin, who until then had kept both husbands in the dark about each other's existence, revealed to Pole her marriage with Guiler, explaining that their relationship had ceased to be sexual. She also informed Pole that she felt obliged to provide Hugh with both emotional and financial support because he had maintained her for most of her life (not only did Hugh Guiler support Nin's daily needs but he also financed the publication of some of her books, gave her money to buy her own press, and helped out—sometimes oblivious to the fact—many of her friends). Pole did not object, and he remained her partner until her last days. Guiler, with whom Nin met more and more reluctantly, excusing herself with her declining health, allegedly remained oblivious to Pole's existence until Nin's funeral, where the two men met. Anaïs Nin died of cancer on 14 January 1977. The obituary in the *New York Times* mentioned Hugh Guiler as Nin's husband, while the *Los Angeles Times* listed Rupert Pole.

DIARY VERSUS *DIARY*

No biographical note about Nin would be complete without a description of the work that contributed greatly to forming her identity, that made her famous, and that was the main source of carefully crafted self-portraits, namely, her diary. When it was published in 1966, it brought her immediate recognition, which, as she reports at the end of volume 6, "erased all the past disappointments" (396). Nin was invited to lecture, to give speeches, to appear on television, and to write blurbs, prefaces, and reviews. The release of her *Diary* therefore constituted a turning point in her literary career.

Anaïs Nin began her diary at the age of eleven in response to two traumatic events: her father's abandonment of the family and the decision taken by her mother to move from Europe to the United States. Her diary, which started as a series of letters to her father in 1914, continued through her lifetime, albeit in various forms, until her death in 1977. Elizabeth Podnieks, who in addition to the customary textual analysis also provides a detailed description of the physical qualities of Nin's original volumes, notes, "There is a gradual shift in the journal as it moved from being a letter to Nin's father to a letter to the world, from a romantic document to a modernist text, and *from a work that was written in order to be published to a work that was written because it was being published.*"[14]

The original diaries from 1914 to 1965 were sold in 1976 to the University of California–Los Angeles for $100,000, and they are available for inspection.[15] The remainder are in the possession of the executor of the Anaïs Nin estate. While going through Nin's diaries from 1914 to 1965, one cannot help but notice a change in their format. Nin kept the diary in book form up to May 1946, and these journals were occasionally interspersed with photographs, paper clippings, and letters. The manuscript journal number 69, covering the period from November 1945 to May 1946, was the last one written in book form. From 1946 on, the diary was written on loose sheets of paper, and the closer one approaches the year 1965, the less of a diary one encounters—the diary was almost entirely replaced by Nin's vast correspondence. So in its later stages, Nin's diary seems more like a collection of letters to and from Nin, rather than a diary as one tends to think of it—a record of daily entries.

Nin also copied and rewrote her diary at different stages of her life. The originals together with the copies were kept in various places. Bair relates that in the 1950s Nin made use of three storage sites for her enormous oeuvre: a bank vault in Pasadena, where she stored half of the original journals; her friend's basement, where she stored the other half; and Bekins Storage in Arcadia, "where she kept the first revised copies typed by Virginia Admiral [a young painter whom Nin commissioned to copy her journals in the early 1940s], as well as the second series of revised copies typed mostly by Lila Rosenblum [a young student and friend of Nin's], with occasional assistance from Jim Herlihy." The Nin archive contains therefore not only the original version of the published diary but also the rewritten versions of the original. Nin's diary is better thought of as an enormous textual collage made up of revised and embellished copies of her diary as well as other texts, such as letters, lecture notes, and newspaper articles.[16]

The published diaries—seventeen volumes in total, to date, extending from 1914 to 1974—subdivide into three series. The first series to be published consists of seven volumes (cited here as *Diaries 1–7*) covering Nin's life from 1931 to 1974, most of which appeared during Nin's lifetime. These volumes were heavily edited, and the extent of this editing is investigated in chapter 2. Nin herself (with the collaboration of her agent, Gunther Stuhlmann) managed to revise six out of seven volumes. After her death, Rupert Pole and Gunther Stuhlmann took over the revision of *Diary 7,* which appeared in 1980. Another series, known as *The Early Diary of Anaïs Nin,* started to be published shortly after Nin's death; it contains four volumes presenting Nin's early life from 1914 to 1931. Having thoroughly examined the manuscripts of the early diaries, Podnieks notes that these were published with few alterations and are a better reflection of Nin's original than are the other two series.[17] One has to bear in mind, however, that the first volume was translated from French, as Nin kept her diary in that language until 1920.

The last series, referred to as unexpurgated diaries, originally consisted of four tomes: *Henry and June* (1986), *Incest* (1992), *Fire* (1995), and *Nearer the Moon* (1996). These four installments cover the period from 1931 through 1939 and include the material that was left out of the first two *Diaries* of the first series. Although these diaries were advertised as unedited, the comparison between them, the first series of the *Diary,* and the manuscripts reveals a great extent of editorial manipulation. Recently two more volumes of the unexpurgated *Diary* were published—*Mirages* in 2013 and *Trapeze* in 2017. The first one covers the years between 1939 and 1947; the second narrates Nin's life from 1947 to 1955. Both installments differ considerably from the previous unexpurgated volumes. The biggest change involves a revamping of the format. Unlike the other four unexpurgated journals, these two are divided into thematic chapters, each with its own separate title. This change in layout was a decision of a new editor. Whereas the previous unexpurgated volumes were edited by Rupert Pole, Gunther Stuhlmann, and John Ferron, the editor of Harcourt Brace Jovanovich, *Mirages* and *Trapeze* were edited by Paul Herron, the founder of Sky Blue Press, which releases an annual magazine, titled *A Café in Space: The Anaïs Nin Literary Journal.*

The next two chapters are largely devoted to Nin's self-marketing in and through the diary. There are two significant reasons for starting the analysis of Nin's celebrity with the diary. First, separating Nin the public persona from Nin the *Diary* persona is virtually impossible, as she became the director and star of the *Diary;* in a sense, she became her *Diary*. Second, the published version of the diary was the first medium that launched a set of representations of Nin, which later would be either reinforced or contested as Nin's visibility in the public increased. But before I concentrate on Nin's diary, a few words of introduction to the phenomenon of literary celebrity are in order.

one

Literary Celebrity, the Modernist Marketplace, and Marketing the Diary

> I was thinking of Fame, of that mysterious and sublime power which raises one man above his fellow creatures and stamps him as an individual, a personality and an extraordinary being.
>
> —Anaïs Nin[1]

Writers, just like any other public figures, can achieve celebrity status. Joe Moran, the author of *Star Authors: Literary Celebrity in America,* points to an interesting paradox around the contemporary notion of authorship: whereas academia has proclaimed the death of the author, nonacademic culture has been increasingly fascinated with its writers. Loren Glass in his study *Authors Inc.: Literary Celebrity in the Modern United States, 1880–1980* provides a very effective illustration of this paradox. He notes that the very proponents of the death of the author, Roland Barthes and Michel Foucault, have been elevated to legendary status as authors themselves. So while academic criticism has attempted to remove the author from the text as the governor of meaning, thus allowing multiple readings and empowering the reader, popular interest in the figures of writers has skyrocketed. Writers have always held a special appeal: it has long been an established practice (dating back to at least the nineteenth century) to send them on book-signing or lecture tours and to turn their birthplaces into pilgrimage sites. One of the most recent manifestations of this fascination is turning writers' lives, rather than their works, into cinema blockbusters.[2]

Glass maintains that marketable "personalities" of writers have for a long time been considered as significant as the quality of their literary production. Moran provides a characteristics checklist for literary celebrities. For him, celebrity authors are the ones who "are reviewed and discussed in the media at length, who win literary prizes, whose books are studied in universities and who are employed on talk shows." If we take into consideration the fact that Nin was described as "one of the most frequently interviewed of twentieth-century authors," that in 1976 the *Los Angeles Times* proclaimed her "Woman of the Year," and that in 2010 *Esquire* placed her among "The 75 Greatest Women of All Time," along with Sappho, Joan of Arc, Queen Elizabeth, Marie Curie, Marilyn Monroe, Gloria Steinem, Aretha Franklin, Janis Joplin, and Meryl Streep, we can see that Nin definitely qualifies as a celebrity author, especially if she is situated against the American culture of the late 1960s and early 1970s.[3]

Although Nin may not be readily recognizable nowadays in the way that, for example, Meryl Streep is, worldwide recognition, as Jeffrey J. Williams points out in his essay "Academostars: Name Recognition," is part and parcel of the Hollywood model of stardom, which cannot always be brought to other star systems, because doing so fails to consider the distinctiveness of various types of fame. Commenting on academic fame, Williams notes, "The celebrity draws his or her power not from culture at large but from his or her particular audience." Therefore, in casting Nin as a celebrity author, we must take into consideration both the specificity of literary celebrity and the particular cultural and historical context that contributed to the elevation of Nin to the status of a star.[4]

According to Moran, literary celebrity differs significantly from other types of celebrity mainly because of its precarious position between literature, still frequently associated with "high" culture, and the marketplace, which has been frequently blamed for bringing this "high" culture down. He argues that a celebrity author is the one who is both commercially successful and capable of remaining a cultural authority, in other words, able to maintain a balance between being an artist and being a star. Nin, as will become evident in the course of this book, managed to maintain such an equilibrium. Her self-presentation as an extraordinary artist, as exhibited in her *Diary*, was later softened by Nin herself in interviews and lectures during which she presented herself as "one of us"—a ploy frequently used by stars to suggest intimacy with their audiences. Nin's presentation of herself as an Everywoman was essential to her public persona at a time when women were searching for role models.[5]

Regarded from this perspective, Nin's self-presentations in the *Diary* become a significant component of her celebrity. Arguing that literary celebrities are partly produced through their own writings and their self-marketing strategies, Moran highlights the complicity of authors in constructing their own image. A central argument of his study is that "authors actively negotiate their own celebrity rather than having it simply imposed on them." Nin was an active agent in creating and distributing her image, and she can be regarded as a powerful formation force in the production/consumption dialectic, which, as many cultural critics (such as Richard Dyer and P. David Marshall) indicate, is typical of celebrity development.[6]

Nin's self-constructions on the pages of her *Diary* are, however, just one aspect of the making of her public persona. A "star's image," as eminent film studies scholar Richard Dyer notes, "is also what people say or write about him or her, the way the image is used in other contexts such as advertisements, novels, pop songs, and finally the way the star can become part of the coinage of everyday life." The coproducing role of readers/viewers in creating the celebrity image is therefore paramount. P. David Marshall, the editor of *The Celebrity Culture Reader* and author of many articles on media and cultural studies, explains it thus: "To make sense of celebrity culture inevitably leads us to a study of how an extended industry helps construct the celebrity as a text—what we could call the cultural economy of celebrity production—as well as how audiences transform, reform, and remake these texts and meanings."[7]

In his seminal study, *Stars,* Dyer puts texts that constitute a star image into four categories: promotion, publicity, films, and criticism and commentaries. These categories can be easily adapted to discuss Nin's celebrity. Films that feature a given star correspond in a way to Nin's *Diary* because, as I have already indicated, it contains a carefully constructed character. Dyer's "commentary and criticism" can be taken to correspond to evaluations of Nin's works by scholars. "Promotion," Dyer remarks, "is probably the most straightforward of all the texts which construct a star image, in that it is the most deliberate, direct, intentioned, and self-conscious." In the case of film stars, promotion involves studio announcements, fashion pictures, ads, and public appearances. In the case of Nin, it entails blurbs, advertisements of books in the press, and book-signing tours. Publicity, as Dyer observes, is not, or at least does not appear to be, deliberate image making, and it includes interviews, gossip columns, and articles—in brief, "what the press finds out." Focusing on literary celebrity, Moran reveals, however, that nowadays many of the marketing strategies that fall under the category of publicity (such as reviews, cover stories, and interviews) are in fact carefully managed by publishing houses, which can go as far as securing a book review or prearranging an interview with the author.[8]

Nin is not only a literary celebrity but also a *female* literary celebrity, and gender, as many critics point out, is an essential factor that determines how a writer is represented in the marketplace. Although academia for some time now has attempted to conceptualize gender not in terms of two opposite binaries but rather in terms of fluid and unstable identities, in popular consciousness the woman/man dichotomy is still very ingrained and was even more so back in the 1960s. The fact that Nin is a woman writer is crucial to the way she has been portrayed and received.

Charlotte Templin in her study of Erica Jong, *Feminism and the Politics of Literary Reputation: The Example of Erica Jong,* provides a historical overview of the response to literary works authored by women writers and demonstrates that the assessment of women's writings in terms of their lives has been a common practice. Following Joanna Russ's argument that women writers, especially in the nineteenth century, were judged on the basis of what is appropriate for a woman, Templin asserts, "Jong's sin is not being a proper woman," and she further explains, "The one period during which criticism of her softened was when she became a mother, which happened during the writing of her novel, *Fanny*. Not only was *Fanny* well-received, but journalistic articles about her at this time portrayed a new Jong: the happy mother and suburban matron." Motherhood is a particularly crucial element in portraying and judging women writers, and Nin is no exception. The harsh criticism of her abortion, discussed in chapter 4, proves the case.[9]

Toril Moi is another critic who regards gender as a significant variable that determines the response to a writer's works. In the part of her study *Simone de Beauvoir: The Making of an Intellectual Woman* devoted to an analysis of Simone de Beauvoir's reception, Moi shows that Beauvoir's status as an intellectual woman involved in politics has provoked much hostility from the reviewers. Moi claims that what a woman writer thinks, says, or writes becomes of secondary importance and that she is frequently reduced to a personality, to who she is. A similar phenomenon is apparent in the case of Nin. Although Nin and Beauvoir stand for extremely different types of femininity—while Beauvoir is frequently accused of being "unfeminine," Nin is often regarded as the essence of femininity—they are both regularly discussed in terms of their looks, characters, and lives. Moi also points to another interesting fact, namely, that Beauvoir's multivolume autobiography has been frequently regarded as evidence of relentless narcissism, which, Moi argues, is not the case in reviews of male autobiographies. Accusations of self-absorption have also been made against Nin and her *Diaries*.[10]

Likewise, Brenda Silver in her examination of Virginia Woolf's iconic status makes gender one of the focal points of her analysis. She emphasizes the role of the women's movement in the canonization of Woolf and indicates that discussions on Woolf often become a pretext to articulate "fear of feminization" or "fear of feminism." The response to Nin and her *Diaries* similarly serves as a departure point for cultural debates about femininity and, to a lesser extent, feminism.[11]

NIN AND THE MODERNIST MARKETPLACE

The position of Nin as a modernist writer is still very precarious. In her 2003 monograph, Helen Tookey points out that Nin has been largely overlooked in modernist scholarship. She demonstrates that Nin's name appears in general outlines of the period but that Nin's works are rarely subject to in-depth examinations.[12] Although some of the studies devoted to Nin consider her place in modernism, a review of scholarly books published after 2003 that specialize in comprehensive introductions to the modernist period confirms Tookey's observation and indicates that Nin is still obstinately disregarded by those critics who examine modernism in general.

It might be tempting to think of Nin's failure in the modernist marketplace in terms of some inherent qualities of her books, to regard her writing as not sufficiently modernist or, worse, not good enough, but neither is the case. As for the first potential charge, two arguments can be brought to dismiss it. First of all, Nin's works, as many of her critics have demonstrated, are very much in line with certain modernist ideals. Second, in recent years there have been numerous attempts to broaden the traditional modernist canon. As Kevin Dettmar explains, "[M]odernism was never really just one thing, never really unified," and as a result we tend to talk about *modernisms* rather than *Modernism*.[13] We may refute the second charge with the commonly agreed-upon idea that (broadly understood) culture influences our tastes and establishes literary values that determine what is deemed good or bad. In other words, what is regarded as good or bad literature is culturally bound, serves specific purposes and audiences, and can change with time.

This is, however, a contemporary, postmodern view of literary value—a result of critical dismantling of traditional modes of thought, modes that, in many instances, were established by modernists themselves who insisted that certain works of literature are more important, valuable, serious, and literary than others. As Aaron Jaffe aptly illustrates in his study *Modernism and the Culture of Celebrity,* modernist authors controlled the marketplace by promoting only certain authors and establishing a well-regulated economy of scarcity and originality—"an economy in which a sparse selection of literary names of the past becomes a means of conferring value on select modern works-of-art." They were involved in establishing standards of what should count as literary and valuable. The creators of this promotional system—predominantly male writers—need to be held responsible, at least partially, for Nin's failed career in the modernist marketplace. The gender bias of the modernist milieu is well illustrated by Jaffe, who, in comparing the status of men writers with the status of women authors, asserts that "the literary reputations of women modernists were poorly served by the restrictive promotional system . . . for which men like Eliot, Pound, Marsh, et al. served as gatekeepers." Later, the process of selection and canonization of modernist works was taken over by scholars. New Critics, who exerted an incredible influence on academia from the 1940s on, played a significant role in establishing the modernist canon, from which they excluded many women writers.[14]

Despite the fact that it was not the culture of modernism that put Nin on the literary map, she was greatly interested in and deeply influenced by the modernist movement. When she arrived in Paris in late 1924, the spirit of modernism had already taken hold. Always an avid reader, Nin gradually immersed herself in modernist literature. Her *Diary* serves as an invaluable record of her changing attitude toward contemporary writers. For instance, Nin was initially unimpressed with Marcel Proust, noting in October 1926 that she hoped "not to read [his works] again." Two years later, however, Proust constantly occupied her thoughts. In one entry she recorded, "I have so much sympathy for Proust and so much admiration. What intellectual energy, patience, and lucidity." Apart from Proust, Nin also read and commented in her diary on Sherwood Anderson, Ford Maddox Ford, Aldous Huxley, D. H. Lawrence, Amy Lowell, and Katherine Mansfield.[15]

She also kept up with the latest literary developments by reading the Parisian literary journal *transition*—which Mark S. Morrisson deemed "the most famous of all American expatriate modernist magazines."[16] Founded in 1927 by Eugene Jolas and his wife, Maria McDonald, it ran until 1938 and enabled the circulation of experimental literature and the exchange of modernist ideas. Nin devoted a few of her diary entries to *transition*, making note of its huge significance to her. On November 1930, she observed, "Reading the last number of *transition* has been tremendous for me. I read all these things after I have done my work and then find an affinity with modernism which elates me" (*ED 4*, 359). A month later, she described the magazine as "the island I had been steadily sailing to—dreaming of—but I was not so very certain of its existence. I thought I would have to build it up alone. No. Here is my group, my ideas, my feelings against banal forms" (*ED 4*, 370). Nin felt that she had much in common with modernist expression.

Many Nin critics have noted this affinity and tried to restore Nin's place alongside modernists. The first one to do so, albeit to a limited extent and rather unintentionally, was Suzanne Nalbantian. Her *Aesthetic Autobiography: From Life to Art in Marcel Proust, James Joyce, Virginia Woolf and Anaïs Nin* is admittedly interested in the analysis of the transformation of life into art rather than the exploration of the modernist movement and Nin's place in it; nonetheless, it does link Nin with the big names of modernism.

In 1998, another study was published, this one more firmly dedicated to the exploration of Nin's place within the modernist framework. *Anaïs Nin and the Remaking of Self: Gender, Modernism, and Narrative Identity,* by Diane Richard-Allerdyce, aims to prove that "Nin is an important Modernist writer, deserving recognition within the literary canon." Helen Tookey's monograph sets a similar goal: "[T]o reassert Nin's place within the feminist-modernist nexus, to show that there are clear links between Nin's works and that of other, now 'canonical,' women modernists." Both studies succeed in achieving their aims, although each one in different way and with a different purpose. Richard-Allerdyce focuses mainly on "Nin's affinities with a psychoanalytically informed Modernism" to examine the ways in which Nin used the creative process to work through traumatic experiences. Helen Tookey, in turn, analyzes Nin's writings within the broader cultural context of modernism. She points out how certain social trends and cultural developments characteristic of the first half of the twentieth century influenced Nin's aesthetics. For that reason, her study is more useful here.[17]

Tookey undertakes the analysis of Nin's relationship with modernism in four case studies. In the first one, she discusses Nin's fascination with *transition* and shows that the aesthetic agenda of the magazine has many parallels with Nin's own concept of an ideal poetic language. Tookey then moves on to Nin's preoccupation with dreams and the unconscious—realms significant for both Freud and some surrealists such as André Breton—thus indicating another point of convergence between Nin and her modernist contemporaries. In the third case study, Tookey tackles two issues: Nin's attempts, inspired by D. H. Lawrence, to create a sensory language; and her efforts, in line with modernist experiments, to fuse different art forms. In her final case study, Tookey investigates Nin's fascination with film by drawing parallels between Nin and other modernist writers such as Virginia Woolf and H.D. (Hilda Doolittle), who also regarded this medium as offering enormous potential for a literary expression. All in all, from Tookey's analysis Nin emerges as a writer who not only was conversant with modernist ideas but also actively shaped the discourse of modernism.

Another study that contributes greatly to resituating Nin in the modernist period is Elizabeth Podnieks's *Daily Modernism*. In a chapter devoted to Nin, Podnieks, like Tookey, mentions modernist figures (Proust, Lawrence, Freud) and phenomena that influenced Nin's views and writings. Podnieks, however, does more than that. She proposes to regard the diary as a genre as "a classic modernist text" that allowed women writers to define themselves and argues that modernism "had to mean more for women than for men, because in 'making it new,' women were being innovative in terms not only of how they wrote but of how they lived and conceived themselves."[18]

My own interest in Nin in relation to modernism is quite specific and informed by recent studies that discuss modernism in terms of the marketplace and celebrity culture. A traditional view of modernism, as many scholars point out, understands it as resistant to economic pressures and the commodification of art. In the introduction to their collection of essays, Kevin Dettmar and Stephen Watt note that "critical accounts of modernism and modernist writing frequently excavate, or are theorized across, a chasm or 'great divide' between modernism . . . and the larger marketplace." The "great divide" they reference here alludes to the concept developed by Andreas Huyssen in his highly influential study *After the Great Divide,* in which he famously declares that "modernism constituted itself through a conscious strategy of exclusion, an anxiety of contamination by its other: an increasingly consuming and engulfing mass culture."[19]

Dettmar and Watt, together with numerous other scholars, do not agree with this oppositional model of high versus mass culture. Instead, they show how modernist writers were implicated in popular culture and explain why modernists and their supporters endeavored to maintain the illusion of this division and their own indifference, or even antagonism, toward mass culture and the market. They claim that "modernist writers and many of their first-generation proponents in the academy wanted for us not to think too deeply about their work in light of marketing and market concerns. For such an interrogation would tend to contradict notions of the aesthetic purity of the modernist artifact."[20]

As could be expected, such an interrogation is carried out by contributors to Dettmar and Watt's volume *Marketing Modernisms,* who, along with a steadily increasing number of scholars, examine the complexities and ambiguities of the modernist encounters with the marketplace and claim that the apparent disregard for mass culture was in fact just another marketing strategy. Dettmar and Watt provide a broad definition of marketing—one that encompasses both material and intellectual production. In an attempt to reveal marketing tactics, contributors to Dettmar and Watt's volume identify several strategies that modernists employed to market and disseminate their writings, such as the establishment of small presses, the publication of limited-edition books, and the foundation of literary magazines. They also analyze texts that have usually been outside the area of interest in modernist studies, such as reviews, prefaces, essays, and introductions, exposing their promotional function.

Nin not only employed the same techniques of self-promotion as many of her contemporaries but also used modernism itself to create her image and further her career. Her published *Diary* is full of stories and anecdotes about famous modernists, and Nin presents herself as a writer who takes to heart the modernist motto "Make it new."

THE IGNORED GENRE OF THE DIARY

Despite the fact that women kept diaries for many centuries—as Margo Culley and Harriet Blodgett make evident in their studies of, respectively, American and English women diarists—serious critical interest in their output did not emerge until the 1980s. In a way, women diarists were doubly excluded—by virtue of their gender and by virtue of the genre they practiced. Laura Marcus explains, "Not only were women autobiographers self-evidently outside the 'Great Men' tradition with which many autobiographical critics operated; generic definitions served to exclude forms of 'life writing' such as diaries, letters and journals, often adopted by women and those outside mainstream literary culture."[21]

The omission of women and forms of daily inscription was arguably due to historical developments in autobiography criticism. Sidonie Smith, a noted life-writing scholar, divides the history of autobiography studies into three waves. She explains that the first theorists of autobiography were influenced by Georg Misch's multivolume *A History of Autobiography in Antiquity* (1907), translated into English in 1951. Misch regarded important public personae—reputed leaders and famous personages—as "the 'representative' and appropriate subjects of what he designates as autobiography." As a result, by the 1960s certain autobiographical texts—such as the confessions of St. Augustine and Jean-Jacques Rousseau and Benjamin Franklin's autobiography—achieved canonical status and became subjects of scholarly debates. And although Misch helped establish autobiography as a valid subject of study, his aid in shaping the canon of great autobiographical works came at a price. His focus on the representative value of autobiography and on prominent individuals meant leaving out other forms of life narratives (such as diaries, journals, and letters) and people who did not achieve the status of eminent individuals (such as women, slaves, and the colonized).[22]

Misch along with other first-wave critics treated autobiographical narratives as a verifiable record that reflected the writer's life more or less successfully, and they did not question the relationship between the author, the narrator, and the narrated I. This relationship between the life lived and the narrated one was problematized by the second-wave critics, represented by Georges Gusdorf and Francis R. Hart. They suggested that autobiographical narratives are acts of creation rather than straightforward records of past events, thus elevating autobiographies to the status of literary genre. But just like the first-wave scholars, they were mainly preoccupied with the lives of great people.[23]

Early feminist critics of literary autobiography concentrated on the absence of women writers from the canon by recovering autobiographies of distinguished women. They too, however, frequently ignored other forms of life narratives. It was only the critics of the third wave of autobiography criticism, informed by postmodern and postcolonial theories, who challenged Misch's identification of autobiography with greatness and individuality, and these critics broadened the range of autobiographical texts by including forms of writing that had been considered trivial and marginal and by focusing on stories of "common" people.[24]

In the 1980s, studies devoted solely to diaries started to emerge. For instance, Margo Culley's *A Day at a Time: The Diary Literature of American Women from 1764 to the Present* was published in 1985, and it was followed three years later by Harriet Blodgett's *Centuries of Female Days: Englishwomen's Private Diaries*. Diaries were also given a proper critical consideration, and theorists began demonstrating a great diversity of diary forms and structures as well as the multitude of roles that diaries serve for their authors. In their edited volume entitled *Inscribing the Daily: Critical Essays on Women's Diaries,* published in 1996, Suzanne L. Bunkers and Cynthia A. Huff thus comment on the change of status of the diary in academic circles:

> Within the academy, the diary has historically been considered primarily as a document to be mined for information about the writer's life and times or as a means of fleshing out historical accounts; now, however, the diary is recognized by scholars as a far richer lode. Its status as a research tool for historians, a therapeutic instrument for psychologists, a repository of information about social structures and relationships for sociologists, and a form of literature and composition for rhetoricians and literary scholars makes the diary a logical choice for interdisciplinary study and a prime exemplar for interrogating the future direction of academe.[25]

Most studies devoted to the diary genre tend to assert that the diary, like any other autobiographical narrative, is not an uncomplicated record of reality but a construction of it. However, this tendency to view diaries as constructs, so prominent in academe, is not necessarily reflected in the outside world. Many readers take the veracity of diaries for granted and choose to believe that diaries are truthful reflections of a person's daily existence and that they capture the essence of their creator. Diaries are commonly regarded as the most private and honest of autobiographical writings, written for personal purposes rather than publication. Even some scholars perpetuate this common misconception. For instance, the prominent feminist and literary critic Elaine Showalter in her book *A Jury of Her Peers: American Women Writers from Anne Bradstreet to Annie Proulx* states that she decided to omit diaries, together with letters, journals, recipes, and wills, from her discussion because her objective was to focus on women who had written for publication.[26]

Despite its title, *The Diary of Anaïs Nin* does not conform in many respects to its generic standards—for example, the entries are very elaborate and only roughly dated—which led many critics to wonder how best to characterize Nin's endeavor. The need to define the published journal was especially pressing among its early critics, who either were denied access to the original or were allowed, like Sharon Spencer, a limited and private viewing. Subsequent critics, who had access to Nin's archive, gave up attempts to provide Nin's published *Diary* with an appropriate label. They focused instead on the complexity of her oeuvre as a whole.

In the early stages, the *Diary* was frequently classified as a hybrid form somewhere between autobiography and fiction. For example, in her study of Nin's works, *Collage of Dreams: The Writings of Anaïs Nin,* Sharon Spencer acknowledges that parts of Nin's *Diary* were rewritten and edited, and she maintains that the *Diary* "is neither a diary in the usual sense—a candid, uncensored record of the events of a life—nor is it a work of fiction like the frankly autobiographical 'novels' of writers like Leiris, Celine, or Henry Miller." From Spencer's account emerges a common view of the diary as a truthful and unedited record, a concept that has since been challenged by many diary critics.[27]

Benjamin Franklin V and Duane Schneider in their *Anaïs Nin: An Introduction* propose to distinguish between the original diary and the published version although they never had access to the former. They encourage readers to bear in mind the three following points when reading the *Diary:* "(1) editorial responsibilities in creating the *Diary,* and the implications of these responsibilities; (2) the question of genre, that is, to what extent is the *Diary* 'pure notebook or journal' and to what extent has it been consciously structured, rearranged; and (3) the function of time, composition, and organization upon the finished product." Consequently, they point to the contributions of Gunther Stuhlmann in the editing of it; they ponder how the thirty-year gap between the actual writing of the diary and its editing might have influenced its form and content; and they propose to regard Nin's *Diary* as "a new and created work of art," "a piece of literature."[28]

For another Nin critic, Nancy Scholar, Nin's work is "part autobiography, part journal"—a view that echoes Lynn Bloom and Orlee Holder's claim that Nin's *Diary* is "a hybrid form, alternately functioning as diary, writer's notebook, and autobiography." This tendency to regard Nin's *Diary* as a form of autobiography or a work of art, also apparent in some reviews of the *Diary,* might be an attempt not only to best describe Nin's work and its internal attributes but also to put value on Nin's writings at a time when the diary form was still highly undervalued. Laura Marcus thus explains the frequent comparison of autobiographies to novels: "[B]y establishing a rapprochement between autobiography ... and the putatively more secure category of the novel, critics felt able to remove the troubling ambiguity of the aesthetic status of autobiography." Perhaps Nin critics felt similarly obliged to justify their literary interest in this disregarded genre and did so by associating diary with autobiography, which at that time was slowly making its way into academia.[29]

Nin's *Diary* has triggered several debates, two of which are particularly important for this study, namely, What is the role of Nin's diary, and How does she fashion herself in its pages? These issues tackled by Nin's critics mirror in many ways general discussions about the diary as a genre. They demonstrate how perspectives on the diary have changed and how diaries and their roles have been conceptualized over time. Consequently, by looking at the critical writings on Nin, we gain an insight into major trends in Nin criticism while simultaneously learning how the research field of life writing has evolved.

Sharon Spencer is one of the first critics to summarize aptly the various roles the diary performed in Nin's life: it served as a record, as a companion and confidant, as a writer's notebook, as a fount of ideas, as a springboard for fiction writing, and as a space where the writer could practice her craft and express herself freely. Despite these multiple purposes that Spencer attributes to the diary, she construes the diary as something external to Nin. This rather straightforward explanation of the roles of Nin's diary reflects the shortage of critical resources available for critics of life narratives at the time when Spencer was completing her study (the 1970s).[30]

While Spencer regards the diary as external to Nin, Helen Tookey, the author of the most recent monograph on Nin, entitled *Anaïs Nin, Fictionality and Femininity: Playing a Thousand Roles,* conceives the Nin-diary relationship as being much closer. Her main argument is that "for Nin the diary is not simply a 'record' of lived experience; rather, the 'life' and the writing impact on each other in a process of mutual feedback, creating a life lived, as Nin puts it, 'within stories.'" A similar treatment of the diary as a process that helps build up Nin's identity is also offered by Elizabeth Podnieks, the author of *Daily Modernism: The Literary Diaries of Virginia Woolf, Antonia White, Elizabeth Smart and Anaïs Nin.* She too considers the diary as a space where the construction of the self takes place. The first Nin critic to point out that by creating her diary Nin created herself is Nancy Scholar. In her study, entitled simply *Anaïs Nin,* Scholar observes that Nin "came to know herself as she composed her own image, and that knowledge altered the person she was or would have been." The views of these academics have undoubtedly been influenced by the developments in life-writing studies, which have increasingly emphasized a close, mutually constructive relationship between authors and their life narratives.[31]

To contribute to this discussion on the various roles of the diary, I suggest that Nin's diary was also a powerful marketing tool. The diary, which at some point acquired a legendary status in literary circles, became Nin's bargaining card. However, I do not reduce it solely to this function; I conceive the diary as a very complex phenomenon, and casting it in this single role would unfairly diminish the multiple roles it played throughout Nin's lifetime. I therefore believe that the various functions noted by Nin critics are not mutually exclusive. I do question, however, some of the roles that scholars have ascribed to Nin's diary. In chapter 4, for instance, I investigate Nin as a trauma survivor and her diary as a site that helped her in dealing with alleged sexual abuse.

Another debate regarding Nin's *Diary* that I hope to revive in this and the following chapter is the construction of her self. The claim that Nin created a character in her *Diary* is not a new one, and several of Nin's critics have pointed to this fact. Nin's *Diary* has been frequently regarded as representing Nin not as she is but the Nin persona. This claim gained even more ground as theories of autobiography advanced and the creation of the persona started to be perceived as an inherent characteristic of any life narrative. As a result, critics began to comment on Nin's persona not only in the published *Diary* but also in the original one.

Focusing mainly on the published *Diary,* Nin's early critics, Franklin and Schneider, regard each volume as a journal-novel, with Nin as the main character surrounded by other minor characters. They wonder whether the success of the first diary influenced the editing of subsequent volumes. They ask whether Nin consciously or unconsciously portrayed herself in a certain way in the first volume and then changed the portrayal in subsequent volumes. Nancy Scholar also points to Nin's conscious intentions to present herself to the public in a specific manner. She remarks that "the reader must consider the legend Nin wished to create in these pages of a courageous, independent woman struggling to forge her own identity and art."[32]

While the early critics emphasized Nin's self-presentation in the published *Diary,* later critics, influenced by expanding autobiography criticism, began to regard the creation of the self as an inherent element of any self-writing project. "Narrative," as Paul John Eakin argues, "plays a central, structuring role in the formation and maintenance of our sense of identity." He also notes that in forming our sense of self we rely on models of identity that are supplied by the culture we live in. Influenced by the latest theories of autobiography, Podnieks analyzes Nin's diaries from the interdependent perspective, "which would admit that the self is always in part invented by and perpetuated through its linguistic and textual configurations but also by its social, cultural, and historical contexts." Tookey echoes this view and argues that Nin "creates narratives and self-representations which are neither entirely fictional nor entirely historical." According to them, Nin's self-constructions are partly invented and partly influenced by the times she lived in. And although the forms of self-representation available to women at a given historical time do not interest me as much as the self-portraits Nin made available in the published version of her *Diary,* I wish to emphasize that to analyze these self-portraits effectively, we must take into consideration two time horizons: when Nin wrote her original entries and when she prepared the diary for publication.[33]

MARKETING THE DIARY

Although Nin was not famous before 1966, her diary had acquired legendary status in literary circles long before it was published, as Edmund Wilson's and Karl Shapiro's reviews attest. The opening sentence in Wilson's 1944 *New Yorker* review of *Under a Glass Bell*—twenty-two years before the first *Diary* appeared in print—announces, "The unpublished diary of Anaïs Nin has long been a legend of the literary world, but a project to have it published by subscription seems never to have come to anything." Shapiro's review of the first volume of the *Diary* in *Book Week* in 1966 begins in a strikingly similar way: "For a generation the literary world on both side of the Atlantic has lived with the rumor of an extraordinary diary." The diary that developed into a legend, or was constructed as one, among literati became Nin's bargaining card. The marketing function of the diary emerges most clearly from the presentation of Nin's attempts to rewrite her work and to have it published.[34]

Shortly after her arrival in Paris in the winter of 1924, Nin began first reading and then copying her early journals. In January of the following year, she noted, "Still affected by the spirit of my old journals, and the Self I found in them, I walked out this morning and saw Paris in a more gentle and sympathetic way" (*ED 3*, 90)—a passage that merits a brief explanation because it hints at Nin's uneasy attitude toward the City of Lights and reveals her recurrent need to revisit her diary, especially during turbulent and emotionally difficult times, and the relocation to Paris proved to affect Nin's sense of self in a profound way. Despite the fact that France was the country of her birth and that she was looking forward to moving to Paris with anticipation, once she arrived there from New York, she had mixed feelings about the place. On some days she loved the city and on others she could not stand it, but for the most part her initial stay in the French capital was marked by distress. The displacement forced her to face new values, different customs, and earlier unacknowledged feelings. What turned out to be the most problematic for Nin was the relaxed attitude of the Parisians toward sexuality.

Gerald Kennedy notes that Nin's "profound ambivalence towards Paris . . . mirrors an ongoing psychological conflict" and adds that Nin projected onto Paris many of her internal struggles, such as "with suppressed desires and disturbing temptations."[35] Indeed, Nin's diary from this period abounds in comments on sensuality, and Paris, in Nin's view, represented the physical aspect of love that repulsed her. "Paris est plain de saletés" (Paris is full of filth), she observed, "and for that I hate it" (*ED 3,* 149). The encounter with Paris threatened the boundaries of her identity and made her realize her own vulnerability. Rereading the diary provided her with a sense of coherent self and equipped her with the strength necessary to confront a new culture.

Regardless of whether these rereadings also helped her realize the value of her diary or whether Paris—"A 'Magnet,' a 'Mecca,' and an 'incubator,' a 'hothouse' for writers"[36]— augmented her literary inspirations, the fact is that in the 1920s Nin began a lifelong process of editing and preparing transcripts of the diary. Initially, she treated her diary as a mine of ideas and stories that could be of use in her fictional writings. In August 1925, she recorded that she had "copied more excerpts out of . . . journals with the hope of making a worthwhile piece of work out of them" (*ED 3,* 152). She also expressed her fears over her potential inability to move beyond writing in her diary. She did not want to be like Amiel, "who wrote nothing but his journal" (*ED 3,* 152), and she was determined to transform her daily entries into fiction. But a few years later, the diary became her "life's real work" (*ED 4,* 433) and in October 1931, she observed, "A strange life I'm leading, because copying out the first part of my Journal I seem to be spinning the whole web out from the beginning while at the same time working on the end."[37] Making transcripts and rewriting the existing volumes while at the same time producing the new ones would engage Nin for the rest of her life.

Meeting Henry Miller in 1931 was a turning point in both her personal and her professional life. Miller and Nin became lovers and literary collaborators. Although it is easy to get an impression that their collaboration was imbalanced, with Nin putting more into their relationship than Miller—while they both encouraged each other's writing, corrected, and commented on each other's works, Nin also supported Miller financially, financed the publication of *Tropic of Cancer,* and even gave him her own typewriter—the period of the 1930s saw intensified writing activity on Nin's part. Whereas during sixteen years from 1914 to 1931 she penned thirty volumes of the diary (an average of two diaries per year), in half of that time, in the years from 1931 to 1939, she produced thirty-two volumes (an average of four journals per year).

Miller was an incisive critic of Nin's diary, in both senses of the word. On the one hand, treating her *Diary* as a bad habit, he discouraged her from writing it and tried to induce her to write more fiction. But when she persisted, he did his best to provide constructive criticism of her work. For instance, while commenting on the early version of Nin's diary in one of his letters to her, dated October 1932, he stated, "What you are trying to do is a piece of art that is perfect in itself as art and yet retains the imperfection, the *human* fragmented, chaotic characteristics of a diary written on the spot in white heat. . . . It's a problem. It's like soldering two kinds of metals that refuse to be fused."[38] Yet he offered a solution—"the technical trick . . . of maintaining the illusion, for the reader, that he is perusing an intimate journal, but doing your story with infinite care, infinite pains." In the rest of the letter, he listed techniques that could help Nin create an appealing and well-written story. He recommended her to chart out the key themes of the diary and expand them, to get rid of short and ambiguous lines, and to avoid too abstract and too dramatic phrases. Miller therefore strongly encouraged her to compose a well-constructed work that retained the spontaneous character of a journal. Reading the first six installments of the published *Diary,* one easily notices that she took his advice seriously.

In that same period, Nin was also determined to make her journal public. As early as 1933, she showed the diary to William Aspenwall Bradley, a literary agent, who, as Bair observes, "with his Russian wife, Jenny, formed the most famous international literary agency in France for half a century." Though he expressed considerable enthusiasm for the diary, in the end he pronounced it, as Bair reports, "unpublishable." Nevertheless, the acquaintance with Bradley must have been very informative for Nin, and his comments definitely influenced her future rewritings of the diary. Nin quoted their conversations regarding her journal extensively and scrupulously noted down Bradley's observations.[39]

During one such discussion, Bradley read from her journal, pointing out the passages he considered effective and identifying those he believed too dramatic or too extreme. Nin wrote down one of his remarks regarding the thirty-second volume of her journal: "Henry [Miller], he says, doesn't come off as a character—it's overdrawn, overwritten, over-intense, exaggerated, inhuman." Although in the beginning she resented his comments, she later observed, "Bradley's virulence has had the effect of accentuating my awareness of the *note* quality of the journal. It is mostly notes which my enemies may say I present as literature. My life has been one long note taking—sum total: little writing. I owe him this realization." As a consequence, at the beginning of the 1930s, Nin began to acquire a new awareness of the literary potential of the diary and began to regard it not only as her private companion but also as a creative endeavor that required serious work.[40]

When Nin began to perceive her diary as art, her writing became more conscious and deliberate. On the first page of Journal 54, which is in a big A4 format, unlike the previous journals, which are in an A5 format or smaller, Nin noted, "Not the small notebook I could hide. A larger, honest, expansive book given to me by Henry, on which I spread out beyond the diary. . . . It lies on my desk like a real manuscript. It is a larger canvas. No marginal writing done delicately, unobtrusively, but work, assertion."[41] She therefore began to regard her diary writing as a piece of work, a creation.

The process of revising the diary went on for most of the 1930s but intensified, particularly in 1936 and 1937. Journals covering these years are full of entries referring to her work on the diary. In a letter to her cousin Eduardo Sanchez, Nin explained her occupation in the following way:

> I took volume 45 of the first trip to New York and I made it bloom like a hot house camellia, I Proustanize, only dynamically. For example, [take the] page [where I describe when] Miriam came to be analyzed. She is my favorite patient. Her confession touched me. "What confession?" Suddenly I sat down and I wrote the whole confession, naturally and diary-like, but full and

complete, like a geyser. Inserted it. By the time I was through there were no more "notes," but a full smooth book, a book, not a notebook. I wrote up Rank that way, filled out, enriched.[42]

Nin expanded stories, remade portraits, and filled her rewritten copies with details she did not record before, in order to shape her diary into a coherent book. She worked on it as if it were a novel, yet at the same time she tried to preserve its journal-like, spontaneous quality.

She also began to present her diary as an artistic undertaking to others. For example, in a 1937 letter to Jean Paulhan, a French writer, critic, and publisher who expressed an interest in the diary, Nin highlighted the novel-like quality of her journal. She explained, "Each volume contains, in a sense, a novel, an incident, a drama." The diary was therefore described as an intentional piece of writing that went beyond what one would expect of a diary, namely, a collection of private notes. In the same letter she also listed experiences that were described in the diary:

> Separation from father and trip to New York; A year as a painter's model to support mother and brothers; A year as mannequin; Trip to Havana with wealthy aunt and presentation to society. Society life, luxury; Marriage in Havana and first novel on artists and models; Trip to Paris; Spanish dancing studied. Appearance on stage; Book on D. H. Lawrence and new worlds entered through it; Seeing father again, reconciliation; Love affairs—about fifteen of them; Two psychoanalysis fully described, in which I seduce my analysts; Birth and death of a child; Playing at being analyst myself in New York, with hundreds of confessions, and incidents, a bursting of full life; Book of *House of Incest*.[43]

At that particular time, Nin was quite willing to share the most intimate details of her life (note, however, the absence of a love affair with her father). A glimpse at the above list offers a good indication of the events she regarded as marketable and interesting for her future audience. Nin portrayed herself as an independent woman who tried by various, usually artistic, means (as a model for painters, as a writer, as a dancer, as an analyst) to earn her living, as well as a worldly figure who traveled extensively and moved between various societies. Being a good advertiser, she also created the atmosphere of mystery and sensation, saying that her diary contained fifteen love affairs, the seduction of her psychoanalysts, and her patients' personal revelations.

Jean Paulhan was one of several people in the mid-1930s interested in the possibility of making the diary public. Another was Denise Clairouin, the literary agent, who initially wanted "all the diaries to be published" (*Diary 2,* 107) but quickly changed her mind and started to doubt the possibility of the diary ever appearing in print: "People can't bear such nakedness. . . . The childbirth story will immediately be censored" (*Diary 2,* 167). Clairouin nonetheless sent the diary to the British publishing house Faber and Faber, which rejected it "with a great deal of reluctance" (*Diary 2,* 206). Maxwell Perkins of Scribner was another person to whom Clairouin showed Nin's work. At his request Nin prepared an abridged copy of six hundred pages, and although, as Nin noted, Perkins was "thunderstruck" by what he read, in the end, he too declined to publish the diary (*Diary 2,* 268).

In 1937 another attempt and, needless to say, another failure to publish the diary took place. This time Henry Miller got involved and set out to publish Nin's childhood diary, which he greatly admired. Miller was convinced that the publication should begin with the very first volume. (It is worth mentioning that throughout her life Nin's efforts concentrated alternatively on her childhood diaries and the ones dating back to the 1930s, and Nin even secured the preface to the planned childhood journal from Otto Rank.)[44] In November 1937, Nin and Miller sent out a circular saying that Henry Miller was going to publish Anaïs Nin's diary *Mon Journal* in the original French in a limited number of 250 copies. The book was supposed to be printed by the Imprimerie Ste-Catherine in Bruges, Belgium. The front endpaper of Nin's fifty-fifth journal, covering the period from September to November 1937, contains a list of the subscribers to this intended publication. So few people were interested, however, that the project eventually failed. That was possibly the last attempt to publish the diary in Europe, as Nin moved back to the United States in 1939, at the outbreak of World War II.

Between 1940 and 1941, Nin was represented by John Slocum, Henry Miller's agent, who, as Bair reports, showed the diary to every publishing company in New York.[45] Around the same time, Nin also sent the diaries to the Boston publisher Houghton Mifflin. She must have sent the diaries including her sexual adventures, for the commentator who evaluated the diary noted, "When the author does prepare it for publication my advice would be cut out the redundancy rather than sex." And then he or she elaborated: "In fact, I'd trim lightly here and with an eye merely on the law. The erotic element is part of its uniqueness." Sex and scandal were, therefore, considered marketable. However, at the same time, the publisher did not like the self-reflexive nature of Nin's journal and remarked that "such morbid preoccupation with one's inner life will seem trivial. My guess is that it is a book to see light about five or ten years after the war is over."[46] Nin's explorations of her personal life seemed petty in the light of World War II.

When the Japanese attacked Pearl Harbor in 1941, the United States entered the war, which had already been ravaging Europe for over two years. The war dominated every facet of life in the first half of the 1940s, while its reverberations were felt far beyond the war years. "Popular culture in the 1940s," as Robert Sickles observes, "was fueled and shaped by the war and one can't look at many aspects of the decade without seeing them as in some way connected to or resulting from the war effort."[47] The cultural climate of the early 1940s was unfavorable for intimate revelations of a woman who was preoccupied with personal rather than national struggles.

Nin continued to work on the diary in the 1940s, revising and copying her earlier volumes. She indexed some of her journals, and the index to her diary covering the period from December 1940 to July 1941 is full of entries that mention her work on the diaries. Bair provides a detailed description of how Nin approached the rewriting process:

> First, with the original diaries beside her, Anaïs rewrote by hand all those parts that she thought were publishable. This included almost everything but the incest with her father and most of the entries about her brother Thorvald. Then she gave the rewritten volumes to Virginia Admiral, who typed them onto "easily transportable" rice paper. Each separate diary volume was then inserted into its own cardboard folder, secured by brass tacks. The diaries she rewrote by hand were locked away with the originals, and the typed copies were made available to selected readers. And so, when Anaïs offered to let someone read the "original" diaries, she was really showing those she had hand-copied from the true originals. Mostly, however, she showed the typed copies, all the while insisting each was transcribed word for word from the originals.[48]

Nin also devoted a lot of time to reading her diaries and pondering on their nature, trying to find a suitable technique for recomposing them. She recorded her observations on the rewriting process, undoubtedly to make her revisions more effective in the future. As a consequence, the manuscripts are full of reflections on the process of diary editing. In February 1940, for example, she attempted to regroup her diaries and to analyze their content. She tried to see them as a coherent opus. She thus commented on her own journals:

> Journals 32–33–34—They recreate a state like opium smoking where one little incident, one caress, one scene produced enormous diffusions—The writing is all about feelings produced, enormous expansion in

sensation, removed from reality. . . . 35 to 45—later diaries are focused on human drama—movement—the writing is lighter. 45–50—The focusing gains in intensity. In the last 50 to 60 there is fulfilled climax and fusion of the dream, the mirage and human life. They flow together.[49]

Or, to give another example, the MS Journal 65 (November 1941–October 1942) contains Nin's suggestions for drawing coherent portraits of people mentioned in the diary. It is a seven-page entry in which Nin cites examples from her previous diaries and writes about the need to discover and capture each person's "hidden demon," gestures, and aura.[50] The work on the diary became, therefore, more and more self-conscious, and her reflections definitely facilitated the final construction of her self-portrait, as well as the portraits of others in the published version of the diary.

In the 1940s, Nin also started to produce an expurgated version of her journal by deliberately excising the scandalous material. In October 1940, she recorded, "Henry is reading the 'abridged' diary from which all the love affairs are extracted—nothing left but the outer relationships with Allendy, Rank, Artaud etc."[51] So the journal that the public read in 1966 started to take shape in the early 1940s.

Between 1942 and 1945, Nin was more occupied with printing her fiction on the press she established with Gonzalo Moré than with revising the diary. With her husband's financial assistance, she bought an old treadle press in 1942, installed it in a studio at 144 McDougal Street, and named it Gemor Press. She was supposed to be responsible for setting the type, while Gonzalo Moré, her lover and collaborator, was to be in charge of operating the press. She managed to print her two collections of short stories (*Winter of Artifice* and *Under a Glass Bell*) and her novel *This Hunger*, yet, as Philip K. Jason suggests, "the Gemor undertaking was, from the beginning, more than a scheme to advance Nin's career." He explains, "Numerous Gemor titles were issued besides Nin's own, and other, non-Gemor printing jobs were sought." Nin devoted a lot of her time and energy to work on the press, but after the initial enthusiasm, she found the venture neither financially nor emotionally gratifying. In a letter to Caresse Crosby dated in the fall of 1944, she complained, "We never made a profit though we worked two of us 6 and 7 hours a day—and I found the work detrimental to my health—I've lost all the good of the summer."[52]

Henry Miller tried to persuade Nin to print the childhood journal on the press and even offered to send her one hundred dollars each month to make the publication possible.[53] Despite his encouragement and the promised financial assistance, the project never came to fruition. Miller soon withdrew his generous offer because the patron who had provided him with the money had stopped his pecuniary support. Besides, printing the voluminous diary on a hand press was not feasible; the collections of short stories proved challenging enough.

Although Nin eventually lost the press through debts, her engagement with it indicates a strong self-promotional zeal and marketing acumen. The following provides insight into how Nin went about her business: "Of 500 *Winters* [*Winter of Artifice*] I gave away 100, sold 250 and 150 are left. I'm only printing 300 of *Under a Glass Bell*. Most of the subscriptions were obtained by my writing pressing letters, telephoning etc." Nin was therefore the driving force behind her marketing campaigns. However, the continuous lack of success wore her down, and in the same entry she recorded, "The support has been infinitely small, not sufficient to sustain me either spiritually or materially. I am going to surrender."[54]

Apart from *Under a Glass Bell,* which was praised by Edmund Wilson, her other works got mainly unfavorable reviews. This must have contributed to the depression that plagued her in the early 1940s. Journal 66, covering the year from October 1942 to October 1943, contains an index with as many entries about working on the press as ones saying "early to bed," "terrible depression," or simply "depression." After the release of *This Hunger,* Nin noted, "I fell into a suicidal depression. Had to face criticism of my book."[55] She came back to the diary, but this time mainly to find the solace in it: "Diary is obviously the diary of neurosis, the labyrinth, and I am in it again, drawn inward."[56]

The novels published by commercial publishers did not fare any better. In 1946, Gore Vidal, whom Nin had met the year before, secured the contract with E. P. Dutton—the publishing house he worked for at the time—for her two novels. Dutton published *Ladders to Fire* (1946) and *Children of the Albatross* (1947) and even reprinted the extended version of *Under a Glass Bell and Other Stories* (1948), but the majority of the reviews were rather negative. Nin's works were frequently criticized, as Jason notes, for the rejection of social conventions of realism, self-centered and unconvincing characters, flaws in the structure, and a style that was too abstract or too elaborate.[57]

The political climate after World War II was not favorable for the type of writing represented by Nin. As Lawrence Schwartz explains, American art and literature became at that time part of the ideological battle with the Soviet Union and communism. In the postwar period, the United States emerged as an economic world leader and soon began setting the cultural trends. During the initial years of the Cold War, American literature became a platform for erecting a homogenous American identity and a cultural weapon, although prominent literary critics of the era propagated an aesthetic method that "seemed to be apolitical but," as Schwartz points out, "was not."[58]

With her autobiographical and experimental writing, Nin could not have fared worse. What was considered publishable in the United States in the late 1940s did not correspond with what she had on offer at that time. But despite the fact that her novels were released during unfavorable times, she did not give up and was determined to be noticed. Bair comments that many people who knew her at that time described her as "a steel hummingbird . . . determined to be famous." Bair adds, "Her efforts to promote her novels attest to this fact. She wrote to every college and university that had previously hosted her, asking for invitations to speak again, and also to universities where she knew no one, frequently sending her photographs and books." Despite Nin's active involvement in the promotion of her works, however, her fiction sold poorly, and Nin once more turned her attention to the diary and "began another round of rewriting."[59]

As early as 1953, Nin also became determined to sell manuscripts of the diary because of her worsening financial situation. Bair estimates that the income of Nin and Guiler for the year 1954 was $522, while their expenses amounted to as much as $25,000. As a result, Nin "vowed to pursue the 'fantasy' of selling the diaries until it became a 'concrete fact.' Each time she wrote to a college or university to request a lecture engagement, she also sent a list of the diary's contents and the names of some of the persons who figured in it, hoping to entice a library to buy it."[60] In 1955 she decided to "devote the rest of [her] time to preparing diaries for publication, no more novels."[61]

In 1957, Nin met Gunther Stuhlmann, who would become her lifelong agent, editor, and friend. When her initial collaboration with Stuhlmann did not result in any immediate ventures, she wrote in 1961 to Alan Swallow, the owner of a small independent press in Denver. She explained her situation and asked him whether there was a possibility of cooperation between them. She suggested a few undertakings that might be beneficial for both of them: either to reprint *The Winter of Artifice,* "which has been out of print for a long time and which I get orders for," as she noted, or to print her unpublished manuscript *Seduction of the Minotaur* (she guaranteed to sell one thousand copies) or to do a collection of her novel *Cities of the Interior.* The diary served as the bargaining card, for she wrote, "There is one added factor, that I have always said whatever publisher puts out my novels I will give an option on the diaries (for the future)."[62]

Alan Swallow reprinted most of her fiction in the 1960s, none of which had any significant success. Both he and Gunther Stuhlmann kept looking for a publisher for the diary. As Bair notes, "James Silberman, of Random House, was the most interested among the many to whom Gunther offered the diaries."[63] However, Silberman wanted to condense the material so that the first volume covered a much larger span of time than Nin had planned. He tried to convince her that "[t]he very least that should be encompassed in a single volume is the entire thirties."[64] (The thirties were eventually covered in two published volumes, not one, as Silberman wanted.)

Silberman also thought it was necessary to produce a book that would strongly affect the audience, would live up to the expectations that had been built up around the diary for so long, and would be of a comparable caliber to Simone de Beauvoir's memoir. To accomplish these aims, Silberman wanted to cut down some personal and reflexive material and have more sketches of people instead. "In other words," as Stuhlmann related in a letter to Anaïs Nin, "he is looking perhaps for more 'portraits,' more 'action' and he seems to feel that 'condensation' will 'speed up,' make the book more 'solid.'" Nin reacted quite strongly to Silberman's suggestions, and in a reply to Stuhlmann's letter, she wrote indignantly, "A diary is not an action film. . . . What greed, too, and entre nous, there is more in my diary than in the diary of Simone de Beauvoir. . . . [Hers] is deadly dull." She also added that she wanted to preserve the integrity of her diary and did not agree to shorten her manuscript. Eventually, the project was dropped.[65]

Peter Israel of Putnam was another editor who saw the manuscript of the diary. Putnam had earlier published Miller's letters to Nin, which Nin had edited and to which she held copyright, but in the end Putnam too declined the diary. In a letter to Nin, which she quoted in a letter to her husband Hugh Guiler, Israel lavished a lot of praise on her writing, admiring her self-revelation and the skillfully drawn portraits in her diary; however, at the same time, he expressed some doubt as to "whether these pages are commercial or not." His main concern was the fact that Nin was relatively unknown in the literary marketplace, and he worried whether the confessions of an obscure individual would appeal to readers. He mentioned that he decided to show the diaries to his wife to get another opinion. In the letter to Hugh, Nin expressed her annoyance:

> As you can see, with the prise [*sic*—praise] there is still the commercial reservation. He will now try it on his wife, on the salesman, on the doorman, the elevator man, the night watchman, the cleaning woman, the delivery boys, the telephone girl, and then he will ask me to make it sound like candy, and like Simone de Beauvoir, and like Mary Mac Carthy [*sic*—McCarthy] and yet keep it clean for the *Ladies Home Journal,* and perhaps rewrite it in the third person, make Allendy a negro physician, my father a taxi driver, for human interest, and instead of a dead child, write about nine children . . . and throw in a few more famous names, but be sure and do not do name dropping as Charlie Chaplin did.[66]

Despite her frustration, Nin was perfectly aware that the publishers wanted a best seller. They tried their best to forecast what the public might like, and they made writers adjust their material accordingly so that it reached the largest number of people. By then, Nin also knew that the power of her diary was not in her self-revelations but in the characters who were portrayed in it, since both Silberman and Israel emphasized the importance of her eminent acquaintances. That is why whenever the manuscript of the journal was sent to publishers, it was accompanied with a register of the famous people included in the diary. Later such a list would be sent to reviewers, and at some point Nin would even suggest using the list of characters, which she considered "a good publicity attraction," "as a map within the Diary, or end paper," for she believed "it would sell books."[67]

Alan Swallow, who tried to find a copublisher for the diary, showed it, among others, to William Morrow. When Nin was rejected by Morrow, she wrote in a letter to Swallow that she wished he were rich enough to print her diary on his own, adding immediately, "But you know, it is not the money, as I will get money from every country in Europe, it is the fact that we will get no reviews, as with the other books." If this remark is read together with the *New York*

Times critic Nona Balakian's observation on the situation in American publishing that she had shared with Nin a year earlier, a clearer picture of the functioning of the publishing industry emerges: "[T]here is a terrible snobbism in this country about publishing with the 'right' publisher. What I mean is, unless a writer is published by the leading publishing houses (Knopf, Random, Harpers, Harcourt etc.), he [sic] is either completely neglected or treated in a light way—unless of course he has something sensational or fashionable to say." Nin knew perfectly well that unless her diary was published by one of the leading publishers, it would probably be doomed to obscurity and that being published with a prestigious firm would guarantee, if not success, then at least reviews and publicity.[68]

In the meantime, Nin kept editing the manuscript, working closely with her brother Joaquín, who contributed greatly to the accuracy of their family story, and with Henry Miller, who offered advice, corrected some details, and demanded a few changes. She finalized the editing of the diary on 18 May 1965, announcing in a letter to a friend, "The diary is now completely edited, retyped, ready to go. It has been accepted everywhere but the U.S."[69] A few months later that year, Hiram Haydn of Harcourt Brace offered her a contract, and thus the first volume of the long-marketed *Diary* was published in 1966.[70] But before it was finally released, Nin in a manner characteristic to herself had been scrupulously supervising the production of her *Diary*. "I have to watch Harcourt Brace like a hawk," she wrote in a letter to her husband Hugh Guiler on 8 December 1965, and she further clarified, "They had [the] date of Diary as big as my name, which as a friendly bookshop suggested, will drive away the young. For the sake of truth it has to be there, but not in marquee size letters on the black background. These people really don't know their business."[71] She therefore played an active part in every stage of the marketing process.

The story of Nin's publishing effort is interesting in several respects. First of all, until the 1960s there was no room in the American literary market for the type of writing represented by Nin's diary; Nin's revelations were considered too intimate and self-absorbed. Even at the beginning of the 1960s, the publishers considered the portrayal of the famous people, and not Nin's inward journey, as the main asset of the diary, which in itself is thought-provoking, as confessional poetry had been popular by then and autobiographical novels were on the rise. Perhaps an autobiographical streak was acceptable in more-established genres, such as novels and poetry, but the diary, which by default is personal and confessional, had to demonstrate some other qualities. The history of Nin's publishing attempts also goes against the common assumption that diaries are written for private purposes. Nin's diary was deliberately and consciously created and also shaped by the comments of many people, such as Henry Miller, William Bradley, and the editors of big publishing houses. Nin frequently revised it, treating it as art and trying to find the best methods to shape it, which concurs with Lynn Z. Bloom's conclusion that diaries of professional writers are always public documents.

two

Public Promotion of the Private Self
Anaïs Nin's Self-Constructions in the Diary

> The very process of the diary resembles that of a painter making a series of sketches each day in preparation for a final portrait.
>
> —Anaïs Nin[1]

Nin and her diary are so closely intertwined that the analysis of her public persona would be incomplete without the examination of the self-projections included in the published *Diary*. The *Diary* introduced Nin to a larger audience, brought her recognition, and launched her image into the sphere of media and society. The published version of the diary made available certain representations of Nin that would later be either reinforced or contested as Nin's visibility in the public increased. Taking a closer look at the intricate relationship between Nin the person, Nin the diary (the manuscript version) persona, Nin the *Diary* (the published version) persona, and Nin the public persona is therefore worthwhile.

NIN THE PERSON VERSUS NIN THE DIARY PERSONA

Although Anaïs Nin left us with 35,000 pages of the manuscript of the diary and seventeen published volumes easily available to anyone, getting to know the "real" Anaïs Nin is impossible, for at least two reasons. First of all, there was no one "real" Anaïs Nin. Taking the postmodern view of identity as fluid, unstable, and impossible to fix, I assume that no one has an essence, a true and coherent core that is there to be discovered. People and their identities are multifaceted and changeable and thus impossible to pin down. The second reason is related to the nature of language and the writing process. Language was the medium in which Nin chose to capture and convey her-*selves*. And as she observed in the following passage, she became aware that expressing her-*selves* effectively and completely in writing was impossible:

> It seems to me now that when I write I only write consciously or at least I follow the most accessible thread. Three or four threads may be agitated like telegraph wires at the same instant, and I disregard them. If I were to capture them all I would be really . . . revealing innocence and duplicity, generosity and calculations, fear and courage. *The whole truth.* I cannot tell the whole truth simply because I would have to write four pages to the present one. I would have to write always backwards, retrace my steps constantly to catch the echoes and the overtones because of the vice of embellishment, the alchemy of idealism which distorts the truth every moment.[2]

Nin therefore recognized the complexity of human experience and the impossibility of capturing it in words. She knew that writing embellished and distorted the reality and that any attempt to communicate the "truth" was doomed to fail because the "truth" was complicated and multidimensional. She grappled, therefore, with the question tackled by the theorists of autobiography, who consider the relation between the reality and the record of it, between the real-life person and the text persona.

In her study of American women's diaries, Margo Culley urges us to remember that "diaries and journals are texts, that is[,] verbal constructs" and that "all diarists are involved in a process, even if largely unconscious, of selecting details to create a persona." In a similar vein, Felicity A. Nussbaum notes, "The diarist pretends simply to transcribe the details of experience, but clearly some events are more important to the narrative 'I' than others." Lynn Z. Bloom believes that the process of recording daily life is even more complex in the case of professional writers. She argues that "for a professional writer there are no private writings," and she demonstrates that writers shape even their most intimate writings, such as diaries, with an audience in mind, thus creating public documents. This observation particularly resonates with Nin's diary practice because Nin consciously worked on her diary long before it was published. Nin's diary therefore contains not the "real" Anaïs Nin but the Nin persona.[3]

There is also another interesting dimension of the relationship between the real person and the diary persona. Writing about American women diarists, Culley observes, "Some evidence exists that the persona in the pages of the diary shapes the life lived as well as the reverse." Similar observations emerge from discussions of Nin's diary by both Elizabeth Podnieks and Helen Tookey, who claim not only that Nin constructs the text and textual persona(e) but also that Nin's own identity as a person is affected in the process of self-writing. "The writer of any life text," Podnieks observes, "necessarily creates herself in the process of self-documentation."[4]

While it is impossible to measure effectively how Nin's identity was influenced by her self-presentations in the diary, there is some textual evidence that Nin's diary writing had a significant impact on her life. "I really believe," Nin observed, "that if I were not a writer, not a creator, not an experimenter, I might have been a very faithful wife.... But my temperament belongs to the writer, not to the woman."[5] This comment provokes a fascinating question, namely, to what extent the need to experience is triggered by the need to have something interesting to describe. When one wants to write, especially a story of one's life, as Nin did, one wants to have something interesting to write about, and a housewife's existence usually does not provide captivating stories. Therefore, the possibility exists that writing incited Nin to experiment with her life.

What is more, bearing in mind the fact that Nin shared her diary and tried to publish it as early as the 1930s, we can speculate about how her diary writing was guided by the awareness of the audience and by the need to present herself in a particular way. Margo Culley emphasizes the importance of an audience, whether real or imagined, conscious or unconscious: "The presence of a sense of audience . . . has a crucial importance over what is said and how it is said." And she adds that many diarists suppose some kind of audience, even if it is the diary itself, addressed often as "Dear Diary." Nin's audience beginning in the 1930s was real rather than imagined as she shared her diary with various people, including her relatives, friends, and prospective publishers, and this needs to be remembered while analyzing Nin's self-presentations. In this regard Nin's diary differs from the diaries of people who never engaged in bringing their daily inscription to public light and whose diaries either remained unpublished or were published posthumously.[6]

It would be neither possible nor advantageous to determine to what extent Nin the diary persona reflects Nin the real person, if only for the simple fact that Nin the "real" person is impossible to capture. As a result, the original diary contains her self-made portraits rather than reproducing Nin the person. The selves recorded by Nin did not reflect the real-life Nin but were Nin's interpretations, or representations, of herself. These interpretations were strongly influenced by society, culture, and the times she lived in.

NIN THE DIARY PERSONA VERSUS NIN THE *DIARY* PERSONA

Before Nin's *Diary* reached its readers, it went through a process of double construction.[7] Nin first had to choose what to put in her original diary, and she frequently admitted that giving a full account of herself and her life was impossible.

"I sometimes doubt that this can be considered a complete record of a life," Nin wrote about her journal and explained, "Not because I have not written every day, but because I have not written *all* day, every hour, every moment.... The moment I catch and fix, when I can spare a few minutes and sit down to write, is only one of the thousands which go into the making of a day."[8] Once she selected what should go into the diary, she needed to decide how to "frame" it—that is, how to capture her experiences in writing—and she devoted a lot of time and energy to invent the best technique for her diary (as discussed in the previous chapter). Then the second stage of the construction process, the conscious and deliberate preparation of the diary for publication, took place. Nin had to select parts of the material, rewrite them by either elaborating or condensing them, and adorn them with photographs to make them more appealing for her potential readers.

How this process of double construction unfolded can be clearly seen in Nin's account of her friendship with Henry Miller. In the first six volumes of the *Diary*, Nin presents their relationship as only friendship and literary collaboration, while the unexpurgated volume *Henry and June* and Nin's biographies reveal that they were also engaged in a very passionate sexual affair. Nin therefore changed the content of her diary by either concealing certain facts or presenting them in the way she thought appropriate. Apart from manipulating the content of the *Diaries,* she also changed the form and style of her writing by editing her entries. A comparison of the original and published account of her first meeting with Henry Miller exposes significant differences between the two versions. Here is the passage from the original:

> I'm singing, singing, and not secretly but aloud. I've met Henry Miller. When I first saw him stepping out of the car and walking towards the door where I stood I went blind, in my usual way. Blindly, I *looked* at him with a second vision. I saw a man I liked. I saw a mouth which was at once intelligent, animal, and soft, strange mixture. Then my eyes opened and I saw

a man who was likeable, not overbearing, but strong, a human man, who was [intelligible word] aware of everything (In his writing he was flamboyant, virile, animal, magnificent). "He is a man whom life makes drunk" I say that inwardly "He is like me."⁹

And here is the corresponding entry from *Diary 1:*

> When I saw Henry Miller walking towards the door where I stood waiting, I closed my eyes for an instant to see him by some other inner eye. He was warm, joyous, relaxed, natural.
> He would have passed anonymously through a crowd. He was slender, lean, not tall. He looked like a Buddhist monk, a rosy-skinned monk, with his partly bald head aureoled by lively silver hair, his full sensuous mouth. His blue eyes are cool and observant, but his mouth is emotional and vulnerable. His laughter is contagious and his voice caressing and warm like a Negro voice.
> He was so different from his brutal, violent, vital writing, his caricatures, his Rabelaisian farces, his exaggerations. The smile at the corner of his eyes is almost clownish; the mellow tones of his voice are almost like a purring content. He is a man whom life intoxicates, who has no need of wine, who is floating in a self-created euphoria.¹⁰

In this case, Nin elaborated the notes taken after the actual meeting with Henry Miller on 3 December 1931. The original entry served as a rough draft that Nin expanded and embellished. To every original sentence, Nin wrote two or three, thus making her text clearer for her audience, as in the fragment in which she explained that she tried to grasp Henry intuitively, with her "inner eye." The original entry in which Nin wrote that she went blind might have been confusing for the readers, whereas the published version makes perfect sense. In rewriting the original, Nin also employed literary devices, such as similes and elaborate epithets, which increased the readability and attractiveness of the published *Diary*.

Interestingly, a very similar description of Miller appeared in a letter Nin sent to him three months after they met and shortly after they embarked on their sexual adventure. On 9 March 1932, Nin wrote,

> How did I single you out? I *saw* you with that intense selective way—I saw a mouth that was at once intelligent, animal, soft . . . strange mixture—a human man, sensitively aware of everything—I love awareness—a man, I told you, whom life made drunk. Your laughter was not a laughter which could hurt, it was mellow and rich. I felt warm, dizzy, and I sang within myself.[11]

On the one hand, this repetition of words, phrases, and ideas gives us an insight into Nin's creative process. The comparison of the original entry to the passage from a letter shows that while she was recycling similar vocabulary in making Miller's portrait, she nonetheless made efforts to find the best descriptors and to polish her sentences in order to best capture his essence. On the other hand, the juxtaposition of all three fragments reveals how her various rewritings enriched the final shape of the *Diary*. Nin could draw on these different versions to create the ultimate portrait of Miller in the published version.

Yet aesthetic concerns were not all that influenced the final shape of the *Diary:* there were also personal and legal considerations. Nin had to consider what she wanted to and could reveal. She produced a very sanitized self-portrait in which she got rid of controversial material, such as her sexual affairs and incestuous relationship with her father, and some unflattering details, like a nose surgery that she underwent in her thirties. Portraits of others were also retouched. Miller, for instance, who contributed significantly to the revision of the final draft, corrected his own description and advised Nin on how to construct portraits of other personages so as not to anger them, because he was perfectly aware that Nin would have to obtain releases from people whom she wanted to include in her *Diary* if they were still alive.

The following excerpt from the letter to Hiram Haydn not only describes how Nin procured necessary permissions but also gives an insight into revisions that were made to volume 1:

> The minor characters are all done flatteringly and will not question anything. Zadkine is a historic figure, Duchamp, Allendy and Rank are dead, we took out Rebecca West who is very difficult, others do not appear under their real name, Fred [Alfred Perlès] was written up by Henry [Miller], and by himself and as he wrote such a distorted story about me he will lie quiet ... Fred lives in Greece, and it would take months to get a release and he is not badly portrayed as Henry asked me to take out what could bother him.[12]

As is evident from the above passage, some people did not agree to be portrayed in the *Diary*. Apart from Rebecca West, Nin's close cousin Eduardo, her brother Thorvald, and her husband Hugh Guiler refused to appear in Nin's published journal. Nin dealt with this difficulty in various ways: she removed such troublesome individuals, as she did in the case of Rebecca West, excluding her from volume 1; she portrayed them in a more complimentary light (for instance, she brought back Rebecca West for the second volume, mentioning her briefly and describing her only in superlatives); she invented fictional characters based on real-life people, as she did with her cousin Eduardo, whom she replaced with Marguerite, describing her in *Diary 1* as "a dark haired girl" whom Nin "met . . . at the home of my neighbor" (74); she used other *Diary* characters, attributing to them words and actions that were originally spoken and done by somebody else (for example, many events that she experienced with her husband, such as the visit to the brothel described in *Diary 1,* were portrayed as if she had lived through them with Henry Miller). All these amendments had a great impact on the form and content of the final text.

There was also a question of audience, which must have played a crucial part in determining the material selected for publication. Margo Culley stresses the importance of an audience to the diary writing. By my arrangement of levels of self-construction, she refers to the first level: writing in the original diary. In the second level of self-construction, that is, in the process of final editing, the audience comes to the forefront. Because readers' reactions (in the form of letters and reviews) to the consecutively published *Diaries* were available to Nin, she must have taken them into consideration while arranging the material, elaborating or consolidating it, and making it coherent, readable, and contemporary. The *Diary* is, therefore, multilayered, consisting of Nin's version of her life as she saw it at the moment of writing, rewritten at various stages, and finally "cropped" to suit the audience and legal requirements.

As a result, six volumes of the *Diary* that appeared during Nin's lifetime launched highly manipulated representations of Nin, easily available to anyone who was willing to read her narrative. Although the volumes promised to be the most private documents, they were in fact the most public façade of Nin. In revising them for publication, Nin carefully crafted her portrayal, and as a result, while reading the six installments of her *Diary* one can discern the best defined and most distinctive self-portraits.

NIN THE *DIARY* PERSONA VERSUS NIN THE PUBLIC PERSONA

P. David Marshall's division of star performance into two dimensions—the textual and the extratextual—may help us understand the connection between Nin's *Diary* and Nin the public persona. For Marshall, the "textual" refers to the star's performance in the domain s/he represents. Thus, for an actor it would be acting in a film, for an athlete it would be playing a sport, for a musician it would be singing at a concert, and in the case of Nin, the "textual" would be writing. Then there is the "extratextual," which stands for the performance of everyday life of public personality. According to Marshall, these two dimensions produce public personality, or celebrity. Consequently, he posits that to make sense of the star involves not merely the analysis of the primary text (for example, film performance, or, in the case of Nin, her *Diary*) but, first and foremost, the study of magazine profiles, television interviews, and fans' involvement in the celebrity reception.[13] For these reasons, this chapter deals with Nin's self-presentation in the *Diary,* whereas the next one examines Nin's participation in public life and her reception by various media.

As a result of the correlation between these two dimensions, Nin becomes in a sense the living embodiment of the persona that she created in the *Diary*. On the one hand, Nin created herself in the *Diary,* and thanks to its success she managed to promote herself through it. On the other hand, by publishing the heavily edited *Diary* and launching certain images of herself for the public, Nin was forced to live up to the expectations of the audience, thus building her public persona on her *Diary* character and also on the public reception of this character.

With the publication of each volume, Nin released self-presentations of herself that she had to maintain once she appeared in front of her fans. By publishing the *Diary* and insisting that it contains a genuine self and her real life story, Nin had to enact the persona she created in the *Diary*. This phenomenon has been noticed by Elyse Lamm Pineau in her thought-provoking essay "A Mirror of Her Own: Anaïs Nin's Autobiographical Performances." Analyzing unpublished audiotapes of Nin's lectures, interviews, and discussions, Pineau identifies "continuity between her autobiographical and performance personae" and regards Nin as the embodiment of her *Diary*. Pineau also notes, "Performance marked the culmination of Nin's autobiographical project, for it provided an ongoing, public, and collective enactment of her *Diary* persona on college campuses nationwide." This ability to re-create her *Diary* identity contributed significantly to Nin's popular success after 1966.[14]

Public Promotion of the Private Self

NIN'S SELF-PORTRAITS IN THE *DIARY*

The release of Nin's *Diaries* in the 1960s and 1970s coincided with the rise of the women's movement. Several of Nin's critics, such as Philip Jason, Diane Richard-Allerdyce, and Helen Tookey, have pointed out the importance of feminism to the success of her *Diary*. Tookey, for instance, has remarked that the "context of second-wave feminism enabled ... [Nin] to situate herself as a woman artist who had struggled for emancipation, for recognition, for her own identity." Nin's *Diaries*, however, must have struck a chord not only with the women's movement but also with other elements characteristic of the era—identified by Arthur Marwick in his 1998 study *The Sixties: Cultural Revolution in Britain, France, Italy and the United States, c. 1958–c. 1974*—such as the importance of the young, the emergence of the "underground" and the "counterculture," idealism, and frankness in books and behavior. My argument is that while Nin's ideas about femininity were frequently at odds with the position taken by feminists of the 1960s and 1970s, her portrayal of herself as a supporter of the young and a participant of Bohemia must have appealed to the young generation and the hippies, who, as Elizabeth Wilson points out, were the new bohemians. Nin's text, although originally written a few decades earlier, reflected many concerns and fascinations of the 1960s generation.[15]

Although Nin started the diary as an eleven-year-old in 1914 and although at different stages of her career she made plans to publish her childhood journal, the first volume that was eventually released, in 1966, covered the period from 1931 to 1934 (the years she spent in Paris). She likely would not have achieved the same recognition had she released the story of her early days. Despite the fact that Nin's early journal is a valuable record of her teenage years, marked by struggles in a foreign country, it probably would not have had the hold over her audience that the Paris years had. After all, at the time of the publication of the first *Diary*, Nin was not an established figure in the literary marketplace, and reading about the adolescence of a little-known personality would not have been as appealing as reading about Nin's acquaintance with Henry Miller, which constitutes a great part of volume 1. In choosing the opening date, Nin did not opt for her early days in Paris, either. She arrived in the French capital in 1924, and her arrival might have served as another logical opening point for her published journal. Instead, she decided to begin her *Diary* when her personal and professional life accelerated: in 1931 she published her study of D. H. Lawrence and met Henry Miller, along with other well-known personages. The choice of the opening date was therefore a well-thought-out and strategic decision.

The first installment of the series, *The Diary of Anaïs Nin, 1931–1934* (hereafter *Diary 1*), gives an intimate picture of a bohemian coterie in France, features Henry Miller together with his eccentric wife, June, and describes Nin's commencing adventure with psychoanalysis. Writing and psychoanalysis are therefore two leading themes of *Diary 1*, and they frame Nin's self-presentations. Because of the simple fact of being the first in the series, and therefore probably the most frequently read one, *Diary 1* was incredibly influential in shaping Nin's further career. First of all, because it sold, it made the publication of further volumes possible. Second, it launched the first set of representations of Nin. The story of Nin's life in Paris between 1931 and 1934 contained in the first *Diary* and later elaborated in two unexpurgated volumes, *Henry and June* and *Incest,* has been frequently exploited in popular culture. The Miller-Nin-June trio captured the imaginations of readers especially powerfully, and as a consequence, Nin's relationship with Henry Miller became one of her most recognizable "characteristics." For these reasons, the present analysis centers on Nin's self-portraits in *Diary 1,* while later volumes are brought into consideration only when an indication of how these portraits developed or changed is necessary.

The second installment of Nin's journal, *The Diary of Anaïs Nin, 1934–1939,* published a year after the first one, in 1967, continues the story of Nin's life in Paris. With the third volume, the setting moves across the Atlantic, and volumes

3–6 cover the years Nin spent in the United States. *Diary 3* begins in 1939 after the outbreak of World War II with Nin's departure from France and her arrival in New York. *Diary 6* ends with Nin's announcement of the publication of the first volume in 1966. Volumes 3–6 are far less coherent than the first two installments. While *Diary 1* and *Diary 2* are well constructed and read more like a novel or an autobiography than a diary, with the third part this semblance of coherence begins to dissipate: Nin inserts many articles and reviews and frequently quotes her correspondence. In *Diary 3* and *Diary 4,* Henry Miller's letters prevail. In his letters, which are usually full of praise toward the addressee, Miller mentions how much Nin's help means to him, lists other enthusiasts of Nin's writings, and encourages her not to give up her literary work. In *Diary 5,* the role of Nin's admirer and supporter is taken over by another writer, James Herlihy.

Nin's *Diary* always bridges at least two cultural perspectives: the times when the *Diary* took its first shape (for example, the 1930s, in the case of the first installment) and the times when it was revised, published, and read by the public (thus, "the sixties," understood here broadly as the period stretching beyond an actual decade and encompassing the years 1958 to 1974). Consequently, while analyzing Nin's *Diary* and her self-portraits included in it, we must take into account both discourses that accompanied the production of her text and cultural contexts that enabled its successful consumption, because "to 'read' a text or a work of art," as Lisa Rado argues, is to "eavesdrop upon, to hear snatches of a much larger cultural interchange." In the rest of this chapter I trace how the culture of modernism, psychoanalytic discourse, the myth of the bohemian artist, and interwar perspectives on femininity and creativity shaped Nin's self in the diary. I also try to explain why Nin's *Diary,* rejected for three decades, found its audience in the sixties.[16]

Naturally, Nin's self-portraits, just like the cultural discourses that shaped Nin's journal and influenced its success, are not limited to the ones discussed below. It would be extremely difficult, verging on the impossible, to present all self-portraits and to disentangle all cultural exchanges that contributed to the creation of Nin's self and to point out how these corresponded with the culture of the sixties, so only the most prominent portraits and the most obvious cultural references are examined.

Nin the Writer

The first volume of the *Diary* can be divided into four parts according to the people who prevail in them. Thus, the first part features Henry Miller and his wife, June; the second introduces the psychoanalyst René Allendy; the third describes Nin's acquaintance with the French poet and actor Antonin Artaud and recounts Nin's reunion with her father; and the fourth one is largely devoted to her other analyst, Otto Rank. This division, with a new character introduced at regular intervals, was undoubtedly intentional. It was a result of a long editing process (described in the previous chapter), and the following comment made by Nin about the revision of the first installment may serve as another proof that she diligently planned her journal: "The balance is what is difficult to achieve. For instance, there may have been too much of Allendy, yet later it turns out the contrast was necessary to bring out the larger vision of Rank."[17] It must therefore be emphasized once again that Nin took great pains over the revisions of her journal.

The first Nin encountered in *Diary 1* is Nin the writer—a portrait that would be strongly developed in the following five volumes of the expurgated series released during Nin's life. *Diary 1* opens with a description of the French village, Louveciennes, where Nin lives, and Nin's house. Like a skillful novelist, Nin sets the scene for the events that will take place. The first few pages are abundant in literary allusions and comparisons. Nin compares Louveciennes to the village where Madame Bovary died, describes a village character as "one of Balzac's misers," mentions Maupassant's fondness for Louveciennes, and likens people commuting to Paris on old-fashioned trains to Proustian personages (*Diary 1*, 3). The literary ambience is therefore perceptible from the very beginning.

After reading these opening pages, we can clearly see that Nin's *Diary* is not what its label may suggest—a collection of spontaneously penned daily entries—but a well-structured and beautifully written work of literature. Nin's self-presentation as a writer therefore takes place on two levels: first, through the text and texture of the *Diary,* which serves as the best evidence that what readers hold in their hands is the work of a fine writer; and second, through her direct self-portrait of herself as a writer.

As far as the latter is concerned, Nin introduces herself as an aspiring writer. One of the first things she relates is that she has finished her book *D. H. Lawrence: An Unprofessional Study* and that she is not interested in an ordinary life of mending socks, canning fruit, and polishing furniture. She seeks moments of exaltation, and they occur while she is writing (*Diary 1,* 5). Moreover, anyone familiar with the plot of *Madame Bovary* knows that the heroine of this novel is unhappy within the confinement of her marriage. Nin, therefore, implicitly hints at her domestic imprisonment—implicitly because, apart from the preface, her husband does not appear in *Diary 1* (he does appear in later volumes but always under the pseudonym Ian Hugo, never as Nin's husband). However, she also states that unlike Madame Bovary she is not going to commit suicide. Writing prevents her from this tragic step. She presents her writing as the only means to escape "a beautiful prison" of her existence, to bring a state of hibernation to an end, and to start living more fully (*Diary 1,* 7).

Throughout *Diary 1,* Nin talks at length about her attempts at writing. She describes her experiences of composing her prose poem *House of Incest,* the collection of novelettes *The Winter of Artifice,* and the preface to Miller's *Tropic of Cancer.*[18] She also devotes a lot of space to discussions of a writer's nature. She endows writers and artists with a special role and portrays them as special, chosen, and unique. She states that whenever she writes she is in "a state of grace" and experiences "illuminations and fevers" (*Diary 1,* 5). Her creative sensibility brings on "states of ecstasy" that others can only achieve through drugs (37). And although at some point Nin compares writing to pains of childbearing—"No joy. Just pain, sweat, exhaustion"—in general, she presents writing as a very gratifying experience (315).

Providing such idealistic descriptions, Nin contributes to the construction and maintenance of the tradition that has regarded writers as creative geniuses, superior to other people. Nin's idea of an author is grounded in the romantic, and in effect modernist, notion of an artist as a lonely, insightful, misunderstood, and frequently underrated genius, who sets him/herself (although when Nin talks about the artist in general she always uses a male pronoun) against society. And Nin promotes this notion throughout the whole series of her *Diaries*.[19]

In the first volume, Nin also tries to establish the origins of herself as a writer as if to authenticate her occupation. She traces her interest in writing back to her teenage years, quoting, for instance, an entry from her early journal, written at the age of thirteen, which reads, "I should rewrite my arrival in New York," and then she comments, "Even then, I had literary preoccupations" (243). Similarly, while recalling her arrival to America, she recounts that as their luggage was being unloaded, she held on obstinately to her brother's violin case, since she "*wanted people to know [she] was an artist*" (218 [original emphasis]). She also mentions that from a very early age she invented stories to amuse her brothers and that she wrote for a school magazine (219). Such self-presentation creates an illusion that Nin's writing was not a career but a vocation, which again gives her the air of a chosen one, of someone special.

In creating her self-portrait as a writer, Nin also repeatedly draws on discourses characteristic of the modernist period. Nowhere is it manifested more clearly than in the second *Diary*, in which she narrates her gradual move toward feminine writing. Because modernism is synonymous with innovation, Nin's self-portrait is constructed through the use of words that connote invention, experiments, and the discovery of previously unexplored areas. Her attempts to speak on behalf of women, to write from their point of view, give her a sense of importance as she regards herself as a pioneer who embarks on unmarked territory by trying to capture and express what has been neglected by male writers, namely, feminine sensibilities. Her writing is presented as a groundbreaking endeavor. To support her image of an explorer of novel areas, she quotes Lawrence Durrell's letter in which he praises her for creating "a new Art," the art of women's expression, one that cannot be judged by male standards because it is so different from those standards (*Diary 2*, 183). Nin's efforts to find her own artistic voice, a voice of a woman, were appreciated by young women in the sixties who were increasingly aware of social restrictions imposed on them. Determined to forge their own identity, they found in Nin's *Diary* a confirmation that self-expression was possible despite the constraints of a patriarchal society.

Other dimensions of Nin the writer emerge in volumes 3–6, and they too correspond with the modernist notion of a writer: struggling but uncorrupted. In the third installment, Nin expresses her dissatisfaction at the lack of publishing opportunities, but despite being discouraged by the lack of interest in her works, she decides to act. She buys a press and prints her own books. Her preoccupation with the press gives rise to the portrait of a self-sufficient, hardworking, and independent woman writer who takes her fate into her own hands.

Setting up her own press puts her in line with many modernist writers who turned against the literary establishment and decided to print, distribute, and promote their works by themselves. Numerous small publishing houses were established by Nin's contemporaries in the first few decades of the twentieth century. Virginia and Leonard Woolf's Hogarth Press and Shaw Weaver's Egoist Press were founded in London, while Paris saw the emergence of Caresse Crosby's Black Sun Press and Nancy Cunard's Hours Press. Nin soaked up the modernist atmosphere of self-publishing, and her Gemor Press can be regarded as a form of rebellion against the marketplace, against the commercial. It strengthens her self-portrait as a writer who is determined to promote uncompromised art, not tainted by commercial concerns.

The Gemor Press titles were produced with great care and were frequently illustrated with engravings by Hugh

Guiler, who contributed them under the pseudonym Ian Hugo. Philip Jason rightly notes that "Nin and her co-workers practiced, whenever they could, book production as an art form." These beautifully done pieces brought out by Gemor Press are today collector's items. Although they do not fetch as much as their modernist counterparts—a signed first edition of *Ulysses* sells for $60,000 to $70,000—one still has to pay a considerable sum of approximately $3,500 for a deluxe edition of Nin's novel *This Hunger* that was printed in color in a limited number of fifty copies. Apart from Nin's books, works of others were published by her, too, and as Jason points out, "The Gemor Press story is, among other things, the story of creative networking," for Nin cooperated with several writers, artists, and other publishers, including Caresse Crosby, who commissioned Nin to print an edition of Paul Eluard and Max Ernst's *Misfortunes of the Immortals*.[20]

Nin always presents her self-publishing efforts with profound reverence. Wherever she mentions Gemor Press—whether in her *Diary,* in "The Story of My Printing Press," which she contributed to Bill Henderson's *The Publish-It-Yourself Handbook: Literary Tradition and How-To,* or in Robert Snyder's documentary *Anaïs Observed*—she romanticizes her struggles. "The Story of My Printing Press," for instance, apart from a few anecdotes relating the failures and mistakes of novice publishers, contains many passages that idealize the printing endeavor. Nin claims that "setting each letter by hand taught [her] economy of style," thus giving the press a central place in not only the design of her books but also the creation of their content. By emphasizing the great significance of the press, she reinforces her image of the uncompromised writer.[21]

The small press was just one of many publishing practices popularized by modernists; the little magazine was another. Mark Morrisson claims, "Among modernism's major contributions to twentieth-century culture was the little magazine."[22] Little magazines had a key role in shaping the modernist movement. They promoted nonmainstream literature and provided a forum for intellectual debates. The modernist era witnessed the emergence of a profusion of little magazines, the best-known of which were the American *Little Review, Dial,* and *Poetry,* the British *Criterion,* and the Parisian *transition,* with many modernist authors serving as their editors. "Even though individual little magazines often had short lives and small print runs," as Morrisson observes, "the genre has flourished ever since. Already by the middle of the twentieth century, over a thousand different little magazines had been published, and hundreds more have since come into existence."[23] Many appeared during the turbulent 1960s, so there is another affiliation between what Nin described in her *Diary* and the times when her *Diary* was published.

A new technology that emerged in the sixties—photo-offset printing—lowered publication costs, enabling the boom of underground magazines, which became the voice for various social movements. Underground papers covered stories the mainstream media avoided, championed antiwar activism, promoted alternative opinions and lifestyles, and ultimately contributed to the creation of vibrant countercultures. Nin always participated in and supported alternative publishing. Apart from owning her press, she assisted with the editing of a bilingual magazine, *Two Cities,* and contributed many articles to other alternative publications. She was aware that underground publishing of the 1960s continued the tradition that she had helped to shape with her press, which is evident from the following fragment in which she comments on Gemor Press: "We did not use the word 'underground' then, but this tiny press and word of mouth enabled my writing to be discovered." Although *underground* was a relatively new word—Marwick claims that the word *underground* first came into use in New York in 1964—Nin quickly began using it to describe herself. Her self-portrayal as a struggling, independent writer found approval among those who questioned social conventions and sought to explore unconventional lifestyles and alternative forms of artistic expression.[24]

Nin's self-portrait of a writer is constructed gradually and acquires new dimensions in each installment. Nin starts as an unknown writer in search of her own style. As a result of this search, she becomes a writer of feminine expression. Then she portrays herself as a hardworking and determined writer who does not compromise on her writing and buys her own press in order to print her books. But whatever new facet Nin presents to us, her notion of the writer always circles around the romantic/modernist notion of an artist as someone out of the ordinary, unique, and authentic. This vision of a writer is deeply immersed in the modernist period while simultaneously finding echoes in the culture of the 1960s.

Nin the Artists' Friend

Even when Nin does not write directly about herself, her portraits and descriptions of others often refer us back to the artistic and literary sphere, since many of her friendships are with people connected with the bohemian world of Paris and, in later volumes, with artistic circles of New York. Her status of a writer is therefore further authenticated by the relationships she forms.

The first major portrait in *Diary 1* is that of Henry Miller. Before Nin gets to know Miller the person, she reads a sample of his writing, a short article on Buñuel's film, so Miller is first introduced through his writing. Throughout *Diary 1* Nin comments frequently on the nature of his writing, which she finds "flamboyant, torrential, chaotic, treacherous, and dangerous" (10). She also positions herself in opposition to Miller's mode of expression: he is a realist, she is a poet (55). His language of realism, of flesh, of nature, and of the streets contrasts with her elusive, imaginative, intuitive, and poetic writing (55–57). Miller serves, therefore, as a point of reference for Nin's writing style. By comparing her writing to his, Nin sharpens her portrait of herself as a writer, as she can be more specific about what she stands for.

Nin's relationship with Miller in this *Diary*—as opposed to the volume *Henry and June* published twenty years later—is presented as nothing more than a literary friendship: There is no mention of their love affair, no description of sexual encounters, and no passion, apart from the literary one. They discuss literature together, mark passages in books for each other, comment on their literary techniques, and revise each other's writing. They collaborate with and influence each other: "We have much influence over each other's works, I on the artistry and insight, on the going beyond realism, he on the matter, substance, and vitality of mine" (*Diary 1,* 166). What is more, Nin portrays herself as a writer admired by Miller. She writes, for instance, "He still remembers passages in my novel, wants to have the manuscript, to be able to read it over. Says it is the most beautiful writing he has read lately" (*Diary 1,* 56). Miller's comments serve therefore as an indirect endorsement of Nin's works.

The presence of Miller—a well-established but highly controversial literary figure in the 1960s literary marketplace—certainly spiced up the story, contributed to its popularity, and increased its sales. Henry Miller, a writer known to a limited American audience before 1961, hit the headlines when his novel *Tropic of Cancer* was eventually published in the United States, twenty-six years after it appeared in France in 1934. The book that had been censored because of its explicit sexual content became an instant success. As Miller's biographer, Mary V. Dearborn, relates, "Sales were phenomenal: 68,000 copies sold in the first week, and Grove [the publisher] soon had 130,000 copies in print. *Cancer* climbed the best-seller list. The reviews were also generally positive." Miller was celebrated worldwide as a famous author of dirty books—a label, as Dearborn notes, he was not particularly proud of. Nin was aware of the allure of Henry Miller. That is why she decided to publish his letters to her a year before the publication of the first *Diary.* And she was not the only one who traded on Miller's name. In 1962, Alfred Perlès, an acquaintance of both Miller and Nin, published his memoir of Henry Miller, entitled *My Friend Henry Miller.* The number of publications with Miller's name in the title grew steadily in the 1970s and 1980s.[25]

Another writer with whom Nin became friends and another major portrait in *Diary 1* is Antonin Artaud, the French actor, critic, and playwright, whose works and ideas enjoyed a revival in popularity in the United States in the 1950s and 1960s. Particularly inspirational was his theory for what he called a Theatre of Cruelty, which he formulated in a series of essays published between 1931 and 1936 in the *Nouvelle Revue Française,* which were collected as *The Theatre and Its Double* (1938). Artaud advocated an intense theatrical experience that should shock the audience to liberate their emotions and instincts that were repressed by civilization. In practice, it meant a stage performance made up of special lighting effects, elaborate props, symbolic gestures, and inarticulate exclamations, such as groans and screams. Murder, torture, rape, and madness were common themes of such plays. Although virtually unknown in the United States in the 1930s, Artaud's ideas appealed to postwar poets, dramatists, and performers. As Joanna Pawlik, a scholar researching postwar American literature in the context of surrealism and French theory, explains, "Artaud was received enthusiastically by poets such as Allen Ginsberg and Michael McClure, and recruited as a posthumous ally in their distinctive revolt against Cold War oppression, militarism, and conformity."[26] The subsequent generation applauded his contribution to the development of modern drama, and the counterculture of the 1960s adopted him as an icon.

Introduced in the third part of Nin's *Diary 1,* Artaud is portrayed as a tortured, reclusive artist on the verge of madness. His portrait therefore perpetuates the vision of an artist as someone extraordinary, or in this case, even bizarre—the social outcast. His insanity and extraordinariness are even contained in Nin's description of his looks: "A gaunt face, with visionary eyes," "the lean, ghostly figure who haunts the cafés" with eyes "blue with languor, black with pain" (186–87). The fact that Nin manages to get through to him and win his friendship sheds light on her as someone exceptional and sympathetic toward artists and their angst, and thus attuned to the artistic world.

Yet it is not only the portraits of Miller and Artaud that have the potential to attract readers. The Paris of the 1930s is equally alluring. Writing about the Parisian artistic community in the first four decades of the twentieth century, Shari Benstock rightly observes, "Rarely has a time and place so captured the imagination as the Paris of these years. . . . We have romanticized those years, and so have those who lived through them." Indeed, Paris at the beginning of the previous century fascinated people on both sides of the Atlantic equally strongly when the artists and writers of the era were actually creating their masterpieces there, as occurred in the 1960s, when Nin published her *Diary,* and in the 1980s, when Benstock released her study *Women of the Left Bank: Paris, 1900–1940.* Paris continues to appeal to audiences in the twenty-first century, as is evident from the growing number of studies devoted to the period as well as more-popular representations of the era, such as Woody Allen's highly acclaimed film *Midnight in Paris* (2011), which takes the main character on a nostalgic trip to the expatriate literary scene of the 1920s.[27]

Before Nin's *Diary* was released in 1966, several personal accounts of the period in question had already been published. One of the earliest portrayals of the Parisian artistic milieu to appear in print was Gertrude Stein's *The Autobiography of Alice B. Toklas.* Writing in the guise of her lover's "autobiography," Stein recounted her life as a writer, a patron of arts, and a hostess of the popular artistic salon. After its release in 1933, numerous other memoirs followed, many authored by American writers. Robert McAlmon chronicled the 1920s in his autobiography *Being Geniuses Together* (1938), which was later revised by Kay Boyle and reissued with supplementary chapters in 1968. In 1953, Nin's friend Caresse Crosby—cofounder of the Black Sun Press, which printed works of such renowned authors as T. S. Eliot, D. H. Lawrence, Ezra Pound, and William Faulkner—published her recollections of the Paris period in *The Passionate Years.* A few years later, Sylvia Beach, the owner of a bookshop that was very popular among expatriates, described her time in the City of Lights in a memoir that bore as the title the name of her famous establishment, *Shakespeare and Company* (1959). Two years before the publication of Nin's

Diary, in 1964, Ernest Hemingway's *A Movable Feast*—a set of portraits, anecdotes, and reflections on 1920s Paris—appeared. All these reminiscences, together with a plethora of diaries, journals, letters, and autobiographical novels set in the French capital, laid the ground for Nin's *Diary,* in the sense that they kept interest in that time and place alive. In choosing the opening of the *Diary,* Nin and her publishers capitalized on the popular fascination with the artistic scene of Paris at the beginning of the twentieth century.

The portrayal of the Parisian artistic milieu allows Nin to inscribe herself in the tradition of writers and artists who created in the City of Lights in the interwar period. In the *Diary,* Nin provides her own story of these years, an alternative story, because despite a considerable number of accounts from the period, she is absent from the personal memoirs of people such as Stein, Hemingway, and Crosby. This absence is caused not by malice but by the fact that most of these authors were oblivious to Nin's existence. Even Caresse Crosby, who later became friends with Nin, did not refer to Nin in *The Passionate Years,* but she did not do so for a simple reason: they did not know each other at the time. Unsurprisingly, when in one of her letters to Crosby Nin reveals that "the only thing which estranged me and hurt me was your not once referring to my work in your autobiography, nor whenever you listed writers you had known," Crosby, astonished, replies, "How could you have made such a mistake. I didn't write about you in *The Passionate Years* because it is written only up to 1940. We hadn't even met and we did not know each other in the Paris years."[28]

Nin resided on the outskirts of literary Paris—both literally, as she lived in Louveciennes, a village located in the suburbs of the city, and figuratively, as she did not move in the prominent literary circles of the time. She was not a regular visitor on rue de l'Odéon, where two important bookshops and gathering places for artists were situated: Sylvia Beach's Shakespeare and Company, faced by Adrianne Monnier's La Maison des Amis des Livres. She never frequented popular salons, such as those established by Natalie Barney and Gertrude Stein, which were attended by the likes of Ezra Pound, T. S. Eliot, James Joyce, Djuna Barnes, and Ernest Hemingway.

Yet in her *Diary* she portrays herself as belonging to another artistic group: the group of a smaller caliber that included Henry Miller and Alfred Perlès. Nin recounts their discussions, frequently pertaining to literature and their own writings, and depicts the fervent atmosphere of creation that accompanies their meetings. Her journal is full of fragments, like the following one, which romanticize the encounters of the trio:

> I love those long nights of talk at the café, watching the dawn arrive.... I carry a few pages of Fred's book [*Sentiments Limitrophes*], delicate as a water color, and a few pages of Henry's book which is like a volcano.... I live by improvisations, impetus, surrealist whims. Great things are going to grow out of all this.
>
> I feel the fermentation. I look at the workmen carrying their tools and their lunch boxes, and I feel that we are working too, although they may not think so when they see us sitting at a café table with a bottle of wine, talking. (*Diary 1*, 93)

Although Nin did not belong to the world created by the key modernist luminaries, the *Diary* gave her an opportunity to put her name on the literary map of Paris. Constructing her self-portrait, she capitalized on the reputations of those who gained some recognition before her, like Miller and Artaud, while simultaneously creating an alternative version of 1930s Paris, thus challenging the dominant myth (still very powerful in the 1960s) of a single modernist movement.

Other *Diary* installments also contain famous names. The second volume continues featuring Henry Miller but also introduces other well-known characters, such as the writers Lawrence Durrell, Theodore Dreiser, Waldo Frank, and Eugene Jolas, the painter Hans Reichel, and the Wagners. The number of personages increases dramatically in volume 3, which contains the portraits of France Steloff, the owner of the cult New York bookshop Gotham Book Mart; Dorothy Norman, the *Twice a Year* magazine editor; the artists Yves Tanguy and Salvador Dali; the writers Robert Duncan, Sherwood Anderson, Kenneth Patchen, André Breton, Richard Wright, and Max Ernst; the actors Luise Rainer and Canada Lee; the photographer Alfred Stieglitz; the composer Edgar Varès; and the art collector Peggy Guggenheim. Volume 4 includes the independent filmmaker Maya Deren; the literary critic Edmund Wilson; the writers James Agee, Gore Vidal, James Merrill, and Tennessee Williams; and the sculptor Noguchi. Volumes 5 and 6 are dominated by portraits of James Leo Herlihy and the experimental filmmaker Kenneth Anger, but there are also brief references to such popular actors as Charlie Chaplin, Gregory Peck, Marilyn Monroe, and Jayne Mansfield, as well as the Beat poet Allen Ginsberg. On the one hand, these encounters reflect Nin's life at those given moments. On the other, because of the very sketchy nature of certain portraits, as in the case of Charlie Chaplin and Marilyn Monroe, it is hard to resist the impression that they were included because their names enriched the index.

Also noteworthy is the fact that with each volume of the *Diary,* Nin's attention shifts from her self-portrait to the portraits of others. A very significant declaration appears in *Diary 6:* Nin decides "to retire as the major character of this diary," and she names her journal as "*Journal des Autres* (Diary of Others)."[29] She makes more-elaborate portraits of her friends and acquaintances, sometimes providing quite thorough stories of their lives. Yet Nin's portraits of others work to define her as well. For instance, in the third and fourth volumes she recounts her acquaintance with young and unknown artists and stresses her attachment to, understanding of, and appreciation of the young. She writes, for instance, "I like the adolescent world, yes, because they are still vulnerable and open. They are a relief from tight, closed, hard, harsh worlds."[30] She compares their spontaneity and flexibility to the maturity and rigidity of people of an established public position, such as the literary critic Edmund Wilson. She finds the world of the latter "oppressive, definitive, solidified," as opposed to the "fluid, potentially marvelous, malleable, variable, as-yet-to-be-created" world of the young (*Diary 4,* 95). She thinks that the younger generation understands her better, appreciates her writings, and prevents her from getting corrupted by reality. Describing her young friends as innocent and fluid and emphasizing her connection with them, Nin reinforces her self-portrait as a pure and unsoiled artist.

Nin's idealistic portrayal of the young must have positively affected her audience, which consisted, as Gunther Stuhlmann notes in the preface to *Diary 4,* mostly of young people. Her descriptions tapped into the youth culture, which was growing in size and prominence in the 1960s. Edward J. Rielly claims that "[t]he decade of the 1960s can be considered . . . the decade of youth." The postwar generation of baby boomers reached adolescence and young adulthood in the 1960s, and the number of Americans between ages of fifteen and twenty-four increased by over ten million. Their presence was so manifest that, as Rielly notes, "*Time* magazine named the 'Twenty-Five and Under Generation' its Man of the Year" in 1966. Nin's positive depiction of the young was another aspect of her *Diary* that found reverberations in the times when her journals were published.[31]

The Bourgeois versus the Bohemian Nin

At the beginning of *Diary 1,* Nin leads a rather conventional, bourgeois lifestyle with which she is not particularly satisfied. As the text progresses, she becomes more and more drawn into the kind of life represented by Henry Miller—the bohemian life of the artist. Consequently, toward the end of the first journal (351–52), she states that she is divided into three selves. First, there is the domestic, bourgeois Anaïs, who lives in Louveciennes and leads a luxurious life, spending her free time writing, translating her early diaries from French to English, going to concerts, meeting distinguished people, undertaking psychoanalysis, and dreaming of a fuller existence. Second, there is the bohemian Anaïs, who enjoys the artistic way of life, is a friend of Henry Miller and Alfred Perlès; bereft of her Louveciennes servants, she peels potatoes and grinds coffee but also discusses art and literature in Parisian cafés. Third, there is the Anaïs who is about to try an independent living by becoming a psychoanalyst in America.

Nin is therefore in-between—neither totally bourgeois nor wholly bohemian. In a way, she epitomizes the perpetual conflict between the bourgeois and the bohemian. Bohemians, as Elizabeth Wilson observes, emerged in response to the rise of bourgeois society and defined themselves against it.[32] In the *Diary,* Nin deliberately contrasts these two worlds that represent different attitudes, values, and beliefs. The bourgeois world is embodied by Nin's father and her psychoanalyst Dr. René Allendy. It is the world Nin tries to leave behind, despite both men's disapproval of her links with the bohemian community. The former urges her "to give up the parasites, the Bohemians, the failures," while the latter compares her presence in the bohemian world to "a flower on a dung pile" (*Diary 1,* 250, 162). Nin, however, becomes more and more attracted to the bohemian way of life and presents Henry Miller's world as more authentic and sincere than the world of her father, which was built on appearances.

Nin's attraction to the bohemian society and her rejection of bourgeois values are a way to authenticate her artistic sensibilities. Her idea of a writer as someone special corresponds with "the bohemian myth—the idea of the artist as a different *sort of person* from his fellow human beings," which, as Wilson explains, "is founded on the idea of the Artist as Genius developed by the Romantic movement in the wake of the industrial and French revolutions. The romantic genius is the artist against society." And since "dissidence, opposition, criticism of the status quo" are central to the myth, on a few occasions Nin pictures herself as a rebel.[33] For instance, while reporting a conversation with one of her acquaintances, Nin presents herself as an independent woman who has resisted social roles, saying, "I have rejected all conventions, the opinion of the world, all its laws" (*Diary 1,* 186). She also recounts her rebellion against Catholicism, which she repudiated at the age of sixteen when her prayers for the return of her father were not answered, and the rebellion against the bourgeois life of her father, which she considers superficial. And finally, she associates with rebels: with Henry Miller, who rejects the traditional lifestyle; with Antonin Artaud, who rebels against classical theatre; and with Otto Rank, who opposes the ideas of his famous teacher, Sigmund Freud.

Nin's defiance of bourgeois society also manifests itself in her unusual dress and the design of her house. Elizabeth Wilson claims that many bohemian women devoted themselves to arranging beautiful interiors and were preoccupied with making original clothes: "For maximum effect upon their urban stage the bohemians needed a *mise en scène,* theatrical sets and costumes for the performance of revolt and identity." Wilson claims that interiors and dress were loaded with meaning, expressing both personality and taste. And there was not one single costume code: some bohemians dressed in black, while others wore colorful attire.[34]

Nin too pays a lot of attention to both the décor of her house and her clothes. She insists that the latter must resemble and represent her, because they communicate to others who she is. She wears unusual clothes and often invents her own outfits: making dresses out of Spanish shawls, adding fur to winter shoes. Her dress constitutes an essential element of her original identity and has a symbolic meaning for her, as she admits: Dress "had, first of all, a poetic significance: colors for certain occasions, evocations of other styles, countries. . . . It was a sign of individuality. . . . I wanted striking clothes which distinguished me from other women" (*Diary 1,* 111). She pays similar attention to her surroundings. The second volume, for instance, contains descriptions of her houseboat at the quay of the River Seine, where she is surrounded by social outcasts: rag pickers, hobos, prostitutes. By decorating the houseboat, she creates an ambience of a very cozy place where, as Nin maintains, everyone wishes to stay. It is unusual, artistic, and colorful, and people who come to visit her are enchanted with it. Conrad Morricand—a poet-astrologer who reads horoscopes for her and her friends—is amazed by the houseboat and thinks of it as "an opium den" (*Diary 2,* 125). This unusual abode stands for freedom and an alternative way of living. Including such descriptions in her *Diary* is another way of portraying herself as an artist.

Nin's rebellions are, however, rather minor: she does not reject completely the bourgeois lifestyle, and many elements characteristic of bohemian living—such as sexual transgression, extravagant behavior, poverty, and the abuse of drugs and alcohol, which are typically associated with the bohemian myth—do not form part of her self-portrait. Yet these aspects do characterize her associates. For instance, Henry Miller, her best friend and literary partner, is portrayed as an embodiment of the bohemian artist who devotes himself to literature and pursues an unconventional life. Nin presents Miller as the ultimate writer "who dodged jobs, responsibilities, ties. He freed himself of all tasks but one: to write" (*Diary 1,* 257). His bohemianism expresses itself not only in his commitment to his writings but also in his way of life. This "blurring of life and art" is essential to the bohemian myth, as Wilson explains. "The bohemians brought into play all those aspects of daily life that were *not* central to the production of works of art. . . . [such as] dress, surroundings and relationships. By doing so they challenged the bourgeois insistence that art was a realm apart."[35]

Miller is devoid of any possession, undisturbed by poverty and shabbiness, happy as long his stomach is full and his thirst quenched. He looks scruffy and frequently borrows clothes. He embraces all experience and is interested in the ugly and the sick. By introducing Nin to seedy places of Paris, he makes her a more conscious observer of street life (*Diary 1,* 77–78). Apart from Miller, there are other characters, such as June Miller and Antonin Artaud, who fit the definition of the bohemian better than Nin does. June, Miller's wife, is a very eccentric figure. Clad in tattered clothes, she flaunts her bisexuality, indulges herself in intoxicants, and talks profusely but elusively. Artaud, in turn, is an impoverished writer "in conflict with a world he imagines mocking and threatening" (*Diary 1,* 187).

In creating her image, Nin recycles the myth of the bohemian, drawing on it and contributing to it at the same time, because the myth, as Wilson observes, is inseparable from its fictional representation through which it self-perpetuates. In a way, Nin and Miller represent two sides of the same coin, namely, two aspects of the bohemian artist ingrained in popular culture: she, the artist as a special individual; he, the artist as a vagabond and outcast. As Wilson explains it, "[W]hile on the one hand the artist saw himself as a romantic genius elevated above the common run, on the other his fascination with the everyday, the obscure, the forbidden, and the sordid contributed to the perception of the bohemian artist as one who deliberately went 'slumming.'"[36]

Nin's self-portrait as a bohemian is very toned down. She narrates the transgressions of others, like Artaud's drug addiction, but she is rarely involved in unlawful or excessive conduct herself. The only incidents narrated in the first volume that might raise eyebrows are her visit to a brothel with Henry Miller (in reality she went with her husband) and her fascination with June. As far as the latter is concerned, Nin depicts a sensual relationship between herself and June Miller that ends with a long kiss. Their "affair" goes through stages typical of falling in love. First, when Nin meets June, she is thunderstruck. She describes June's astounding beauty and states that she would do anything for her (*Diary 1*, 20). Then, just like lovers tend to do, Nin begins to discover and ponder similarities and differences between herself and June. With each meeting, their relationship becomes more and more fervent, and Nin's feelings intensify. The descriptions of bodily contact and physical attraction start to appear, as, for instance, in the following fragment: "Coming out of the theatre I take her arm. Then she slips her hand over mine, and we lock hands. . . . I was infinitely moved by the touch of her hand" (*Diary 1*, 24–25). Finally, during one of their meetings they confess love for each other. Nin writes, "When I realized what she was revealing to me, I was overjoyed. I overwhelm *her?* She loved me then? June! . . . Let's be overwhelmed, it is so lovely. I love you, June" (*Diary 1*, 31–32 [original emphasis]). After the meeting, as they walk along the streets together, "bodies close together, arm in arm, hands locked," Nin admits to being in a state of such ecstasy that she is not able to talk (32). And when June finally departs for New York, they kiss—a kiss that is more than a usual goodbye kiss between friends: "And she offered her mouth which I kissed for a long time" (40).

Nin provides several descriptions of this relationship that clearly indicate infatuation: "I want to become immersed with her" (24); "I am fascinated by her eyes, her mouth" (25); "I held her warm hand. . . . I could not eat before her" (27). Why did Nin decide to narrate a very intimate relationship with a woman while she cut out all other (heterosexual) affairs? Perhaps this is because the subsequent passages quickly dismiss any homosexual bond. Nin begins to interpret her love for June not as a passionate affair but as a form of alliance between women. Her relationship with June is exonerated when Rank confirms that it was not of a homosexual nature. Anything that goes beyond the norm is very quickly restored to "normality" so that it reflects the required social order. Her adventure with June becomes a controlled transgression—a temporary departing from social standards that allows Nin to present herself as a nonconformist without the risk of being labeled a deviant.[37] Nin incorporates the June episode into her published narrative only because it confirms her heterosexuality while simultaneously providing a titillating story.

Nin therefore presents herself as an insider of the bohemian milieu, but she seems to be more an observer of Bohemia than a fully fledged participant. Her bohemianism is very cautious, studied, and deliberate. She mothers the artists, provides the place for their meetings, participates in their literary conversations, tries to transgress the boundaries in writing, and dresses unusually; yet all her actions included in the *Diary* are within the norm. There is nothing exceedingly shocking or extravagant about them. They are socially acceptable since they are not outrageous or offensive. And whatever "transgressions" Nin narrates in the following volumes of the diaries, they are very moderate, always within the social norm.

For instance, at the end of *Diary 5*, Nin recounts her adventure with LSD, which was, in fact, a monitored experiment conducted in the office of Dr. Oscar Janiger, who, like the more notorious Timothy Leary, researched the influence of LSD on the creative process. Nin describes in great detail what she experienced. She provides a vivid picture of her psychedelic vision, but at the end she comments that in her writing she explores similar states of mind, and she concludes that one does not need chemical alternation to reach the subconscious, at least if one is an artist. She is happy to discover "that this world opened by LSD was accessible to the artist by way of art."[38] In volume 6, Nin considers the pros and cons of LSD. As for advantages, she enumerates LSD's potential to liberate thinking and to allow contact with the inner self. She claims, for instance, that some people could understand her writing better under the influence of LSD. She is, however, against its indiscriminate use. She insists that artists and mystics can access these states of minds without any artificial alterations, and either ordinary people should be taught how to do that or the artist should translate such experiences into his or her art.

Nonetheless, this alternative, if cautious, Anaïs must have struck a chord with the generation of the 1960s, especially with the hippie movement, whose members had little regard for social conventions and were notorious for their indulgence in drugs, such as marijuana and LSD. In terms of percentages, the hippie subculture was a minor phenomenon (Marwick applies the very broad definition of the term to only 0.1 percent of the American population); however, their distinctiveness made them the most visible part of the counterculture, and their "counter-cultural, underground practices," as Marwick observes, "had a lasting effect on the lifestyles and leisure activities of important sections of the population."[39] The hippies continued the tradition of the beatniks, who were popular a decade before, and both generations recycled the bohemian myth that promoted disdain for society and traditional values, encouraged experiments with intoxicating substances, and advocated sexual freedom. The hippie movement thus has its roots in the bohemian culture that Nin depicted so attractively.

Nin's penchant for unusual ethnic clothes, her descriptions of her bohemian friends, her elevation of the youth culture, and her experiments with LSD align her with the counterculture of the 1960s. Another point of convergence between the times she portrayed in her *Diary* and the times when her *Diaries* were read was her pacifist attitude. On numerous occasions, Nin declares her apolitical position. She does not have faith in political action and prefers to remain personal. This lack of interest in political movements is nurtured by the romantic idea of the artist for whom, as Wilson explains, "[a]rt . . . expressed the originality of the unique creative individual, and the artist's duty was to realize himself and his unique vision rather than to create works that expressed the dominant beliefs in society."[40] Nin's rejection of ideologies and political or social movements—be it Marxism in volume 2, communism in volume 3, or, later, feminism—is a manifestation of this ideal. Her belief in the personal is not necessarily egocentric, as many critics have pointed out, but is inscribed in the notion of the artist she believes in.

Nin's disparagement of communism and, more broadly, her declaration of an apolitical nature parallels certain convictions popular among the 1960s generation. Communism had been America's archenemy starting at the end of World War II. In the 1960s, the Cold War was well under way, and the two major countries involved—the USA and the USSR—continued to expand their respective spheres of influence. In 1961, a new powerful symbol of the conflict emerged—the Iron Curtain took shape as the Berlin Wall, which physically separated communist East Germany from the more democratically oriented West Germany and symbolically divided Western Europe from the whole of Central and Eastern Europe, which was under Soviet control. Nonetheless, in the 1960s, Europe ceased to be the main area of interest for two superpowers; as Maurice Isserman and Michael Kazin observe, "[T]he focus of Cold War competition shifted to what was beginning to be called the 'Third World,' the less developed nations of Asia, Africa, and Latin America."[41]

When the third volume of Nin's *Diary,* in which she vents her frustration with communism, appeared in 1969, the United States was in the middle of the Vietnam War. Trying to defend South Vietnam from its communist neighbor North Vietnam, the United States had to gradually increase its involvement. As Edward J. Rielly explains, "Between 1964 and 1968, the United States moved steadily from an advisory role to spearheading the military action against North Vietnam and the guerrilla forces in the South known as the Viet Cong. As 1968 began, close to half a million U.S. military personnel were in Vietnam, and over 16,000 Americans had been killed in the conflict."[42] Anticommunist feelings therefore ran high.

At the same time, however, an increasing fraction of Americans opposed the participation of the United States in the war, and the opposition grew particularly strong after the Tet Offensive—a bloody attack by Viet Cong militia that occurred in 1968 during the Vietnamese holiday known as Tet and took Americans and the South Vietnamese by surprise, as the Viet Cong had proclaimed a cease-fire in conjunction with the festival. Nin's *Diary* with its pacifist attitude fitted in nicely with the growing antiwar movement, with its slogan that was particularly popular among countercultures: Make Love Not War. Nin can be regarded as a proponent of such an attitude. In her infrequent comments on World War II, she always emphasizes her interest in creating an individually perfect world, and in one entry she declares, "Against hatred, power and fanaticism, systems and plans, I oppose love and creation, over and over again, in spite of the insanity of the world."[43] Nin's distrust of social systems and institutions might easily win the approval of the generation of the 1960s.

Nin the Woman

While in the first part of *Diary 1* Nin establishes herself as a writer, in the second one, largely devoted to the psychoanalytical sessions, she begins to develop a self-portrait of a woman in search of herself. Her descriptions of psychoanalysis, first with Dr. Allendy and then with Dr. Otto Rank, which she extensively quotes in the *Diary,* give readers the impression of discovering the "real" Anaïs Nin. Not only does she reconstruct the detailed conversations with her psychoanalysts, but also she practices her own inner psychoanalysis. Her diary becomes, therefore, a space of self-reflection where she exposes what seems to be her most private self.

Nin talks about her fears and anxieties and creates a portrait of a neurotic, sensitive woman who is troubled by her artistic sensibility. She is hypersensitive and in need of love, admiration, and understanding. She also presents her status of a writer as being complicated by her femininity. She admits that she chose to be a writer because of her lack of confidence: "I decided to be an artist, a writer, to be interesting, charming, accomplished" (*Diary 1,* 77, 81). The following passage in which she presents herself as a woman first and then an artist is quite significant (even though Nin's *Diary* contains many contradictory statements and elsewhere she places much emphasis on her role as a writer): "And if I am not a great artist, I don't care. I will have been good to the artist, the mother and muse and servant and inspiration. It's right for a woman to be, above all, human. I am a woman first of all" (*Diary 1,* 223). She portrays herself here in a passive role typically assigned to women, that of a muse, an inspiration. Being a writer and being a woman are presented as incompatible: Nin the artist is hampered by Nin the woman.

The conflict between the writer and the woman comes to the fore in the fourth part of *Diary 1,* devoted to psychoanalysis with Dr. Rank. Nin, who was previously analyzed by Dr. Allendy, finds Dr. Rank, a rebellious disciple of Freud, a more suitable analyst for her needs because of his interest in the artist. Whereas Allendy treated Nin as "an ordinary woman, a full human being, a simple and naïve one" and wanted to "exorcise . . . [her] disquietudes, vague aspirations, . . . [her] creations which sent . . . [her] out into dangerous realms" (281–82), Rank recognizes and authenticates her self-portrait as someone special and creative. He calls her a "myth-maker" and explains her childhood journal entries starting with "I am an orphan"—which she was not—as her need to create herself, her need not to be born of human parents (272). Nin writes that, unlike Allendy, Rank "had not thrown [her] back upon a vague ocean of generalities, a cell among a million cells" (273)—yet another example of her portrayal of herself as a unique individual.

While reading extensive passages of Nin's conversations with Rank, one cannot help but notice that Rank is full of stereotypical notions about women, and his ideas must have influenced Nin's. On the one hand, he puts women's way of thinking and perceiving, which he considers intuitive and personal, on a pedestal. He states that thanks to psychology it was discovered that women "remained in touch with that mysterious region we are now opening up" (*Diary 1*, 276). He compares women's perception to that of the child, the artist, the primitive. On the other hand, he has very pronounced views about the inferior position of women in history. According to him, women never invented anything, they never were great artists (291). And the notable women who did exist thought and wrote like men (276). Alas, such ideas about femininity were common to turn-of-the-century sexology.

As Freud's former student, Rank must have been affected by Freud's theories, including those concerning women. Freud's views were, in turn, rooted in the patriarchal Victorian society, which was full of prejudices about the capacities of women. In his writings and lectures, Freud frequently perpetuated common preconceptions about the opposite sex. For instance, in his 1925 paper entitled "Some Psychological Consequences of the Anatomical Distinction between the Sexes," he declared that the process of the formation of the superego in women could account for "[c]haracter traits which critics of every epoch have brought up against women—that they show less sense of justice than men, that they are less ready to submit to the great necessities of life, that they are more often influenced in their judgments by feelings of affection or hostility."[44] Such views, when voiced by a figure of authority, which Freud undoubtedly was, reinforced the notion of women as passive and morally weaker.

Freud's impact on society and culture cannot be overestimated. Calvin Hall thus describes Freud's significance after World War I: "Psychoanalysis was the rage, and its influence was felt in every theater of life. Literature, art, religion, social customs, morals, ethics, education, the social sciences—all felt the impact of Freudian psychology. It was considered fashionable to be psychoanalyzed and to use such words as subconscious, repressed urges, inhibitions, complexes, and fixations in one's conversation."[45] Even Nin fell victim to this fashion. In one entry she recorded a teasing exchange with her husband—to his confession of jealousy, she was supposed to reply, "My, my . . . a case for Freud [whom I haven't read yet], a real complex."[46] Although Nin had not read Freud's work at that point, she was familiar with his basic concepts, and shortly afterward she began exploring his works, which also must have affected her beliefs.

But not only sexology propagated the inferiority of women. Similar ideas were simultaneously perpetuated in other cultural sites by Victorian scientists, whose influence reached beyond the nineteenth century. Influential anthropologist Paul Broca, for example, measured skulls and brains to prove the intellectual inferiority of women, while Charles Darwin preached that women were biologically weaker, intellectually inferior, and culturally inadequate. His claim that "[i]f two lists were made of the most eminent men and women in poetry, painting, sculpture, music (inclusive of both composition and performance), history, science, and philosophy, with half-a-dozen names under each subject, the two lists would not bear comparison" strikingly resembles Otto Rank's pronouncement (recorded in Nin's diary), "Man was the philosopher and the psychologist, the historian and the biographer."[47] All these men failed to acknowledge that women did not have the same opportunities—a phenomenon that was aptly illustrated by a modernist writer, Virginia Woolf, in her essay "A Room of One's Own." Trying to envision the lot of Shakespeare's imaginary sister, Woolf comes to the conclusion that even if she had had similar artistic aspirations, social expectations would have effectively prevented her from realizing them.

It may seem that French society, popularly imagined as more liberal than the American one, offered women some exciting alternatives to traditional roles. But that was hardly the case. French women at the beginning of the twentieth century inherited stereotypically feminine roles from their nineteenth-century grandmothers. As Benstock observes, "The status of French women has always been deceptive. In their homes, in society, and in the church, their position has remained secure, provided that these institutions found no reason for disapproval. . . . But in terms of real political, professional, economic, and legal power a French woman at the turn of the century was marginal, often overlooked by the system altogether."[48] The position of French women was not, therefore, much different from the position of their peers in other Western countries. Women were responsible for domestic duties, the comfort of their husbands, and care of the children. France was, after all, one of the last countries in Western Europe to grant their women the right to vote. Women affiliated with the artistic community of Paris enjoyed more freedoms—they were not, for instance, constrained by the imperative of heterosexuality and could pursue homosexual relationships—but, as Elizabeth Wilson points out, even this apparent sanctuary of unconventional lifestyles frequently limited woman's role to that of a wife, mistress, muse, salon hostess, or patron.[49]

Immersed in this culture, Nin conceptualizes femininity in rather traditional terms. She frequently juxtaposes masculinity and femininity and gives value to what she considers feminine characteristics. She writes, for example, "The territory of woman is that which lies untouched by the direct desire of man. Man attacks the vital center. Woman fills out the circumference" (*Diary 1,* 184). She therefore sees women as closer to life, maternal, giving, and protective. And she represents herself accordingly. She paints herself as gentle, sensitive, compassionate, and understanding. She emphasizes the fact that she is unable to hate, caricature, or mock and expresses her lack of interest in politics. She strives to create a world of her own, a world that is not affected by the ugliness of the external reality. For example, when she decides to quit the psychoanalytical school, which she took up for a short period of time, she recounts, "I experienced my first knowledge of the monstrous reality *outside*. . . . Doom! Historical and political. . . . And then, with greater, more furious, more desperate stubbornness I continued to build my individual life, as if it were a Noah's Ark for the drowning" (*Diary 1,* 331–32 [original emphasis]).

She also pictures herself as self-sacrificing, putting others' needs above hers. For instance, when Allendy asks her during one of their sessions, "Have you ever wished to surpass men in their own work, to have more success?" she replies that she did not, and she recounts how she made her brother's pianist career possible and how she is currently helping Miller by giving him her own typewriter. And she adds, "I wanted to be married to an artist rather than be one, collaborate with him" (*Diary 1,* 82). What is more, her diary is the search for the father and the guide. For instance, after having finished her psychoanalysis with Allendy, she bemoans the fact that she has no guide: "It saddens me to have become again an independent woman. It was a deep joy to depend on Allendy's insight, his guidance" (194).

At the same time, Nin shows some awareness of the fact that social conditioning turns women into selfless and helpful persons (*Diary 1,* 164–65). She also declares that she does not want to be controlled by men, and she gives her mother as an example of a woman dominated by a man, someone who gave up her music career for the sake of her husband's (110). In another passage in her first *Diary,* she recounts an evening of hysteria, a rebellion, as she puts it, "against my life, against the domination of man, my desire for a free artist life, my fear of not being physically strong enough for it" (309). However, these outbursts of anger are rare, and Nin's concept of femininity generally does not challenge conventional gender roles. Although she occasionally observes the domination of men and yearns for independence, she does not propose any revolutionary solutions. She does not cast away the stereotypical roles that men assigned to women. In the successive volumes of the *Diary,* she cultivates "feminine" qualities, both in her life, by helping others, and in her writing, by attempting to find the feminine mode of expression. Although Nin has frequently been regarded as a feminist icon, her "feminism" was in many respects in opposition to the mainstream feminism of the 1960s and 1970s, which rejected femininity in its traditional guise.

Nin's involvement in the enhancement of her career constituted an important part of her celebrity. Nin very actively participated in the creation of her own legend. She promoted her diary and devoted a lot of energy to see it in print. By publishing the *Diary,* she entered the marketplace. Her *Diary,* like any other book, became a commodity, and in a way, Nin became a commodity herself—she became a marketable personality. Her main contribution to the construction of her public persona consisted in the release of carefully coined self-portraits. These self-portraits, before reaching readers, went through a process of double construction. Nin first recorded her-*self* in the original diary. Then, in preparing the diary for publication, she carefully chose which of the whole spectrum of Nins she wanted to present to the public. Although it would be naïve to assume that Nin had complete freedom in the making of her public self, she did demonstrate a great deal of agency and managed to preserve some integrity by constructing and releasing her portraits as she wanted them to be.

Through the text of her *Diaries* in which she recounted her experiences, Nin crafted her personality. She presented herself in a few highly fashioned textual poses. By highlighting some of her experiences while concealing others, she created a limited number of very neat self-portraits, thus developing a set of self-presentations that she would have to continue to deploy once she began to interact with her audience after the publication of the first volume of the *Diary* in 1966.

three

Public Relations of the Self
Anaïs Nin, Feminism, and Celebrity Authorship

> A book is judged almost entirely by a person's need, and what people respond to is either a reflection of themselves, a multiple mirror, or an elucidation of their time, a concern with their problems, fears, or a familiar atmosphere which is reassuring by its familiarity.
>
> —Anaïs Nin[1]

Although Nin's works were translated into many languages and enjoyed considerable success in France, Italy, Germany, Japan, and the United Kingdom, the Nin persona left nowhere a more durable imprint than in the United States. It was in America that, as Suzette Henke describes it, "an Anaïs Nin cult took root and flourished in the 1960s." It was in America that large audiences would gather to listen to lectures delivered by Nin, who by the 1970s had become "an extremely celebrated writer," as Harriet Zinnes recalled. The prolific years began for Nin in 1966, when volume 1 of her *Diary* was published and caught the attention of intellectuals, academics, and the general public. In volume 7 of the *Diary,* which opens in the summer of 1966 and describes the release of *Diary 1,* Nin recounts the first glimpses of fame: "A month of good reviews, love letters, appearances on television. Has the sniping really stopped? I feel like a soldier on the front, amazed by the silence of the guns, wondering if the war is over. A month which made up for all the disappointments, the poison pen reviews, for all the past obstacles, insults. . . . Suddenly love, praise, flowers, invitations to lecture." Thanks to the success of her *Diary,* not only did Nin's morale soar but also her financial situation was improving. Deirdre Bair records that in 1962 the five books by Nin available then—*Seduction of the Minotaur, House of Incest, Winter of Artifice, Under a Glass Bell,* and *Cities of the Interior*—earned her only $32.56 in royalties. Her annual income rose to $9,500 for 1966, and by the third quarter of 1973 Nin earned $62,000. Her earnings were therefore rising rapidly.[2]

And so was her status. The importance given to autobiographical and confessional literature in the 1970s, the ever-growing women's movement, the rising influence of the young, and the emergence of the counterculture combined with Nin's images of herself as an independent woman-artist that she put forward in the *Diary* turned her into a cultural icon. Nin's name was emblazoned on T-shirts and appeared in crossword puzzles. Her pictures and interviews were published in newspapers and magazines. She made appearances on television, took part in radio programs, and received thousands of adoring fan letters. The popular rock group The Doors made the title of Nin's book *A Spy in the House of Love* their own (to which Nin objected). And in 1970 the first academic/fan magazine devoted to Nin, *Under the Sign of Pisces,* came into existence.[3]

Nin was also awarded many official honors. In 1973, Philadelphia College granted her the honorary degree of Doctor of Fine Arts; in 1974, she was elected a member of the American Academy and Institute of Arts and Letters; in 1975, she was honored by the United Nations in the International Women's Year; and in 1976, she was named Woman of the Year by the *Los Angeles Times.* Nin's works began to be studied in colleges. And Nin herself became a very competent and sought-after public speaker. Although she gave lectures prior to the publication of the *Diary*, the demand for her public appearances increased dramatically after 1966.[4]

During these prolific years, Nin took an active part in the construction of her public image and the management of her career, thus further contributing to the creation of her own legend. She was a very conscious self-marketer and knew the value of a good advertisement. Keenly involved in the process of self-promotion, she frequently sent her books to reviewers, wrote to colleges and universities asking for an opportunity to lecture, and befriended many of her critics. The following excerpt from Nin's letter to her accountant serves as a good example of her marketing awareness: "Harcourt Brace is so stingy with its review and publicity copies . . . I have had to spend almost all my royalties giving copies to excellent reviewers. . . . Every lecture, every foreign contract, every translation, entails gifts, review copies, etc."[5] Nin also continued controlling her image. The previous chapter demonstrates that Nin's *Diary* contains a set of carefully constructed self-portraits. The landscape of Nin's *Diary* is like a French formal garden—ordered and deliberate, with no random elements. During the period of intensified public encounters, Nin, like an adept gardener, did her best to maintain the design of her *Diary* and the shape of her image.

At the same time, as Nin's popularity grew, she had to share the creation of her public persona with her audience. Critics of celebrity culture (such as Richard Dyer and P. David Marshall) point out that celebrity is a common product both of celebrity production—by celebrities themselves and the people responsible for the management of their careers (agents, editors, and publishers)—and of celebrity reception by the public. After 1966, not only were the *Diaries* widely reviewed, but Nin herself became a subject of press articles, interviews, television and radio programs, and even a feature documentary film. By consuming and interpreting the images of Nin, her audience became co-constructors of her public persona. Consequently, Nin developed into a hybrid of self-creation and media invention. This chapter exposes the mechanisms behind this process.

The process of constructing a celebrity is partly universal, as all celebrities are the product of self-invention and media representation, and partly culturally and historically specific—Nin's celebrity is a product of the system of production, circulation, and consumption that was characteristic of the American culture of the 1960s and 1970s. Celebrities were created differently back then than they are in the twenty-first century. Before the widespread use of the Internet, traditional media, such as print, radio, and television, were mainly responsible for maintaining one's fame. For these reasons, "institutional readers"—journalists, reviewers, interviewers, and academics—were especially important to the production of Nin's public persona. They created textual representations that could reach a wide range of readers and were more enduring (and also more accessible) than the interpretations of so-called ordinary readers. "Institutional readers," whose "personal voices," as Charlotte Templin notes, "are magnified by their institutional affiliations," are the ones whose judgments are available to the public. As a result, they have the potential to influence other people's opinions. This chapter therefore deals mainly with institutional readers—reviewers and journalists—and their reception of Nin, as well as Nin's interaction with her public through lectures and interviews. This allows me to examine Nin's celebrity in the process of making.[6]

THE PRESS RECEPTION OF ANAÏS NIN
Nin's Diary on Trial

In the introduction to a bibliography of writings on Nin, Rose Marie Cutting comments on trends in the reviews of the *Diaries*. She says that the first *Diary* received over thirty reviews in 1966 alone (she counts foreign reviews), and according to her, favorable reviews outweighed negative ones by two to one. As for *Diary 2*, there was a decline of interest in comparison to *Diary 1*, but positive opinions outnumbered the negative by three to one. *Diary 3* again received fewer reviews in comparison to the previous volumes, but still there were more positive responses—by two to one. As for volumes

4 and 5, Cutting notes that there was roughly the same number of positive and negative reviews.[7]

Nin's diaries were reviewed in many different publications: influential review magazines (such as *Library Journal* and the *New York Times Book Review*), important journals of opinion (such as the *New Yorker*), and popular magazines (such as *Newsweek*), as well as major American dailies (such as the *Chicago Tribune,* the *Los Angeles Times,* the *New York Times,* and the *Washington Times*). Some publications were very consistent in their opinions. For example, *Library Journal* and the *Nation* assessed the great majority of volumes positively, whereas the *New Yorker* offered only very brief, sardonic, and rather negative comments. Most of the publications, however, recommended the *Diaries* with varying levels of enthusiasm. For instance, the *Los Angeles Times* offered three extremely complimentary reviews (all penned by Robert Kirsch), but these were balanced by two very detrimental ones. Critics also did not agree which of the volumes was the best. Some argued that the first two were the most interesting; others (including those of the *Washington Post*) pointed to volume 4 as the most successful one. William Goyen, reviewing for the *New York Times Book Review,* considered volume 5 "the most unified and shapely," while for Nancy Hoffman in the *New Republic* this volume was not remarkable at all.[8]

The most common evaluation of Nin's diaries was along the lines of successful/unsuccessful writer. Opinions as to whether Nin had succeeded in creating the diary varied. Reviewers were divided into those who considered her *Diary* a work of art and those who saw it as a creative failure. Usually those critics who appreciated the *Diary* treated it as an artistic achievement, and they frequently commented on the fact that it was un-diary-like, whereas those who disliked it accused Nin of lacking in literary craft.

Reviewing volume 1 for the *Los Angeles Times,* Robert Kirsch calls it "one of the most remarkable in the history of letters." He writes that it "becomes an odyssey, more powerful than a novel, though possessed of the same elements, beginnings, a middle, a climax." Karl Shapiro goes as far as claiming that Nin's *Diary 1* "is a new and beautiful kind, shining a strange light on literature itself." Like Kirsch, he finds that the diary has "the full dimensions of the novel (character, 'plot,' exposition, dialogue, causal action, and so on) as well as the normal characteristics of the *journal intime.*" And he adds that Nin's *Diary* "stands the test of the most formal writing without surrendering the charm of authenticity which is usually the sole appeal of autobiographical literature." The last comment is particularly telling, for it reveals a certain anxiety connected with assessing Nin's journal. To praise the *Diary* for its authenticity and intimacy alone seems insufficient, because if it is "just a diary," how can one justify its public existence, and how should it be advertised? Have not thousands of men and women kept their diaries? What, then, makes this one special and worth reading? To overemphasize its formal qualities is like throwing the baby out with the bathwater. If it is too artistic, it risks accusations of being too deliberate, un-diary-like, and even untruthful.[9]

Nonetheless, most critics who commended Nin's *Diary* did so by highlighting its craftsmanship and literary merit. Writing for the *Kenyon Review,* Duane Schneider, the future scholar of Nin's works, regards the second volume as "a well sustained work of art" that distinguishes itself with "the originality of the style, a well-written prose." According to him, "it is as art that the *Diary* commands our attention." In a similar vein, Daniel Stern, who reviewed both *Diary 2* and *Diary 4* for the *Nation,* claims that Nin is in control of her writing, which is well presented and well constructed. He considers her *Diary* the work of a conscious novelist. Responding to volume 4, he suggests, even in the title of his review ("The Novel of Her Life"), that the *Diary* is more than what we usually think about the genre. According to him, Nin's *Diaries* are a "'fictional' representation of the modern era," and thus more like a novel. Similarly, Anna Balakian, assessing volume 4 for the *New York Times Book Review,* notes that Nin's *Diary* is like "no other in the history of letters," and she adds that "the word 'diary' does not do her work justice. If the writing is spontaneous, we see a pattern emerging from the selections that constitute the specific volumes."¹⁰

But Nin's volumes also received diametrically different assessments in which Nin is deemed an unsuccessful writer and accused of being boring, humorless, and too exalted. Writing for the *Christian Science Monitor,* Henrietta Buckmaster claims that there is no discipline in Nin's writing and that Nin lacks the necessary artistic craft. She finds Nin's *Diary* repetitive, stating that the first half of *Diary 1* in particular is "all talk, talk, talk, like a fountain using the same water over and over again." Considering that repetition is a distinctive attribute of the diary genre, one may say that that is a peculiar accusation. Jocelyn Knowles, reviewing *Diary 2* for the *Los Angeles Times,* disparages it as merely a collection of compliments collected in the years 1934 to 1939, adding that "Miss Nin writes without benefit of second thought or evidence of editing. Her idea of a sentence seems to be a series of gushes separated by a series of commas." In the *New York Times Book Review,* Jean Garrigue thinks of "the plotless plot of the [third volume of the] diary" as "the patched quilt of juxtapositions that it was in the first two volumes." She therefore sees the *Diary* as lacking in structure. Evaluating the series of six volumes in the *Village Voice,* Laurie Stone concludes that Nin regards her "passive output" as her major work. This comment reveals Stone's perspective on diary as a genre—diary, according to her, seems to be a mere by-product of life.¹¹

The fact that critics differed so much in their evaluation of Nin's *Diary* and its formal qualities supports Templin's assumption that literary values are constructed and that critics' judgments depend on many factors. Templin maintains that it is impossible for evaluators to "get *outside* experience and values and find a position of objectivity." What decides whether a given literary work is deemed a success or failure are frequently reviewers' attitudes, values, political affiliations, literary preferences, and institutional loyalties. These disparate comments on Nin's *Diary* also illuminate the ambiguous status accorded to life narratives in the 1960s. The genre began to attract some critical interest in the Anglo-American context only in the 1950s, and not only was it a slow start but also critics were very selective in the types of life narratives they discussed. Autobiography—at the expense of diaries, journals, memoirs, and letters—was favored until the 1980s. Yet even autobiography was making only slow inroads into academia. It would not be uncommon, therefore, as Laura Marcus observes, for critics to affiliate autobiographical writings with more-recognized genres. Kate Millett makes a similar observation but one pertaining directly to the reception of Nin's *Diary* in noting that those who consider Nin's work a new kind of novel do so because "novels are respectable and journals aren't." Seen from these perspectives, even positive comments made by critics sound somewhat empty.[12]

Nin was also often evaluated along the lines of insightful/ self-absorbed. Where some critics found a person of great sensitivity, perceptiveness, and honesty (in, for example, reviews in *Books Abroad,* the *St. Louis Dispatch,* and *Newsweek*), others saw only egotism, exaggeration, and delusion (in such publications as the *New Yorker* and the *New York Review of Books*). The former praised her for great perceptions and uncompromising portraits of herself and other characters, admired her for her enormous humanity and sympathy toward her human fellows, and marveled at her power to resist the destruction and corruption of the modern world. The latter derided her dramatic persona of "an injured romantic," as, for instance, the *New York Review of Books* did, accusing her of being "her own best friend" and describing her as being naïve, petty, vain, and hungry for compliments.[13]

Again, these comments are immersed in culture and reflect the growing popularity of the confessional genre on the one hand and a still-powerful suspicion of life narratives as too self-absorbed and devoid of any literary value on the other. Although autobiographical writings were just beginning to receive critical recognition in academia in the 1960s, the genre was increasingly popular with writers and readers. An autobiographical streak could be detected in many literary forms of the period, not only in typical life narratives. In poetry, for instance, the autobiographical impulse was represented by confessional poets, such as Robert Lowell, Sylvia Plath, and Anne Sexton, who wrote boldly about their private experiences and emotions. Also, many well-liked novels of the era—Henry Miller's *Tropic of Cancer* (1961 in the United States), Sylvia Plath's *The Bell Jar* (1963), and Philip Roth's *Portnoy's Complaint* (1969), to list just a few—were inspired by the life circumstances of their authors. At the same time, however, American culture was still influenced by New Critics, who dismissed autobiographical narratives as inferior literary texts or, at best, treated them as marginal material about great works. Sidonie Smith explains, "For the dominant Anglo-American critical tradition . . . autobiographical writing was a suspect mode of 'trivia' or 'personal' writing, the site of writers' flawed notions about their artistic works, and therefore was to be bracketed out of the canon of poetic and narrative texts and critical theory that the implementation of New Criticism enabled in the academy." Assessing Nin's journal, critics not only expressed their views about the qualities of her writing but also participated in a larger debate about the value of life narratives.[14]

Nin's femininity was also on trial. On the *Diary* pages, Nin tried to establish herself as the voice of feminine consciousness, and many reviewers responded to these attempts. Nin was frequently assessed for the femininity she represented: both as a concept and as an embodiment of it. Some reviewers, especially men, perceived Nin as the essence of a woman and the writer of feminine expression. Robert Kirsch, for example, notes in the *Los Angeles Times,* "Of special interest is what she has to say to women. Few women diarists since the 18th century have so eloquently expressed the core of femininity." Of a similar opinion is Professor Harry T. Moore, who writes in the *St. Louis Dispatch,* "The diary is . . . an intense revelation of female experience—the word feminine suggests too many frills and laces on the surface, while this journal really goes to the heart of existence. So, female it is." Although Moore rejects the word *feminine* as an adequate description of Nin, both reviewers seem to refer to the same thing—Nin as an exemplar of true womanhood. Likewise, Saul Maloff, the author of *Newsweek*'s review of volume 2, states that "the reader finally has to admit that Durrell was right the first time—there is something seductive about such relentless femaleness." The piece is accompanied by a photograph of a young Nin sitting on the beach in a swimming costume/summer dress, captioned "Nin: Real female."[15]

For these critics, Nin embodied "femaleness" and "the core of femininity," and their accounts resound with a certain nostalgia for such true womanhood. Their reviews also suggest that femininity is something natural and rooted in the core of existence. Thus, they perpetuated the assumptions of biological essentialism according to which women were/behaved/spoke in certain ways that were distinct from those of men and did so because of natural propensities emanating from their genetic makeup. In the context of the emerging women's movement, such claims can be regarded as an attempt to provide a definition of "proper" womanhood and to signal to other women what it means to be a real woman. Nin was given as an example of womanhood worthy of imitation.

By contrast, many female reviewers distanced themselves from the concept of femininity proposed by Nin. Jean Garrigue, while reviewing *Diary 3* in the *New York Times Book Review*, claims that Nin's insights may be helpful to some women, especially those struggling with rejecting the traditional model of womanhood, but in general she questions Nin's archetypal femininity and her usefulness as a role model for contemporary women. Similarly, Audrey C. Foote, in evaluating volume 6 for the *Washington Post*, expresses her astonishment that "this romantic, delicate very 19th-century lady . . . has become a *monstre sacre* to the young, and particularly to young feminists." Foote believes that Nin's feminism is outdated because Nin fights for women's fulfillment in love and art, rather than sports and career. Jocelyn Knowles, the author of a very negative review of *Diary 2* in the *Los Angeles Times*, is indignant at Nin's attempt to promote herself as the representative of women.

Knowles writes, "Most exasperating is her determination to establish herself as a spokesman for womanhood."[16]

According to the majority of female reviewers, Nin should not be a model for contemporary women (but it is often noted that she is) because the femininity she promotes is at odds with what is regarded as significant for women in the 1960s and the 1970s. The concept of femininity prevalent at that time was influenced to a large extent by the women's movement, which, along with the African American Civil Rights movement and Gay Liberation, was one of the predominant forces shaping the era. The women's movement of the 1960s and 1970s, customarily referred to as the "second wave" of feminism, had, like the first wave, an emancipatory orientation, but unlike the first wave it was to an extent directed against men, who were seen as possessing power and controlling women. *Patriarchy* was a key word used in many feminist debates of the time. A prominent feature of second wave feminism was, as Joanne Hollows points out, a hostile attitude toward traditionally understood femininity. "The identity 'feminist' was predicated on a rejection of femininity," says Hollows, which explains why Nin, considered by many as the embodiment and essence of femininity, was criticized by feminists.[17]

Also, Nin's preoccupation with personal liberation and psychoanalysis as a means of achieving it was in conflict with the social approach and collective action proposed by early feminists. The proponents of liberal feminism—one faction of the feminist movement—were preoccupied with making the public sphere more accessible to women. For them, issues such as free childcare, equal salaries, flexible working hours, equal job opportunities, and access to education, together with free contraception, were at the top of the agenda.[18] Liberal feminism was represented by organizations such as the National Organization for Women (NOW), which was headed by Betty Friedan, the author of the feminist classic *Feminine Mystique* (1963). Another faction of feminism active in the 1960s and 1970s—radical feminism—strongly encouraged a collective, rather than individual, approach as a means of liberation. Radical feminists were responsible for the establishment of thousands of consciousness-raising (C-R) groups throughout the United States. These groups, which consisted of community discussions, were supposed to change women's beliefs about themselves, their relations to men, and their position in society.[19] Nin's insistence on individual emancipation was therefore at odds with the second wave collaborative effort aiming at improving the social status of women.

Reviews and Their Role in Maintaining the Legend of Anaïs Nin

Despite the various levels of enthusiasm expressed by reviewers for Nin's *Diary,* readers acquired similar information in most of the reviews. Consistency of information is especially evident in the case of the assessments of the first volume. Very often, before critics get down to actually summarizing and evaluating *Diary 1,* they provide some background information about Anaïs Nin herself. These pieces of information regarding Nin reveal, however, no more to readers than Gunther Stuhlmann did in the introduction to volume 1, which aptly illustrates the interaction between the production and the reception of the celebrity.

Stuhlmann begins the introduction to the first volume with comments on Nin's legendary status in the literary world. He mentions Henry Miller's laudatory article on the diary, which appeared in 1937 in *Criterion* magazine, in which Miller states that Nin's work will "take its place beside the revelations of St. Augustine, Petronius, Abélard, Rousseau, Proust." Then Stuhlmann discloses the size of the original diary (150 volumes or 15,000 pages of typewritten transcript). And finally, he provides some basic information about Nin's family background, her life prior to 1931, the inception of her diary, and her literary achievement up to the date of publication. Information provided by Stuhlmann (who worked closely with Nin) can be condensed to the following three elements: (1) Nin's status in literary circles and the mention of the long-awaited diary; (2) the story of the beginning of the diary and the size of the original diary; and (3) the account of Nin's origin (family, nationality, childhood).[20]

These elements constantly recur in the reviews of *Diary 1*. Each of the reviews of the first volume includes at least one of these three elements, and some (such as Fanny Butcher's review in the *Chicago Tribune*) have all of them. What readers learn at this stage is therefore very limited and controlled by Nin and people collaborating with her. In effect, those involved in the reception repeat what the production side has given them. The constant reiteration of these three elements perpetuates certain images of Nin and contributes to making her into a legend.

Let us consider the first element that is frequently mentioned in the reviews—Nin's status in literary circles and/or the mention of the long-awaited diary. Some reviews refer to Nin as a legendary or mysterious figure in the literary world. It is very likely that they reiterate here Stuhlmann's words from the introduction: "For more than three decades, Anaïs Nin's monumental diary, or journal, has been the object of much rumor, gossip, and conjecture."[21] And thus, Butcher states that Nin's *Diary* "has become legendary among the literary intelligentsia of two continents." The *Christian Science Monitor* literary critic, Buckmaster, is more suspicious about Nin's position, and she notes, "Anaïs Nin is one of those shadowy figures in the circles of art whose reputation has acquired a mystique. . . . One says knowingly, 'Oh, yes, Anaïs Nin!' without knowing what one is knowing." Thomas Bishop in the *Saturday Review* begins his appraisal in a similar way: "Anaïs Nin has always been a strange, somewhat mysterious literary figure." Such descriptions of Anaïs Nin are in fact constructions of her persona as, at best, legendary, and at worst, enigmatic and vague.[22]

What is more, many reviewers of the first volume speak of Nin's diary as a long-awaited and anticipated work. While it is true that Nin had previously been known to some literary critics, such as Edmund Wilson, and had a small circle of fans, it is hard to imagine that the general public was waiting for the publication of the diary with anticipation. But the reviews give exactly such an impression—as if Nin were a Messiah expected by the world—by writing things like "For a long time, publication of these diaries have [sic] been anticipated" (Kirsch, *Los Angeles Times*); "Miss Nin's rich, rhapsodic, hubris-filled memoir, so solemnly awaited, so piously acclaimed" (Mazzocco, *New York Review of Books*); and "All the while . . . there has been a diary which the world has not seen but has often whispered about" (Moore, *St. Louis Dispatch*).[23]

Interestingly, both positive and negative reviews comment on Nin's diary as a long-anticipated literary work. For example, the reviews of *Diary 1* in both the *St. Louis Dispatch* by the well-known professor of English Harry T. Moore and the *Chicago Tribune* by the retired critic Fanny Butcher indicate this expectancy in their titles: the former is entitled "A Long-Awaited Diary"; the latter, "A Long Awaited Literary Flight." The similar titles, however, are the only thing that these reviews have in common, for their evaluations differ enormously. Their final lines speak for themselves: for Moore, "The book is deep, beautifully done, and always absorbing"; while for Butcher, "With the publication of this portion of the Anaïs Nin diary, a long awaited literary flight to the moon has missed its promised rendezvous." Nonetheless, such statements about the *Diary*, whether positive or negative, play a part in creating an aura of mystery around Nin by perpetuating certain discourses circling around her persona.[24]

As a result, the pattern of responses emerging from reviews of the first volume presents Nin to the public as a mysterious, long-awaited, legendary figure. This pattern is important because it solidifies certain elements of the Nin persona. Examining George Orwell's reception, John Rodden proposes to distinguish between evaluation, "a private act," and reputation, "the cumulative, ultimate consequence of innumerable acts of receiving and approving (or disapproving)."[25] A single review might be insignificant in making the Nin persona, but if the same information is repeated over and over again, then it becomes inextricably associated with her image. Such is the case with the reviews of Nin's *Diary 1*. There is a great uniformity of responses, which recycle the same facts and stories about Nin. Moreover, these facts and stories are provided, and therefore controlled, by people who work closely with Nin. Thus, Nin's celebrity is formed at the intersection of production and consumption.

So what sort of images of Nin circulated in the press in the late 1960s and the early 1970s? Which descriptors, or, to use Rodden's term, "watchwords"—that is, common nouns and adjectives used repeatedly to describe an author—are associated with Nin?[26] Rodden distinguishes between primary and secondary watchwords. For him, descriptions of George Orwell as an "outsider," "loser," and "maverick" are secondary watchwords of the primary watchword "rebel."[27] As far as reviews of Nin's *Diaries* are concerned, many portray Nin as a legendary or cult figure, but while some appraisals give this label a positive slant, others regard Nin as "a woman who is the best exponent of her own cult."[28] The secondary watchwords of the primary watchword *legend* include both positive labels, such as a "heroine," a "myth," and a "prophet," and negative ones, such as "a failed visionary." Another aspect of the Nin persona highlighted in the reviews is her femininity—for some excessive, for others archetypal. Her focus on the self is also frequently reiterated, and whereas some see it as a reason to disparage Nin as a self-absorbed and egocentric writer, "a person of . . . pustular ego," others hail her as "the champion of the feminine inner life" or a "poet of the inner voyage." Finally, Nin's unconventionality often recurs in the appraisals of the *Diary,* in which Nin is portrayed as "the underground goddess," a "princess of the underground," and a "darling of the avant-garde."

These are the portraits of Nin that emerge from the reviews of Nin's *Diary*. It is worthwhile, however, to take a closer look at what does not form part of Nin's image at that time. The most striking absence, in comparison to how Nin's portrait would develop after her death, is sexuality. Contrary to some popular beliefs held today, in the 1960s Nin was not yet lauded as an icon of sexual liberation. This is partly due to the fact that the *Diary* is cautious in its depiction of sexuality. Although it contains some ambiguous passages, such as the account of Nin flashing her breasts to her psychoanalyst, the description of the infatuation with June, and fragments of Nin's erotic stories, Nin's sexuality is not in the foreground. Consequently, reviewers do not emphasize this aspect of Nin's self-portrait either. For instance, when they comment on Nin's erotica included in the third volume, it is usually to commiserate with the poor writer who had to resort to writing pornographic pages to support herself. The fact that the sexual Nin is not singled out for attention is particularly intriguing when we consider that the 1960s is commonly remembered as the decade of the sexual revolution. This omission suggests that either Nin's treatments of sexuality were too weakly developed to be noticed or that the mainstream press chose to avoid the topic.

The Business of Reviewing

Although it may seem that books selected for evaluation are a critic's choice, the reality of the reviewing business is frequently different. Joe Moran argues that reviews, interviews, and cover stories are carefully managed by the publishing houses. Richard Ohmann in his article "The Shaping of a Canon: U.S. Fiction, 1960–1975" quotes a 1968 study that reveals a correlation between the number of advertisements that publishing companies placed in the *New York Times Book Review* and the number of reviews they received from the magazine. He finds that the biggest advertisers got the biggest number of reviews. For Nin the reviewing business was not a secret. She knew, as indicated in the previous chapters, that being published with a prestigious company would guarantee publicity and reviews.[29]

What is important, therefore, is not merely to be reviewed but to be reviewed in the right publication. Ohmann lists the eight most influential review magazines in the United States in the 1960s and 1970s: the *New York Times Book Review,* the *New York Review of Books,* the *New Republic,* the *New Yorker, Commentary, Saturday Review, Partisan Review,* and *Harper's.* According to him, the literary work "had to win at least the divided approval of these arbiters in order to remain in the universe of cultural discourse."[30] Nin's *Diaries* were reviewed by five influential American magazines (as classified by Ohmann). The *New York Times Book Review* assessed all the volumes, and the reviews were rather positive. Additionally, the *New York Times* wrote two reports: one on volume 2 (very brief and scathing), and the other on volume 4 (neutral). The *New York Review of Books* did only one review (of the first *Diary*), and it was rather harsh. The *New Republic* reviewed the fifth and sixth volumes: the former one received a negative appraisal, and the latter one got a neutral assessment. The *New Yorker* included very brief notes on volumes 1, 2, 5, and 6, written in a rather mocking tone. *Saturday Review* pithily mentioned the first volume in an article "Pick of the Paperbacks" and then reviewed volumes 2, 5, and 6. The second volume got a very favorable review from Anna Balakian, and the remaining two received rather negative appraisals.

Although the majority of the cultural arbiters showed little enthusiasm for Nin's work, Nin secured favorable evaluations in what Ohmann considers the most influential review magazine—the *New York Times Book Review*. According to him, "The single most important boost a novel could get was a prominent review in the Sunday *New York Times*—better a favorable one than an unfavorable one, but better an unfavorable one than none at all." The large number of readers of this periodical, reaching about a million and a half in that period, was, as Ohmann suggests, incomparable to any other literary magazine. The *New York Times Book Review* was read widely by intellectuals and academics but also by people who shaped, albeit indirectly, reading preferences, such as bookstore managers and librarians. What is therefore very significant is the fact that Nin's diaries and later her erotica were regularly reviewed by the *New York Times Book Review*. The first volume of Nin's *Diary* got even the prestigious front-page review in this magazine. Penned by Jean Garrigue, the review mainly provided some basic information about Nin and her diary and offered an outline of main events of the volume. At the end, it positively summarized the diary as "a rich, various and fascinating work."[31]

Apart from the prestige of the magazine, the name of the reviewer counts as well because some critics are more esteemed than others. Charlotte Templin and John Rodden, in their respective studies of Erica Jong's and George Orwell's reputations, point to the importance of a writer being supported publicly by another one, especially one who is well-known. Templin remarks, "Recognized writers have tremendous cultural authority and can, as book reviewers or in other ways, single out a new writer for a special kind of attention," and she recounts how significant for Jong's reputation were positive reviews of John Updike and Henry Miller. Yet at the same time, while dividing reviewers into three categories—literary journalists, academic critics, and novelists—she argues that the last group is more prone to extra bias because of the competitive nature of the literary marketplace. She explains, "It would not be unusual for a writer who has asked Jong for a blurb for his [sic] novel—and been refused for any one of a number of reasons—to bear a grudge that would influence his review of a Jong novel at a later date." A writer's power to make or break one's reputation emerges clearly in Nin's relationships with Henry Miller and Gore Vidal.[32]

Not only did Nin portray famous people in the *Diary,* but she also used her well-known acquaintances to forward her career. Nin's most famous best friend was Henry Miller. Both Nin and Miller exploited their friendship to achieve their common goal—to become recognized authors. Their mutual support dates back to the 1930s. During that time, Nin supported Miller financially, gathered money to print his *Tropic of Cancer,* and provided the volume with a laudatory preface. Miller, in turn, tried to help her print the diary, and as early as 1937 he praised it in *Criterion*—an influential modernist little magazine created and edited by T. S. Eliot. Miller's statement—that Nin's diary constituted "a monumental confession which when given to the world will take its place beside the revelations of St. Augustine, Petronius, Abélard, Rousseau, Proust, and others"—was often cited once the diary was published. Cutting observes that Miller's words are "probably the most frequently-quoted encomium to Nin's diary." And although over the years Miller and Nin drifted apart, he always remained her loyal supporter and spoke positively about her writings.³³

Templin considers Miller a prestigious opinion leader, and she points to the vital role he played in promoting Erica Jong's literary career. Miller was a popular, if controversial, literary figure in the 1960s. And before Nin's diary found a publisher, she involved herself in another project, namely, the publication of Miller's letters to her. Miller granted her copyright to his letters in 1962, and his side of their correspondence appeared in 1965 under the title *Henry Miller: Letters to Anaïs Nin*. For the publisher of her novels, Alan Swallow, who was excluded from this publication, the whole endeavor was "trading upon Miller's name."³⁴

Trading it was indeed. How important Miller was for launching Nin's career can be seen in a letter Nin received from her husband Hugh Guiler in January 1965. He wrote,

> Bay offered $500 dollars for your novel, or two of them, if he could get the Miller letters for $600. You remember Peter Owen finally paid $2000 for the Miller letters and Gunther feels you should have at least $1500 for them from Bay. Also, he does not want him to be taking you only as a package with Miller, but feels he should be interested in doing your novels for their own sake. . . . In general Gunther wants to stop anyone from taking you only as a package with Miller, which he thinks is not good for you.³⁵

Two important points emerge here. First, Nin and her agent, Gunther Stuhlmann, were using Miller's letters as bait to entice the publishers. Second, Nin was regarded as Miller's supplement, and Stuhlmann was determined to make Nin into an author in her own right.

Nin herself was aware of Miller's importance to her diary. "He has enormous, almost unbelievable power, because as you know, in America once a name is made, then everything happens," she observed in a letter to her husband in 1965 while preparing her diary for publication. In the same letter, she also mentioned that she and Miller eventually reconciled and he took the diary with him to the hospital to read through it. She noted, "This is a turning point for the fate of the diary." Apart from lending his name to Nin's cause, Miller also expressed positive opinions about her and her works in the media. For instance, in 1966 he penned an article for the *Village Voice* that appeared next to the review of *Diary 1*. Miller presented the *Diary* as an exceptional and candid record of a unique person and commented on the original volumes of the diary that he had seen: "The record is tumultuous, almost unbearably naked, often clairvoyant. . . . It is my impression that no woman has ever written in like manner, and very few indeed are the men who have had the courage to reveal the truth so wholeheartedly." He also paid homage to Nin in the prologue to the feature documentary *The Henry Miller Odyssey,* in which he introduced her as "an author of the now famous Diary . . . an inspiration to, and a protectress of so many striving artists, including yours truly, Henry Miller."[36]

While Miller is an example of how literary support from a known writer may enhance another writer's career, Gore Vidal, Nin's ex-friend, serves as a good illustration of how personal animosity between writers may have negatively influenced Nin's reputation. Vidal wrote a review of *Diary 4* (in which he starred) for the *Los Angeles Times*. It begins with the account of a meeting with Nin during which she asked him for the release of his portrait in volume 4. He implies that she did not show him the entire portrait—"several fine warts were withheld for the current showing." He then reveals some undisclosed details about Nin's life and does so in a very sarcastic way, commenting, for example, that she "played at being a poor artist," while in fact she was married to a wealthy businessman. Eventually, he moves on to an equally sarcastic summary of volume 4.[37]

Vidal's version of *Diary 4* makes Nin look vain and petty. He implies, for instance, that Nin ended her friendship with Maya Deren, a filmmaker, because Deren made her look old in her film. He also insinuates that Nin omitted a lot from the fourth volume, including at least two very meaningful relationships, and he issues a warning to literary historians: "[D]eal warily with Anaïs' 'facts.'" He accuses Nin of both editing out essential elements in her life from the published version and making up certain stories. He writes, "She is dealing with actual people. Yet I would not recognize any of them (including myself), had she not carefully labeled each specimen." He also alleges that her *Diary* was never the honest and secret endeavor that Nin claimed it to be. He quotes Nin as saying, "Writing in a diary developed several habits: a habit of honesty (because no one imagines the diary will be ever read)," and then he comments, "[T]his was written in June, 1946, when I was trying to get Dutton to publish the childhood diary."[38]

For Vidal, as for any creative writer, a review provides a chance not only to evaluate a book but also to show off his imaginative powers and to establish his own authorial persona. His appraisal of *Diary 4* is a piece on its own—funny, witty, and highly readable. In Vidal's case, the review also gives him a chance to distance himself from the portrait of him made by Nin. By deriding Nin, he diminishes her authority. It is highly probable that readers, especially those who admire Vidal and his output, take on his perspective and start regarding Nin as a silly woman who, as Vidal sums her up, "always said 'yatch' instead of 'yacht.'"[39]

The review is accompanied with an eye-catching caricature captioned "Anaïs Nin and Gore Vidal, circa 1945." The caricature depicts Nin and Vidal in bed: Vidal fast asleep; Nin, sitting next to him by the candlelight, is scribbling in what seems to be her diary. The picture therefore quite bluntly suggests that Vidal was not only Nin's friend but also her lover (in both her published and original diary Nin described Vidal as her friend, and, as Kim Krizan rightly notices in her article on the Nin-Vidal relationship, "had Nin had a sexual encounter with Gore Vidal, she would've written about it").[40] Vidal's assessment was a crucial moment in Nin's career—it was one of the first attempts, if not the first one, to provide some serious corrections to Nin's neatly coined image. His review definitely sparked an interest, as Nin was later asked about it in several interviews. The Nin-Vidal relationship also became a theme of the *Village Voice* article "Anaïs Nin vs. Gore Vidal: Bon Mots and Billets Doux." Ann Morrissett Davidon recounts their low-key battles, discusses the nature of their friendship, and wonders how it is possible that two so different individuals with such diverse attitudes and beliefs were once good friends fascinated with each other. And even in 1980—nine years later—Vidal's piece is mentioned in another review. Katha Pollitt, evaluating volume 7 of the *Diary,* refers to Vidal's review, in which he states that Nin "played at poverty," when she asks: "[H]ow else are we to know if her portrait of herself as martyr to her friends is accurate—or, as Gore Vidal has suggested, the fantasy of a wealthy woman who played at Bohemianism?" Gore Vidal's assessment therefore planted the seed of doubt, opened the ground for questioning the truthfulness of Nin's journal, and was an important voice in modifying Nin's image. Whereas the appraisals of the early volumes rarely questioned the gaps in the *Diary,* queries relating to what was left out of the published *Diary* became more and more persistent with later volumes.[41]

There is also another factor that needs to be considered about the reviewing business, namely, Nin's own participation in it. First of all, many of the critics, even these who disliked the *Diary* (such as reviewers from the *New Yorker* and the *New Republic*), agreed that Nin became more mature and less self-focused in volumes 5 and 6. Whether it was a "natural" development of Nin as the person or Nin's response to earlier reviews cannot be determined unequivocally. Nin did admit in the sixth volume of the *Diary* that she retired as its main character. However, it is also a fact that Nin, as Bair notes, collected everything that was written about her, and therefore she knew what reviewers liked and disliked about her *Diary*. It is highly possible that in creating subsequent volumes she responded to criticism leveled at her.[42]

Also, Nin's attitude toward the reviews her works received was far from passive. She often contacted critics either to thank them for favorable comments or to reprimand them for negative ones and to enlighten them about her works. For example, she must have written an accusing letter to Robert Kirsch, the book review editor in the *Los Angeles Times,* for her archive holds his letter in which he thus defends himself: "As a long-time admirer of your work I cannot understand your allegation that I have 'not allowed reputable critics' to review you. I assigned your books to responsible reviewers." Such a reply must have been prompted by her accusing letter to him. Perhaps that is why Kirsch eventually took upon himself reviewing most volumes of Nin's *Diary*. And each of his pieces was an accolade. Later Nin wrote him a thank you letter, saying, "Of all the things which have been said, written about the Diaries, you wrote what has the deepest meaning for me."[43]

Nin also became acquainted with many of her reviewers and critics. Bair remarks, "Through letters, she began friendships with many persons who wrote about her work, including Harriet Zinnes, Wayne McEvilly, Duane Schneider, Benjamin Franklin V, and Nancy Scholar Zee." She also befriended Bettina Knapp, Sharon Spencer, Evelyn Hinz, Lynn Sukenick, Deena Metzger, Daniel Stern, Judy Chicago, and Anna Balakian, and her sister Nona Balakian, who worked for the *New York Times Book Review*. Nin was therefore very skillful in what nowadays is a crucial component of a successful career: networking. Having critics as her friends meant that she could influence their opinions. For example, *Diary 7* contains Nin's letter to Bettina Knapp, reading, "Your review [of the *Novel of the Future*] is wonderful. . . . Do you mind on page 2, line 16, leaving out *'particularly with the creatures of his fantasy,'* as it may be misunderstood. . . . I hope they [the *Village Voice*] take it. It sounds so warm they may suspect a friendship. I hope not."[44]

Finally, many of these reviewers turned into Nin's devoted scholars. Bettina Knapp, Evelyn J. Hinz, Sharon Spencer, Duane Schneider, and Benjamin Franklin V eventually produced full-length studies on Nin's works. The first person to produce a critical study on Nin's work was Oliver Evans. Before he began writing on Nin, he studied Carson McCullers, and Nin reviewed his study in *Books Abroad*. At the beginning of their cooperation, Nin was pleased with his critique of her works. On 11 May 1965, she wrote to Peter Owen, her British editor, "Oliver Evans has just finished a fascinating study of [the *Diary*]. . . . He is the first to write about the Diary, to have total access to it, and the only critic I have fully collaborated with."[45]

Her full collaboration, however, meant constant supervision of Evans's work in progress and a very detailed criticism of it. And Nin never stopped at just criticizing; she also demanded changes. In one of her letters to him, she gave a detailed report on his study and suggested corrections: "Page 20 footnote: 'To the political commitment of the movement, however, Miss Nin has remained steadfastly indifferent.' This may cause trouble later, as the next volume contains my conflict with just such a commitment and dramatization of it. I would perhaps avoid it." In the same letter, she also asked him to refer to her as Anaïs Nin and not Miss Nin, for "Miss Nin sounds like 'Miss Pin,' 'Prim' etc. Is that polite in criticism?"[46]

As Evans's work progressed, Nin became increasingly dissatisfied with it. She accused him of changing his perspective in the last chapter and assessing her work from a realistic point of view. In a reply to her accusations, Evans wrote, "You know I have the greatest admiration for your work. . . . A 60,000 word 'blurb' would be meaningless, and even if I am mistaken in my judgments it is better to be sincere than to be guilty of mere panegyric which no one would take seriously." Deeply disappointed, Nin never spoke about his work positively. When asked at one of her lectures to identify critics who best understood her work, Nin pointed to Evelyn Hinz, and she often gave Oliver Evans as an example of the critics who misinterpreted her works.[47]

Nin the Reviewer

To stay in the spotlight, one may choose to be the author of various media commentaries, as well as a subject. And that is exactly what Nin did. She authored a plethora of different pieces. By writing reviews, press articles, introductions, and prefaces, Nin maintained her fame. Evaluating and recommending others gave her another opportunity to fashion herself.

Nin reviewed several books for the *New York Times;* among them were *The Complete Plays of D. H. Lawrence, Diary of a Century* by Jacques Henri Latrigue, and *Between Me and Life: A Biography of Romaine Brooks* by Meryle Secrest. She also wrote for the *Los Angeles Times,* for which she evaluated a critical study on Carson McCullers by Oliver Evans and two novels (*Miss MacIntosh, My Darling* and *Angel in the Forest*) by one of her favorite contemporary authors, Marguerite Young. Nin's comments were also used as blurbs. She wrote these for *Androgyny: Toward a New Theory of Sexuality* by June Singer, *Knowing Woman* by Irene Claremont de Castillejo, *Midnight Baby* by Dory Previn, *The Motorcycle Betrayal Poems* by Diane Wakoski, *The Painted Bird* by Jerzy Kosinski, *Varèse: A Looking-Glass Diary* by Louise Varèse, and *Woman's Mysteries* by Esther M. Harding, to enumerate just a few. Apart from reviews and blurbs, Nin also provided prefaces and forewords to several books. The poetry collection *Rising Tides: Twentieth Century American Women Poets,* Judy Chicago's *Through the Flower: My Struggle as a Woman Artist,* and Barbara Kraft's *The Restless Spirit: Journal of a Gemini* appeared with introductions by Nin.

The types of books Nin chose to evaluate or recommend further reveal how she constructed her public persona, as they give us an insight into associations Nin was slowly building for herself. As Aaron Jaffe rightly notes, "[L]iterary reputation is in the introducing rather than in the being introduced." Thus, Nin's review of Lawrence's plays highlights her admiration for the author and her understanding of his works and indirectly promotes her own study of Lawrence. Her approval of Marguerite Young's output reflects Nin's own writing style and her fascination with the exploration of the psyche. Young's magnum opus *Miss MacIntosh, My Darling* (1965), running to over two thousand pages written in a poetic, convoluted style, brings to mind the form of Nin's fiction. In endorsing Young's demanding and complex text, Nin authorizes her own fictional works—a strategy identified by Leonard Diepeveen in his article on T. S. Eliot in which he demonstrates how Eliot constructed and instructed his audience in reviews to promote his own writings. "Eliot," Diepeveen claims, "gives his own writing more authority by discussing difficulty in many of his reviews of earlier literature."[48]

Through her reviewing and prefacing practices, Nin consistently crafted her image of a women's representative. Her blurbs for *Androgyny: Toward a New Theory of Sexuality, Knowing Woman,* and *Woman's Mysteries*—all three written by Jungian analysts exploring feminine psychology—are clearly in line with Nin's developing identity as a role model for women, although in a specific way, as the commended works highlight her interest in psychoanalysis and psychological liberation.

Nin was particularly keen on appraising and recommending life narratives. She positively reviewed *Diary of a Century* by Jacques Henri Latrigue and *Between Me and Life: A Biography of Romaine Brooks* by Meryle Secrest. Both works, not accidently, are about French artists—Romaine Brooks, a painter and lover of Natalie Clifford Barney, and Jacques Henri Latrigue, a painter and photographer whose photos became popular in the 1960s. These appraisals establish her as an international figure and highlight the fact that she used to live in Paris.

Nin also supported autobiographical endeavors of young women. She composed an introduction to an autobiography by one of the leading feminist artists of the 1970s—Judy Chicago. Chicago was the author of the popular multimedia installation *The Dinner Party,* the aim of which was to celebrate the female achievements in arts. The two women met at a party in Los Angeles in 1971, and Nin, who had read Chicago's essay "My Struggle as a Woman Artist," encouraged her to develop it into a full-length memoir, which eventually was published in 1975 as *Through the Flower: My Struggle as a Woman Artist.* The theme of Chicago's memoir mirrors the subject of Nin's journal, as it revolves around the artist's development. Both women describe personal and social obstacles they encountered in their lives.

Another young woman endorsed by Nin was Barbara Kraft. Kraft met Nin in 1974 at a creative writing workshop conducted by Nin. Their collaboration quickly turned into friendship, and Kraft became a loyal companion during the difficult last three years of Nin's life, when she battled a terminal illness. Nin persuaded Kraft, then a wife of a well-known composer and musician, to release her diary. *The Restless Spirit: Journal of a Gemini* was published in 1976 with a preface by Nin. Like Chicago's work, *The Restless Spirit* recounts Kraft's fight for individual freedom.

Consequently, through promoting others, Nin constructed a portrait of a woman-focused international figure who was an expert in experimental and autobiographical writing. The works she recommended were in line with her *Diary* self-portraits. She brought attention to the struggles of women artists, accentuated her love for D. H. Lawrence, emphasized the importance of psychology, and underlined her affiliation with writers practicing poetic prose.

Reviewing is an important (if underexamined) process, as Templin indicates, and it is so for at least three reasons.[49] First, it is the first stage in assigning value to literary work. Reviews, especially those written by prominent figures or published in noted magazines, can contribute to the success or failure of a book, influence future critics, and determine whether the academic community will decide to incorporate the book into its curriculum. Second, and more important, reviews constitute a space where contemporary values are displayed and negotiated. And finally, the aspect that is most significant for this study, reviewing is an integral part of the celebrity formation. Reviewers co-construct Nin's public persona by singling out certain aspects of her *Diary* persona for either praise or criticism. But reviewing is just one mechanism of the celebrity construction. Reviews are a response to Nin's *Diary* persona, but this response can receive a limited reaction from Nin. To examine Nin's persona in the process of making, I turn to spaces where Nin was able to negotiate her image more actively, namely, her public performances, particularly interviews.

NIN'S PUBLIC PERFORMANCES

The presence of the author in the public eye has become a crucial element of the modern literary career. As Loren Glass observes, "[T]hrough live readings, interviews, and promotional appearances, authors were increasingly expected to offer up their personalities as a promotional component of their work in the literary marketplace."[50] Nin was aware of the importance of public encounters with her readers and gave many lectures and interviews. They provided her with an opportunity to maintain the image that she launched in her *Diary*. Speaking in public gave Nin a chance to either reinforce or amend the self-representations of the *Diary* and to engage with criticism directed at her in reviews and articles. Although, as volume 7 (published posthumously) reveals, Nin occasionally grew tired of her fame (see the analysis of *Diary 7* in chapter 4), she performed the role of a public author extremely well.

Making Mark Twain a case study for his second chapter, Moran shows how various media reinforced Twain's fame. He demonstrates that newspapers and magazines created representations of Twain that triggered the desire to meet the "real" person, and this desire was then fulfilled through lectures given by the author. The same phenomenon is apparent in Nin's public life. It is a self-perpetuating machine: the more active and publicly visible Nin is, the more the media notice her, and the more the public wants to see her on stage.[51]

Nin began lecturing in the 1940s and 1950s. A real demand for Nin as a public speaker increased, however, after the publication of the *Diary*. Between 1966 and 1973, Nin lectured widely. Bair notes that "Anaïs Nin realized how much her personal appearance enhanced the sales of her books and she did everything she could to capitalize on it, including registering with the respected W. Colton Leigh Lecture Agency." Hinz mentions that Nin was the most active as a speaker between 1966 and 1973, while Noël Riley Fitch records sixty lectures from the fall of 1972 to the spring of 1973 alone. Similarly, while commenting on the interviews given by Nin, Cutting observes that Nin was one of the most frequently interviewed of twentieth-century authors, and Wendy DuBow relates that most of these interviews took place between 1966 and 1972.[52]

Recalling Nin's popular lecturing tours in the 1960s and in the 1970s, Estelle Jelinek writes, "Nin has traveled across the country speaking at colleges and feminist events, sometimes solo, sometimes in conjunction with other women. Always it is she, however, who is billed as the main attraction; it is her picture that accompanies announcements of the events in local newspapers. And it is her performance that the thousands of women, overwhelmingly white and middle class, wait for in awed expectation. Radicals, conservatives, feminists, Marxists, librarians, teachers, housewives, students, poets—all come to celebrate the idol." Her growing fame is what permitted Nin's name to begin to be used for marketing purposes, particularly advertising events, and her picture to be printed in newspapers to lure the audience. But through these public encounters, Nin also promoted herself and her works, which were frequently on sale during her lectures. Sometimes she arranged book selling herself. For instance, before her arrival for a lecture at Southern Illinois University, she sent a letter asking for two favors: not to mention her relationship with her husband, whose films she planned to show, and to make her books available during her visit. This self-serving attitude provoked negative criticism from some critics. Jelinek, for example, strongly criticized Nin for using the women's movement events as a sales opportunity. She states, "I am not impressed with her appearances at fund raising events for women's centers or her promotion of women's journals because I see these . . . as opportunistic efforts to spread her name and sell her books."[53]

Apart from enhancing her visibility, Nin's public appearances also brought her financial gain. In fact, Linde Salber claims that lectures and meetings, not sales of her writings, were the main source of Nin's income after the publication of the *Diary*. Indeed, the more famous Nin became, the more she was able to charge for the lectures and speeches. For example, in November 1963, Nin bemoaned in a letter to her husband Hugh Guiler that "UCLA gives 2500 for three lectures to Carson, Moravia, Tennessee, and here I am at 100 a shot." Ten years later, as Bair reports, she lectured for a minimum fee of $750, and in 1974 she was offered as much as $1,000 for a lecture in Fresno.[54]

A critical study of Nin's performances has been carried out by Elyse Lamm Pineau, who focuses on unpublished audiotapes of Nin's lectures and discussions. Pineau examines how Nin enacted her diary persona during those events. She argues that Nin becomes an embodiment of the legendary self created in the *Diary*. She examines Nin as "a living text" who "speaks from within the text rather than about it, working actively to blur her identities as author and subject." According to Pineau, during lectures, Nin gave the impression that the three layers of her experience—"her lived reality as the writer of the *Diary,* her inscribed reality as the Diary heroine 'Anaïs,' and her performance reality as a celebrity lecturer"—were "in seamless continuity." Pineau's analysis of Nin's opening remarks also reveals how Nin created an atmosphere of intimacy and complicity with her audience, inviting them to share the responsibility for the event, thus giving them a sense of sisterhood and community that was especially important in the early stages of the women's movement. Pineau also identifies two strategies that Nin used to maintain control over the informal discussion that normally followed the lecture (known as *furrawn* [from Welsh], which means "the intimate talk"). Nin demanded from the readers familiarity with her *Diary* and refused to answer questions she considered too personal.[55]

Because Pineau has already provided a very useful critique of Nin's lectures, I focus mainly on the interviews and occasionally refer to the official version of her lectures, *A Woman Speaks,* the existence and shape of which is additional evidence of Nin's active participation in the construction of her public persona and the enhancement of her career. *A Woman Speaks* was edited by Evelyn J. Hinz, one of Nin's critics/friends, and authorized by Anaïs Nin herself.

Published in 1975, it consists of Nin's lectures, seminars, and some interviews, rearranged to fit neatly into the eight chapters into which the book is divided. Three main themes run through the collection. First, Nin emphasizes the importance of a strong inner life. Second, she applies the importance of a strong inner core to women, stating that the women's movement is too focused on the external—legal and cultural—obstacles. She then highlights the inner, psychological barriers (such as guilt, timidity, and lack of confidence) that prevent women from fulfilling their potential, and she insists that women should work first on getting psychologically unrestrained. Third, she stresses the importance of the artist and the creative process to our lives. She regards the artist as the magician who "holds the anti-toxins to cure us when we are shattered." In *A Woman Speaks,* Nin therefore strongly defends her views about the roles of psychology, artists, and the women's movement. The fact that Nin's lectures were collected, edited, and published indicates, once again, Nin's urge to shape and control her image.[56]

Interviews as the Common Ground for Image Making

An interview is an interesting illustration of how a public image of a person is produced. An interview is a space where an image is negotiated between an interviewer and interviewee, where two sides of celebrity making—production and reception—interact. And this interaction is crucial because, as Brenda Silver explains in her study of the Virginia Woolf icon, "The meaning of the star image . . . is never divorced from a production/consumption dialectic in which consumers are potentially as significant as producers." This dialectical process of celebrity construction is nowhere more evident than in interviews: an interviewee belongs to the production side of the celebrity making, while an interviewer, who serves, at least initially, as an audience, a consumer of a celebrity, quickly turns into an active and quite powerful producer of celebrity images. Thus, in interviews the power of creating an image is divided between an interviewee and an interviewer.[57]

The interviews conducted with Nin represent a range of different media. She was interviewed on television, on the radio, and in the press. The press interviews came out in newspapers (such as the *San Francisco Chronicle* and the *New York Post*), magazines (such as *Everywoman, Mademoiselle, New Woman, Ramparts Magazine,* and *Vogue*), and journals (such as *Chicago Review, Helicon Nine: A Journal of Women's Arts and Letters, Moving Out: A Feminist's Literary and Arts Journal, New Orleans Review, Shantih: A Quarterly of International Writings,* and *Twentieth Century Literature*). It becomes quickly apparent that the medium of an interview and the audience for which it is intended determine to a considerable extent the content and style of an interview and consequently the image of Nin.[58]

The content of the interviews can be broadly divided into nine most frequently recurrent themes:

- the story of Nin's life
- the diary
- Nin's growth as an artist and a woman
- Nin and other artists
- Nin's writings and work routine
- psychoanalysis
- the women's movement
- Nin's current status and her good relationship with students
- love, sex, and sexuality

These various topics are not, however, distributed evenly through the interviews, and what is in a given interview depends greatly on the medium used and the audience at which the interview is aimed. While some subjects, like "the diary" or "Nin and her relationship to other artists," can be encountered in any type of interview, other themes are almost exclusive to certain media outlets. For instance, interviewers for newspapers and magazines tend to focus on Nin's life story, while interviewers for literary journals almost never ask Nin about that subject. Conversely, interviews in newspapers and magazines rarely present Nin's writings in detail, whereas journals devote a lot of space to thorough discussions of Nin's novels, writing style, or her daily writing routine. As another example, while Nin's attitude toward, and her status in, the women's movement are widely commented on in the majority of the interviews, those in journals (with the exception of the feminist *Moving Out: A Feminist's Literary and Arts Journal*) and newspapers (with the exception of the *San Francisco Chronicle*) ignore this topic altogether.

The interviews differ not only in their content but also in their style. In this respect, the interviews that are turned into articles—that is, those that instead of taking the form of question and answer have been turned into unified texts—are the most outstanding. Nin's statements have been paraphrased or inserted in the form of direct quotes, but the main part of such converted interviews consists of an interviewer's descriptions and impressions of Nin. This dramatically changes the presentation of Nin. The interviews turned into articles usually include more comments on Nin's appearance, dress, voice, and demeanor than standard question/answer interviews do. The vocabulary included in the converted interviews is also considerably different. The language used is vivid and full of elaborate epithets, striking comparisons, and witty remarks. All the newspaper interviews and one magazine interview (from *Mademoiselle*) fall into this category. If the converted interviews represent one end of a style continuum, the journal interviews represent the other. The journal interviews are generally composed in a very professional manner. There are no jokes, catchy phrases, or sharp comments. They focus on literature—on Nin the writer, her literary output, and her writing style.

Take, for example, the way in which Nin is introduced in *Chicago Review* and *Mademoiselle*. The former includes a short introductory note on Nin before proceeding to questions/answers. The note reads as follows: "Although her works survived in relative isolation for many years, Anaïs Nin has now become a resonant voice for many readers, especially women, primarily through her published *Diaries*. The collage of her life in Louveciennes and Paris . . . , of her work as a lay analyst with Otto Rank in New York, and [of] the world of writers and artists in America is the rich substrate for her novels." This very eloquent and rather formal introduction differs noticeably from the opening paragraph of the *Mademoiselle* interview, which begins in the following way: "She sits erect in her chair, hands folded in her lap like a well-behaved child, 20-year-old legs crossed at the ankles. Nothing has prepared me for her—neither her pictures nor descriptions by writers who've seen her recently. In 1970, Anaïs Nin is the same size and shape as during her years in Paris in the '30s." This tone and style are maintained throughout the rest of the article.[59]

The subjects tackled by *Chicago Review* and *Mademoiselle* are also poles apart. The former concentrates mainly on Nin's literary achievements, while the latter includes, for instance, three paragraphs devoted to clothes that Nin wears—a topic traditionally associated with the women's magazine. As a result, *Chicago Review* introduces Nin the writer, whereas *Mademoiselle,* in an attempt to relate Nin to its readers, highlights the fashion-conscious Nin. This shows that an interviewer, frequently guided by the interests of an audience for whom the interview is intended, is likely to focus on those aspects of the celebrity that correspond with their readers' likings. Consequently, consumers of various media outlets encounter different Nins.

As another example, in an interview for *Everywoman,* the women's magazine, many questions posed to Nin by Karla Jay regarded women and the contemporary issues of interest to them. Nin was asked, for example, whether she believed that her diary would help women develop new literary forms, instead of imitating those of men; who her favorite woman writer was; and in what ways women's liberation had affected her life and consciousness. In an interview with Jeffrey Bailey in the *New Orleans Review,* whose intended audience is classified by education rather than gender, Nin was asked an entirely different set of questions, and women were not the center of the discussion. The subject of women's liberation simply appeared in the course of conversation, and we may assume that Nin was asked more about this issue only because it came up. The interviewer himself seemed to be more interested in Nin's famous friendships, her house in Louveciennes, her life in 1930s Paris and in 1940s New York, and her writing routine. Each of these interviews therefore produces *a* Nin public persona with certain highlighted attributes and characteristics. While the interview with Karla Jay produces Nin the women's representative, the interview with Jeffrey Bailey brings into being Nin the writer. Nin thus exists in various guises for various readers. The Nin they will remember largely depends on where they have encountered her.[60]

As for Nin's contribution to making her persona through interviews, despite the fact that she was not in charge of the questions posed to her during an interview, she was able to control and manipulate these questions to her own advantage. She could actively negotiate the image that interviewers were trying to craft for her through their questions. For instance, at some point in the interview for the *New Orleans Review*, Bailey asked Nin the following question: "How do you react to the criticism . . . that you are self-obsessed; . . . [critics] seem fond of using the term 'Narcissistic.'" On the one hand, simply by bringing up this common accusation against Nin, he perpetuated a certain image of Nin, Nin as a narcissist, but on the other hand, because it is an interview, and not an article or a review, Nin had an opportunity to defend herself. And she did, by answering, "I laugh at this criticism because I think it comes from Puritanism. I think it comes from the Puritan conception that looking inward is neurotic, . . . that writing about yourself is immodest." The image of Nin created in the interviews is therefore jointly constructed between Nin and her interviewer.[61]

Interviews and Forging the Identity of a Women's Representative

Because the portraits of Nin created in interviews are a joint creation of Nin and her interviewers, it is worthwhile to investigate Nin's developing identity of a women's representative and the role of interviews in that process. In his study *How Our Lives Become Stories,* Paul John Eakin makes a general claim about narratives and their role in shaping our identity, stating that "narrative plays a central, structuring role in the formation and maintenance of our sense of identity." To put it simply, how we talk or write about ourselves determines to an extent who we are. This point can be illustrated by scrutinizing interviews with Anaïs Nin at different stages of her career. These various interviews not only document the change in Nin's identity, a change that might be considered highly strategic, but also help this change to happen because interviews that prompt us to tell the story about ourselves help to shape our, or in this case Nin's, identity.[62]

The first interview of interest here is a radio interview from 1965, when only Nin's novels were available and the first volume of the *Diary* was being prepared for publication. Introducing Nin, the interviewer, Frank Roberts, announced that they were going to discuss the recently published letters from Henry Miller to Nin and her *Diary* that was to appear soon. And indeed these issues are the main focus of their conversation. Nin recounts how she met Miller, how their friendship began and developed, how she managed to get to know the side of Miller that had been hidden from the world. As far as Nin's relationship to the women's movement is concerned, there is not a single mention of it. And while this may be explained by the fact that the movement was in its budding stage, another element of this talk is striking, namely, the way in which Nin presented her *Diary*. She recommended it as the completion of the Miller letters, saying that "the diary adds to the letters. What is not in the letters is here."[63] Thus, her *Diary* was presented, or in other words, advertised, as a source of extra information about Miller and other well-known personages, rather than a work on its own. As a result, the major image of Nin that this interview puts forward is Nin as Henry Miller's associate.

Whereas in later interviews Nin would emphasize her struggle as a woman and an artist as the main theme of the *Diary,* in 1965 she maintained that the major asset of the *Diary* was the portraits of people she knew. Nin said, "I sometimes jokingly call the diary 'the diary of others' because everyone's association with a diary is that it's a self-portrait. My diary contains very large portraits of major characters and many minor characters." And even when the interviewer prompted her to perhaps rethink her statement by saying that "this diary is a self-study as much as it is a study of others," Nin insisted, "It certainly is me in relation to others, but I do feel that I have a gift for bringing out others, what you might call a feminine gift; therefore, the person that I'm relating to is as complete as my own personal growth." She therefore almost erases herself, and her mention of "a feminine gift" suggests that Nin attended to others before she attended to herself; she implies that in making portraits she gave as much as attention to others as she did to herself. This presentation of the *Diary* would be completely modified in later interviews.[64]

In another radio interview, conducted by Clare Loeb in 1970, and entitled, tellingly, "Anaïs Nin on Women's Liberation," Loeb introduced Nin as "an authority and a considerable oracle" on women's liberation, and she explained that Nin had been invited to the studio to express her opinion on that subject matter, which indeed constitutes a large part of the discussion. Thus, five years after the previously discussed interview, in which Nin's relation to the women's movement did not come up, Nin was proclaimed an expert on the subject.[65]

However, as becomes evident in the course of the interview, Nin's ideas on the emancipation of women were not necessarily in accord with the ideas represented by the women's movement, which by then was in full swing. At that stage of her career, Nin perceived inner inhibitions as the main problem for the development of women, and she suggested self-examination as the main solution to those interior obstacles, while the women's movement, especially organizations such as NOW (the National Organization for Women), highlighted the social difficulties and championed collective action and political reforms as an answer to these problems. Nin also believed that cultural and social restraints allowed women to develop some positive qualities, such as compassion, and in voicing such beliefs, she reinforced the stereotype of women as caregivers and nurturers, whereas the movement tried to distance itself from such labels, seeing them as harmful for women's status.

Nonetheless, the fact remains that despite Nin's disparate opinions, she did take part in the discussion about the women's movement, thus both contributing to the discourse on feminism and describing herself in terms of it. Also, her interlocutor, apart from directly characterizing Nin as a specialist on women's liberation, makes numerous attempts during the interview at connecting Nin to the movement. It is evident when Loeb tries to reconcile Nin's idea of individual and psychological liberation with the social and political outlook of the movement. At some point in the interview, Loeb comments, "Certainly it's become well understood that nothing can happen politically without a transformation in consciousness. I guess that's what consciousness-raising is about. But again, no matter how much consciousness-raising one has, can we really be affected without some kind of introspection." This observation, which was supposed to bring together Nin's psychological approach with the social approach of the movement, is a great example of the powerful role of an interviewer in co-constructing a celebrity persona. Nin made use of the language her interviewers employed to clarify her position in and toward the women's movement.[66]

This is apparent, for instance, in the way Nin presented her *Diary* during this particular interview. It was no longer introduced, as was the case during the interview with Frank Roberts, as the story of others; now it was the story of Nin's struggles and the exemplar of the inner self-examination. She says, "The value of the diaries lies in their being a notebook of this very difficult journey, of peeling off what you have been taught, how you have been conditioned." The presentation of the *Diary* as an exploration of her growth and a testimony to her fight with obstacles, rather than as a sourcebook of famous friends' portraits, is the recognition of her real audience and their needs.[67]

When Nin was talking about her in-press *Diary* in 1965, she did not know who her readers would be and what would appeal to them. And because her publishers had always emphasized the portraits of the famous as the main asset of the *Diary,* Nin seemed to adopt their views. By 1970 she knew who read her and what was appreciated about her writing. Her main audience consisted of women and the young who identified with her personal liberation. And although Nin's views on many issues differed from the views of the women's movement, she did appropriate parts of the discourse of the movement and started to present herself and her *Diary* using language that was characteristic of the women's emancipation of the 1960s. She embraced identity that both her interviewers and, more generally, her readers created for her. Her audience was therefore instrumental in constructing her public persona, in the sense that they prompted Nin to become who they thought she was.

In 1971, in another radio interview, Nin was asked to explain her position toward the women's movement. She provides this brief account of her changing relationship with the movement:

> [A]t first . . . I was a little amazed by the mass, group movement. . . . But then I met some very remarkable young women, and I began to learn from the movement things I didn't know, things outside of the range of my experience. I learned from them something that the individual struggle doesn't teach you—that is, how do you solve these problems. If I was the victim of an abortion, how do I manage that? I realized these women were answering and solving some of these problems. . . . I became really very much interested. Finally, I have connected with the women's liberation movement in Harvard. We had a long talk where we tried to make a bridge between two ways of approaching liberation: one psychological and the other social.[68]

In this interview, Nin presents herself as a person who managed to connect with the movement. Her initial attitude toward the movement is described as one of surprise, followed by curiosity, and then by understanding. Although Nin did not compromise on her ideas, she was willing to accept some of the views of the women's movement and negotiate a common ground. This short excerpt also indicates that through interaction with her audience, Nin acquired a better understanding of the movement, and with each interview she became better equipped to talk about that subject. As a result, Nin was able to find a common language with the movement and pictured herself as a part of it. She therefore took on the role that was created for her by her audience—the role of the women's representative. Interviews played a central role in this process: they gave Nin an opportunity to form, express, confront, and rethink her ideas, and thus they contributed to the process of making and remaking her identity.

I do not mean to imply, however, that this process of acquiring a new identity was linear and chronological or that Nin went from presenting herself as a nonfeminist one year to depicting herself as a full-fledged women's leader another year. Nor do I want to suggest that from 1970 on, Nin was regularly identified as a women's representative. This process was, of course, much more complex and erratic, and different interviews stressed various aspects of her persona at various points. But there certainly was an evident tendency on Nin's part to acknowledge the importance of the women's movement, or at least certain aspects of it, just as there was a lot of eagerness among some interviewers to situate Nin against the feminist background.

Nin's acceptance of the women's movement seems to be a very clever step that can be regarded as one of Nin's strategies of self-promotion. The women's movement could bring Nin more readers, if only by recommending her books, inviting her to lecture, or writing about her in their magazines. It can be therefore said that Nin appropriated some feminist ideas to her own advantage. This new identity—Nin the representative of women, Nin the feminist—was used, for example, to advertise Nin's works. However, the same applies to the women's movement, which also appropriated Nin. As a relatively new social force, it needed famous "faces" to support and promote it. And because Nin was very popular with the young and women, in shoring up the movement, she could attract new followers. She was therefore of use to the women's movement as its supporter. Nin and the women's movement thus formed a symbiotic relationship.

A good example of such symbiosis and mutual gain is apparent in an interview for *Second Wave: A Magazine of the New Feminism,* which is a partial transcript of the discussion between Nin and members of the Boston-based organization Female Liberation. The discussion took place a day after a sponsored evening with Anaïs Nin organized by this group. The joint effort to understand each other's viewpoints can be clearly seen. At the beginning of the talk, the participants of the discussion tried to explain their attitude toward Nin and her writings. One of them, Nancy Williamson, says, "We tried to describe [during the event that was open to the public and preceded the discussion] how we see you and your work in relation to the women's movement. We know that there is hostility, that what you say about individual responsibility is misconstrued to exclude collective action." They therefore attempt to clarify any misconceptions concerning Nin's approach to an organized effort as if they wanted her to be more in accordance with the movement's ideals; they try to salvage Nin for the movement.[69]

And when later Nin asked whether they found her writings useful and what else she could do for the movement—a question that itself is a very symbolic gesture toward the movement—Williamson replied, "What we hoped would happen last night was to bring you together with the women's movement in a situation where people from a variety of places would be present. It wasn't just a movement event." Another participant, Evelyn Clark, added, "Our job is to create ways to broaden the movement." And Williamson further elaborated "The magazine [*The Second Wave*] is one of the ways we've created so far. And bringing you here is another." Perhaps because of Nin's ambivalent position toward feminism and her ambiguous status within the women's movement, Nin was able to attract an audience that normally would not be interested in the movement. People who came to such events might do so not because of their interest in the movement but because of their interest in the celebrated author of the *Diary*. Nonetheless, it gave the organizers an opportunity to introduce their ideas to new audiences and to spread their message. Nin's name was thus used to attract a wider audience and possibly to recruit new supporters of the movement.[70]

So, on the one hand, some groups within the women's movement considered it beneficial to engage Nin in women's liberation. As a result, articles on or interviews with Nin could be found in such feminist press as *Ms., off our backs,* and *Second Wave. Ms.* magazine, for instance, reprinted fragments of Nin's *Diary* on a few occasions, and Nin's name appeared on two of their petitions: "We Have Had Abortions," a petition that was part of a campaign to legalize abortion; and "Petition for Sanity," which argued for the freedom of sexual choice. In addition, after Nin's death, Alice Walker, a renowned writer and a regular contributor to *Ms.*, provided a very personal, if critical in parts, obituary. On the other hand, Nin noticed the impact of the movement on women and its significance to her own career. She became more willing to embrace some of the movement's ideas and even went so far as to declare herself a feminist in one of her lectures, saying, "I don't know what a 'radical feminist' is, but I *am* a feminist."[71]

Nin also started to write on feminism. In 1972, she wrote two articles on the women's movement. One, entitled "Notes on Feminism," was written for the *Massachusetts Review;* another appeared in the *New York Times* with the title "Liberation: A Simultaneous Happening." The former carries the message that Nin conveyed in many of her lectures, some of which are included in *A Woman Speaks*. She begins by saying that her contribution to the women's movement is psychological. She maintains that political problems can only be solved by emotionally strong and mature individuals, and that is why she stresses self-development. She also believes that women are more humane and sensitive than men and that they should nourish these qualities. Finally, she suggests that instead of imitating men, women should create and define the world on their own terms.[72]

The latter article, perhaps more significant because of the status of the newspaper in which it was published, was Nin's attempt to explain the origins of the movement. Nin attributed the liberation of women to psychoanalysis, the organized political effort of the women's movement, and the formation of consciousness-raising groups. Estelle Jelinek later criticized Nin for this article in the feminist journal *off our backs*. She was indignant that Nin was being given a role as a voice of the women's movement, and she accused Nin of ignorance about the foundations and development of feminism.[73]

This new identity—Nin the representative of women, Nin the feminist—was used to advertise Nin's works. Differences between how the first and the fourth volume were advertised highlight this shift. The first volume was advertised solely through quoting the positive reviews and statements about the *Diary* by well-known people. People whose opinions are quoted include writers Marguerite Young and William Goyen, and critics including Maxwell Geismar, Jean Garrigue from the *New York Time Book Review* (in small print there is the statement that it was a front-page review); Robert Kirsch from the *Los Angeles Times*; Harry T. Moore from the *Chicago Daily News*; Karl Shapiro from *Book Week*. *Newsweek* is also cited. The quotations, unsurprisingly, are full of strong approving words, such as "rich . . . fascinating work," "a fantastic and great book," "remarkable," and "an exalting investigation."[74]

The advertisement for *Diary 4*, apart from using the usual praise by others, foregrounds Nin's popularity among women. The first sentence of the advertisement, in a big bold font, reads, "She was liberated long before women dared use the word," and later she is described as "one of the first women to try psychoanalysis," as well as "the rage of the college campuses, a truly independent, free-thinking woman." A review from the Austrian *Die Presse* describes Nin as "perhaps the most interesting, the most emancipated woman of her world, a very impressive woman in every respect." Nin is therefore advertised this time as a champion of female liberation.[75]

The press also responded to the new identity. For example, the *San Francisco Chronicle,* in reporting on an event called "Female of the Species," claims that Nin's participation caused the sale of all 1,000 tickets for the event and describes her as "the new heroine of San Francisco's ticket-buying women's movement." The *Los Angeles Times* mentions Nin in an article titled "500 Attend Ceremony for *Times* Women of the Year," which describes the event, during which Nin was one of ten women who were honored with the title "Woman of the Year" in 1976. Later, the same newspaper devoted a whole article to Nin, dubbing her "Feminism's Beacon." The *Wall Street Journal* titled its review of *A Woman Speaks* "A Feminist Writes without Hostility," and Nin's *Diary* is recommended in the *Village Voice* article "What Should You Give a Feminist for Christmas," along with Kate Millett's *Flying* and Simone de Beauvoir's *All Said and Done,* as a possible Christmas gift for a feminist.

Press reports, however, do not always regard Nin's involvement in the women's movement positively. The *Village Voice* article "Who Chose These Women, and Why?" assesses an event held at the Edison Theatre on November 1972 that featured Nin and three budding artists. The author, Bertha Harris, finds that putting Nin together with inexperienced artists was a failure, and she calls Nin "a crowd gatherer." She believes that the budding artists would be better off if staged without Nin, who was far too experienced an artist. Harris is also skeptical about the feminist message or the aesthetic value of the whole show. About Nin's performance she writes, "Anaïs Nin lowered her mask, picked up her 'Diaries' and once again there appeared a woman who is an artist, who seeks to be feminist, speaking primarily on the thinking and doings of men."[76]

The new Nin also got various responses from self-declared feminists. For instance, Estelle Jelinek's article, which first appeared in 1974 in *off our backs* under the title "Anaïs Reconsidered," is one of the harshest attacks on Nin. In the article, Jelinek strongly objects to Nin's so-called feminism, and she considers Nin's concept of woman as "an alternate form of sexism." For Jelinek, Nin embodied traditional femininity. She explains that Nin celebrated such traits as female intuition, sensitivity, and ability for compassion, which have usually been used against women. Referring to Nin's *Diary* and her need for playing roles, Jelinek concludes that Nin "is still playing roles. Currently, it is that of a feminist." She accuses Nin of cultivating elitist views and criticizes her emphasis on the artist, her rejection of politics, and her encouragement of an individual struggle. Jelinek concludes her article, "She may be an inspiration and model for the struggling creative artist, but she is not a feminist; in fact, some of her views are outright sexist. . . . Nin is using the women's movement for her own ends—to sell her books."[77]

A diametrically different view of Nin is given by Kate Millett—the author of *Sexual Politics* (1970) and one of the most famous names in the women's movement of the 1970s. Millett wrote an article on Nin for the French newspaper *Le Monde* in 1976, and it was translated and printed in a periodical devoted to Nin, *Anaïs: An International Journal,* in 1992 as "Anaïs—A Mother to Us All: The Birth of the Artist as a Woman." The piece is extremely laudatory. While trying to establish which American woman had the greatest impact on Millett's generation, she writes,

> For if I were to say what writer matters to us most now, is spread over crammed miles of bookshelves, coast to coast, in the little women's bookstores springing up everywhere, or the women's sections now framed off in every trade store, is devoured whole in women's study classes, is carried in ragged denim bags from class to coffeehouse, to part-time job, to meeting, to assignation, to unemployment line, is memorized and corresponded to in arcane illusion, is both basic primer and ultimate grace of sophistication, is mother to us all, as well as goddess and elder sister—it would have to be Anaïs Nin.[78]

Such praise for Nin seems odd, as Nin never liked Millett's works and Millett disapproved of Nin's friend, Henry Miller, and strongly criticized his writings. But Millett praises Nin regardless.

Nin's relationship with the women's movement changed over time, and interviews not only documented but also facilitated this process. Despite the fact that Nin was frequently represented as an embodiment of femininity, the bond between Nin and the movement was formed—a bond that was likely to benefit both.

Getting to Know the "Real" Anaïs Nin

An interview not only represents a joint effort to make a celebrity portrait and helps forge an identity but also serves as a space where a reality-effect is created. A reality-effect, as Marshall explains, is an illusion that through information we receive about the star, particularly out of their constructed world in film, music, or sport, we get to know the real person. The purpose of an interview is to bring the subject closer to an audience, to give an impression that we can get to know the subject intimately. In the case of Nin, interviews are also expected to fill in the information gap about Nin and provide the audience with insights into her present life (her past is included in the *Diary*).[79]

To achieve this reality-effect, some interviewers describe Nin's apartment, dress, looks, or demeanor or provide details of an interview meeting, as, for example, does Susan Edmiston in *Mademoiselle:* Nin "sits primly in her chair. Each time the phone rings—and it rings every fifteen minutes on the average—she rises lightly, effortlessly"; and "She served tea with the thinnest slices of lemon." These observations make Nin more "real" to her readers, but they also accentuate her popularity (her phone rings constantly).[80]

Whereas Edmiston creates a busy Nin, Susan Stocking constructs a "homely" Nin: "She wears no jewelry and shows no sign of her often elegantly robed public self. Instead she slips around in sandals and a simple Indian madras dress that falls lightly to the floor." Stocking's description suggests that during the interview she encountered not Nin the public persona but Nin the private person. Nin has disrobed of her public self, represented by her elegant dress, and presents to Stocking her homely self, clad in a simple dress. Such inserted comments allow the audience to imagine Nin more clearly and give an impression that the audience participates in and witnesses the dialogue. They provide a glimpse into what seems Nin's private, so therefore "genuine," self.[81]

Nin's *Diary* is a frequent theme in the interviews, and Nin often reassures her readers that the *Diary* contains her real self. Unlike the author of fiction, for whom an interview is an opportunity to create a public persona, Nin has to authenticate the *Diary* persona and to demonstrate that the *Diary* persona and the public persona are harmonious. So, when Barbara Freeman begins the interview for *Chicago Review* with the comment "Talking to you right now seems at the same time to be completely natural and yet . . . who am I talking to? There is a difference between a book and a person in the flesh," Nin replies, "There isn't very much with me, because I've always tried to match the work and the life." This is one example of how Nin maintains the illusion that she and the *Diary* are one. In another interview she claims that the diary is not literary, thus implying again that it is genuine. She also states in several interviews that the diary was kept secret and for that reason it is an expression of her true self.[82]

Interviewers' comments also help create an illusion of authenticity. One of the interviewers, Evelyn Clark, says that she was surprised by the directness and honesty of the *Diary*. She says that "it doesn't have any of the constructions of literature." Another interviewer calls the *Diary* "the repository of the authentic [Nin]," and yet another claims that "Anaïs Nin has told the world more about herself than most of us would tell our most intimate friends." Erica Jong, a popular novelist in the 1970s, is quoted calling Nin "that great truthsayer." Nevertheless, some interviewers question the image of Nin's *Diary* persona as genuine, truthful, and consistent with Nin the person, and thus Nin the public persona begins to fracture.[83]

Such is the case in an interview by Carol Getzoff of the *Village Voice,* which, like many other interviews turned into articles, follows a structure typical of a celebrity profile or a feature interview as identified by Baum:

    A. The meeting of journalist and star in either domestic setting or café.
    B. The description of the casual dress and demeanour of the star.
    C. The discussion of their current work—which is essentially the anchor for why the story is newsworthy.
    D. The revelation of something that is against the grain of what is generally perceived to be the star's persona—something that is anecdotal but is revealing of the star's true nature.[84]

Getzoff begins her article by recounting the circumstances of the meeting with Nin. She describes her arrival at Nin's door with cookies from Bruno's Bakery and recounts how she was welcomed by "Anaïs, gracious with smiles." Then she provides a detailed account of Nin's appearance: "Her hair is honey colored, done up in the back. She wears whitish makeup that lies like a cover over the lines in her face. . . . Her dress, long with a plunging neckline, is made of a brightly colored Indian cotton. It shows her to be sexy and soft at the same time." After that, she narrates their conversation. Getzoff says that they have decided to concentrate on the present because Nin's past is well-known through her *Diaries*. The fourth part indeed reveals Nin's "true nature." What is revealed in this particular interview, however, is far from Baum's anecdote, as Getzoff seriously questions the authenticity of Nin's portrait in the *Diary*. She relates how Nin claimed that her diary was her anchor and her secret space in which she was able to record her angry self who despised housework. Getzoff notes that she cannot imagine Anaïs Nin slaving in the house, because the *Diary* presents a "much more exalted creature." She comments, "I begin to wonder if the woman I know from the diaries is a full and honest portrait of the woman sitting before me." She therefore questions what Pineau termed the "seamlessness" between the Nin diary persona and her public persona.[85]

She is not the only one. Other interviewers expose Nin's persistent refusal to discuss her present life and her determination to keep it as secret as possible. Susan Stocking, for instance, in her interview converted into an article for the *Los Angeles Times,* talks about the ways in which Nin tried by all means to preserve her privacy, forbidding Stocking even to describe her house. She observes, "She gives us the past, but not the present." Three interviewers also asked Nin about Gore Vidal's controversial review of *Diary 4,* mentioned in the previous section. Full of hostile comments, the review revealed several details from Nin's life that she had tried to keep secret, and it denounced Nin as a poseur and cheat. Nin dismissed all of Vidal's accusations and said he was the one who had lied. Nonetheless, the seed of doubt was sown. By entering the public sphere, Nin was no longer able to control tightly her portraits and from then on her image would multiply.[86]

The (Extra)ordinary Nin

Nin presented herself in the *Diary* as a unique individual, an artist. In his study of fame, Leo Braudy remarks that "a famous person has to be a socially acceptable individualist, different enough to be interesting, yet similar enough not to be threatening or destructive." Similarly, Dyer observes that "what is important about the stars, especially in their particularity, is their typicality or representativeness." As far as Nin's presentation in the interviews is concerned, on the one hand, there are many descriptions of her persona as extraordinary, even exotic. On the other hand, she is described and, perhaps surprisingly, describes herself as being ordinary, as doing all the usual things that other people do.[87]

Unlike in her *Diary,* in the interviews Nin's extraordinariness clusters not around descriptions of her artistic vocation but rather around descriptions of her looks and her origin. In an interview-article entitled "Portrait of Anaïs Nin," Edmiston writes, "Her face is *sui generis* [from Latin meaning unique, of its own kind]: immense, round, aquamarine eyes, almost unreal, like the glass eyes of a doll. . . . Her hands, like her legs, are so youthful it's almost eerie—as if she'd made an illicit bargain in time." Many of these descriptors point to the peculiarity of Nin's appearance, so that altogether this fragment makes Nin into an unreal, unearthly creature.[88]

Another interview-article, this time by Fern Marja Eckman of the *New York Post,* likewise makes Nin into someone unusual, "swathed in ankle-length black gown and white-lined swirl of shepherd's cape, her face serene and ageless, looking not unlike a medieval saint enshrined in a niche." Her smile is akin to "a stone madonna's smile that curved her lips but left the rest of her features immobile." This account depicts Nin as supernatural, still, and distant. It gives the impression of an inhuman and artificial figure. Nin's otherness is also highlighted when her origins are mentioned. For instance, Edmiston writes that "she was raised in Paris and New York, the daughter of a Danish mother and Spanish father—whose separate elements, as in a subtle blend of spices, cannot be distinguished." Nin is therefore frequently made into the exotic, supernatural, and eerie other.[89]

Moreover, as Nin's reviewers did, Nin's interviewers often referred to her as a living legend, as a Pacifica Radio presenter observed: "[Y]ou have become a legend in your own time, a mythical figure." Three other interviewers made similar observations. Studs Terkel on the radio station WFMT-FM in Chicago, in his first question posed to Nin, comments, "Her life is almost a legend . . . and yet very real indeed." Eckman begins her article entitled "The Non-legend of Anaïs Nin" with a remark: "There was Anaïs Nin, literary legend, cult heroine, darling of this generation's undergraduates . . . ready and waiting for a 10 a.m. interview." And Barbara Freeman asks Nin in the *Chicago Review,* "[W]hy you, more than other writers, have been made into a myth, a legend to be worshiped?"[90]

Nin herself tried to soften this aura of extraordinariness. She either denied being out of the ordinary, as she did in an interview with Eckman, saying that she did not like to be made into a legend, because it dehumanized her. She portrayed herself as an ordinary woman who did "all the things that people do. . . . I keep house, I sew my hems, I mend stockings. I cook" (note that all are perfectly "feminine" activities). Or she expressed her dislike of being idealized but showed at the same time an understanding of people's need for legends and symbols. In the radio interview with Studs Terkel, she observes, "I think we need legends probably, and we make them up as we go along." This comment also suggests that Nin was conscious of the inherent constructed nature of a legend and the fact that it is made up of readers' expectations.[91]

A legend, however, has ambiguous connotations. As Elizabeth Wilson explains,

> The word "legend" is itself a warning signal of the problems inherent in the identity. It implies a larger-than-life figure, a genius among Lilliputians, yet at the same time it is a good-humoured, but tongue-in-cheek word, an affectionate smile at the endearing eccentricities of "colourful characters," subtly inviting demolition of the very heroes it appears to celebrate. At the same time it hints that the "legend" is a fiction, concealing a more truthful, hidden "reality," "the real" individual behind the myth.[92]

Wilson's interpretation of the word is relevant because it points out the simultaneous elevation and destruction of the Nin persona, or, in fact, that of any celebrity.

Once Nin's popularity grew, her carefully created *Diary* portraits were subject to negotiations. The Nin public persona became a product of self-creation and media construction. To an extent, Nin continued to maintain control of her image. She was a skillful self-promoter and networker, as the section on the reviews reveals, and she persisted in influencing others so that their portraits of her were in line with her self-presentation. She also modified her image and her identity to suit the needs of her audience. Her embracement of a new identity as a representative of women, created for her by both her readers and members of the women's movement, serves as a good example of that. It has to be acknowledged, therefore, that Nin was expert in marketing herself and knew how to take advantage of favorable cultural times to enhance her public standing. Nin's embracement of her new identity also shows the malleability of identity, which rather than being a stable entity emanating from a psychic interiority is constantly reconstructed.

However, in the years of her public visibility, Nin partially began losing power over her image. Examination of the press reception of Nin reveals that while some commentators reiterated Nin's self-portraits and presented her, as she and her editors did, as a legendary woman writer, others, such as Gore Vidal, challenged her neat self-presentation by revealing intimate details of Nin's life, thus dealing blows to her reputation. This serves as a potent reminder that once a person enters the public sphere, she is forced to relinquish control and to let her image proliferate. Still, despite the fact that her image began to crumble, during the most prolific years of her literary career, Nin was mainly regarded as a writer and a representative of women, as obituaries of her illustrate. The *New York Times,* for example, entitled its obituary "Anaïs Nin, Author Whose Diaries Depicted Intellectual Life, Dead"; the *Los Angeles Times* obituary title is "Anaïs Nin Dies: Noted as Writer and Feminist"; and the *Washington Post* announcement is similarly titled "Author, Diarist, Dies at 73." They lauded Nin as, first and foremost, the author of the famous journals "widely known for their view of the perspective of a Western woman and artist struggling to fulfill herself," as an "influential novelist, diarist, lecturer and central figure in the women's rights movement," and as "a woman of great determination." Not a single obituary mentioned Nin as a high priestess of sexual emancipation. Only after her death did serious corrections to her self-portraits emerge and her image truly begin to acquire a highly sexual character.[93]

four

Success, Scandal, Sex, and the Search for the "Real" Anaïs Nin

> Everyone has an image of himself which conflicts with the image held by others.
>
> —Anaïs Nin[1]
>
> [I]n every individual lies a different vision of the same object: the biographer, the autobiographer, the photographer, the filmmaker.
>
> —Anaïs Nin[2]

There is no doubt that Nin actively constructed her public persona during her lifetime. To an extent, she was also responsible for its construction after her death: while some writers are careful to protect their privacy (for example, Charles Dickens, Thomas Hardy, Henry James, and Willa Cather destroyed their private writings), Nin "exposed" herself: in selling her diary to the University of California, Los Angeles, she must have been aware that it would eventually be available to the public. She also, allegedly, agreed to the publication of unexpurgated diaries, although opinion on this matter is divided among Nin's friends.[3] Ultimately, however, the creation and dissemination of Nin's image after her death were beyond her control, the way she was portrayed lay in the hands of her estate, her editors and publishers, her critics, biographers, and journalists, as well as her friends and fans. Even though Nin's name, persona, face, and signature were used to market and endorse certain products, events, and claims during her lifetime, this process expanded considerably after her death. Nin the author could not control and contain her image any longer, and because of the growing controversy surrounding her persona, she became an attractive and attention-grabbing commodity.

Nin's afterlife consists of several significant milestones that changed the public image that she had endeavored so forcefully to control during her lifetime. The following four dates—1977, 1986, 1990, 1992—and the events associated with them, together with the decade of the 1990s, which was marked by the desire to discover the "real" Nin, gave rise to some prominent new portraits of Nin. Shortly after Nin's death in 1977, the volume of erotic stories *Delta of Venus* was released. Apart from getting Nin onto the best-seller list, it also brought to light an association for her name that, despite always being there, had been in the shadow: Nin became inescapably connected with sex. (Although Nin's novels published in the 1940s and the 1950s dealt with sex quite openly and her *Diary* was not silent about sexuality either, the media images of Nin in the sixties were largely devoid of sexual components.) Then in 1986, twenty years after the publication of *Diary 1* and nine years after Nin's death, the first volume of the unexpurgated diaries, *Henry and June,* was published. Not only did Nin's image gain in eroticism, but it also acquired a new dimension (or rather reacquired its old and for a while neglected dimension), namely, Nin as Henry Miller's friend and collaborator.

The adaptation of this diary to the screen four years later, in 1990, reinforced these two portraits of Nin: Nin as a sexpot and Nin as Miller's sidekick. Because of the media hype that accompanied the release of the movie and because of the film's potential to introduce Nin to new audiences, this event was particularly crucial to Nin's afterlife. Finally, in 1992, the second and probably most controversial volume of the unexpurgated diary series, *Incest,* appeared, initiating another powerful image of Nin—Nin as an incest/trauma survivor. This installment also revealed that what Nin described as a stillbirth in *Diary 1* was in reality a late-term abortion. As will become apparent in the course of this chapter, this revelation in particular disappointed and estranged many of Nin's readers and contributed to the loss of her credibility as a writer and to her fall as a women's representative.

The release of the unedited diaries constituted a turning point in Nin's posthumous reputation. It was during this period that most of the biographical material on Nin was produced. Everyone seemed to want to determine who the "real" Anaïs Nin was, to set facts straight. Or perhaps, if we look at it from a different perspective, everyone wanted to benefit from the rising tide of the "Nin controversy." Biographical writings that appeared on Nin throughout the 1990s are a good indicator of her popularity. Nin became the subject of two biographies in English and one in German, a fictionalized account of her life, and numerous memoirs by her friends and contemporaries. The 1990s can therefore be described as the decade of the search for the "real" Nin.

The first biography in English, *Anaïs: The Erotic Life of Anaïs Nin,* written by Noël Riley Fitch, appeared in 1993. It was followed two years later by Deirdre Bair's *Anaïs Nin: A Biography* (1995). Both biographers are award-winning writers. Fitch writes extensively on expatriate writers and intellectuals in Paris. She is the author of *Sylvia Beach and the Lost Generation: A History of Literary Paris in the Twenties and Thirties* (1983), *Hemingway in Paris: Parisian Walks for the Literary Traveller* (1989), and *Appetite for Life: The Biography of Julia Child* (1997), to name just a few. Bair wrote biographies of Samuel Beckett, Simone de Beauvoir, C. G. Jung, and Saul Steinberg. *Samuel Beckett: A Biography* (1978) won her the National Book Award. Out of these two biographers, only Bair had access to the entire Nin archive. As she recalls in an interview with Paul Herron, before embarking on the project she demanded exclusive access to archival material, which she was granted. These two biographies in particular contributed to establishing Nin as an untrustworthy narrator at best and as a liar at worst.[4]

In 1996, two collections of memoirs were published: one, entitled *Recollections of Anaïs Nin by Her Contemporaries,* was edited by Benjamin Franklin V, a coauthor of the critical study *Anaïs Nin: An Introduction;* and the other, *Anaïs Nin: A Book of Mirrors,* was compiled by Paul Herron. These two books gave Nin's friends, scholars, and family members an opportunity to share their memories of Nin and to assess their relationship with her. Many pieces included in these two collections presented her as an inspiring individual, thus counterbalancing the often unflattering images of Nin generated by Fitch's and Bair's biographies. These collections were not, however, as popular as the biographies, so Nin's portraits in them were disseminated mostly among Nin's fans. Nonetheless, they raise important questions about the relationship between scholarship and fandom, as many people who contributed to them were both Nin's acquaintances and scholars.

The search for the "real" Nin has continued into the twenty-first century. The three most recent biographical accounts were written by Nin's friends: in 2002, Margot Duxler published *Seduction: A Portrait of Anaïs Nin;* a year later, Maryanne Raphael released *Anaïs Nin: The Voyage Within* (2003); and in 2011, Barbara Kraft completed *Anaïs Nin: The Last Days*. Duxler, who is a clinical psychologist and a fiction writer, offered the analysis of Nin's emotional life from a psychological perspective interspersed with her memories of Nin. Raphael composed a biographical novel in the mode of Elizabeth Barillé's, and Kraft provided an account of Nin's final months and her struggle with cancer—a subject largely overlooked until the release of Kraft's memoir.

This growing interest in Nin in the 1990s was also reflected in academia. While between 1985 and 1992 no book-length criticism on Nin appeared, in the mid-1990s new critical studies and new perspectives on Nin and her works began to emerge. These critical studies were mainly psychologically or autobiographically oriented, frequently with a feminist slant. The rediscovery of Nin in the mid-1990s in academia, while partly attributable to the publication of the unexpurgated diaries and the emergence of biographies, was also the result of the rising prominence of psychoanalytic theories in the United States, because Nin's works, heavily influenced by psychoanalysis, lend themselves to such interpretations. Also, new developments in autobiographical theories, mainly driven by feminist critics, played their part in enlarging Nin's scholarship. First of all, earlier ignored genres, such as diaries, letters, and journals, started to garner critical attention in the late eighties. As Sidonie Smith and Julia Watson explain, although theories of autobiography flourished in the 1970s, critics tended to focus exclusively on autobiography and ignored forms of daily inscription.[5] Second, in the early 1990s, theorists of autobiography became interested in memories of sexual abuse and psychological trauma. Because of the emergence of the unexpurgated volumes of Nin's diary, especially *Incest,* which dealt with the incestuous relationship with her father, the range of possible debates on Nin expanded. Studies that dealt with Nin from a combined perspective of autobiography and psychoanalysis—such as Diane Richard-Allerdyce's full-length *Anaïs Nin and the Remaking of Self: Gender, Modernism, and Narrative Identity* and Suzette Henke's chapter on Nin in her *Shattered Subjects: Trauma and Testimony in Women's Life Writing*—helped reinforce the portrait of Nin as a trauma survivor.[6]

NIN AS A SEXPOT
Delta of Venus, *1977*

The most prominent aspect of Nin's posthumous existence is the ever-growing eroticization of her image. The process started off rather innocently with the release of Nin's erotic stories in the volume *Delta of Venus* (1977). Nin only reluctantly agreed to their publication because, as Bair indicates, she scorned them and they "either embarrassed her or made her deeply ashamed (depending on her mood on any given day)." John Ferrone, the editor of the collection, has admitted,

"If the decision had been hers alone, *Delta of Venus* would never have been published." Rupert Pole, later supported by Ferrone, was the one who insisted that the material was worth publishing. Although full of doubts about its literary merit, Nin eventually, as Ferrone put it, "capitulated." She allowed the publication of erotica and let Ferrone rearrange the material the way he thought appropriate. Released a few months after Nin's death, *Delta of Venus,* ironically, got her onto the best-seller list for the first time and provided financial security for her two partners. Two years after the success of *Delta,* another volume of Nin's erotic writings was published, under the title *Little Birds* (1979).[7]

Delta of Venus contains fifteen stories of different length that cover a wide spectrum of sexual experiences. There are heterosexual and homosexual couples, hermaphrodites, and people of various ages and races, and from different walks of life (for example, prostitutes and also priests). There are orgies, instances of masturbation, some S&M elements, voyeurism, and exhibitionism, as well as more-controversial practices such as incest, sex with a minor, necrophilia, and rape. But controversy is not what drew readers to Nin's erotic stories, as the reviews of them demonstrate. Her erotica was mainly appreciated for its sensual language and its depiction of feminine sexuality.

Nin claimed to have composed these stories in the 1940s to order for a wealthy collector who, as she recalled in *Diary 3,* repeatedly told her to "concentrate on sex."[8] In the preface to the first volume of erotica, Nin offered a sort of an explanation-excuse for issuing the material, not anticipating the success it would bring her:

> Here in the erotica I was writing to entertain, under pressure from a client who wanted me to "leave out the poetry." I believed that my style was derived from a reading of men's works. For this reason I long felt that I had compromised my feminine self. I put the erotica aside. Rereading it these many years later, I see that my own voice was not completely suppressed.... I

finally decided to release the erotica for publication because it shows the beginning efforts of a woman in a world that had been the domain of men.[9]

In the article "The Making of *Delta of Venus*," Ferrone confirms Nin's hesitancy about publishing the material, but he also reveals that "the famous collector was a myth," as Nin discovered shortly before her death. Ferrone explains, "'He' was actually an underground business, one of several operating in New York during the thirties and forties, that commissioned erotica and then sold copies of the manuscripts privately." Nin, however, decided to adhere to the version presented in the third volume of the diary. After all, an underground business does not sound as innocent and mysterious as a private collector whom Nin described in the diary as an eccentric individual. And as the examination of readers' comments posted on goodreads.com—a website where everyone can leave their own review of a book—demonstrates, the myth of a wealthy commissioner still persists.[10]

Delta of Venus is to an extent the work of its editor, John Ferrone. He recalls being given 850 pages of erotic stories and almost complete editorial freedom. He quotes a letter received from Rupert Pole saying, "Anaïs says, delete, patch, new titles, whatever." And so he did. He shortened and rewrote Nin's lengthy narratives and provided them with beginnings, endings, and new titles. He writes that "slightly more than half of the 850 pages ended up in *Delta,* and another thirty percent was used in the second volume, *Little Birds.*" He was also responsible for the title of *Delta of Venus.* Although the galleys reached Nin before her death, she was unable to evaluate the edited erotica because of her declining health. Ferrone's extensive involvement in the rewriting process makes the signature "Nin" problematic: to what extent is *Delta of Venus* Nin's and to what extent, Ferrone's?[11]

This is difficult to determine without a detailed comparison of the original papers with the published version—an investigation that is beyond the scope of this book. What is certain, however, is the fact that *Delta of Venus* was a product of its cultural times. It is not a coincidence that stories written in the 1940s were not published until the 1970s. The 1960s and the 1970s witnessed what is nowadays lodged in public consciousness as the sexual revolution. The sexual revolution, as David Allyn explains, had many different manifestations. The invention of the birth control pill, the increased interest in sexual behavior, the relaxed codes of sexual conduct, the growing acceptance of nudity in the media, the battle against censorship, and the decriminalization of abortion in 1973 were just a few among many developments that characterized the decade and contributed to the image of the sixties as the epoch of the sexual revolt. Books such as Helen Gurley Brown's *Sex and the Single Girl* (1962), in which the author admitted to numerous sex affairs; Dominique Aubry's *The Story of O,* the 1945 French novel published in the United States in 1963, which offered "a woman's first-person account of her voluntary descent into a life of sexual slavery and torture"; and Nancy Friday's *My Secret Garden: Women's Sexual Fantasies* (1973), a collection of sexual dreams based on the accounts of actual women, paved the way for the unproblematic publication and the positive reception of Nin's erotica.[12]

Most reviewers of *Delta of Venus* and *Little Birds* assessed both volumes favorably. Nin's erotic writings were repeatedly described as delicate, emotional, sensual, poetic, sensitive, and elegant. Moreover, many commentators pointed out that Nin managed to create an original form of erotica—erotica from a woman's point of view. For instance, writing about *Delta of Venus* in the *New York Times Book Review,* Harriet Zinnes presented Nin as the forerunner of the American tradition of women's erotic writings. She contrasted Nin's erotica with the male equivalents to conclude that Nin invented a new language to describe sexual experiences. Michelle Leber, assessing *Delta* for *Library Journal,* went so far as to describe the book as "full-bodied, feminist erotica."[13]

Not everyone, however, regarded Nin's erotica as an appropriate and successful exploration of female sexuality. For example, Susan Wood, in the pages of the *San Francisco*

Chronicle magazine *This World,* claimed that Nin's erotic writings in no way contributed to an understanding of sexuality, and she urged readers to remember that they had originally been written for a wealthy customer. The *New Yorker,* instead of a review, offered a three-page parody of Nin's stories entitled "*The Delts of Venus* (Selections from Another Volume of Early Writings by Anise Nun)." Its author, Charles McGrath, followed the format of Nin's stories, even offering a preface in which he thus caricatured Nin's motives for writing the erotica: "I was so poor that for days on end I ate nothing but string and leaves." McGrath made fun here of Nin's explanation that a lack of money forced her to produce erotic stories.[14]

Curiously enough, none of the reviews, whether favorable or not, discussed the problematic nature of Nin's erotica. After all, it is difficult to overlook that some sexual practices verge on perversions that are banned if visualized in the media and illegal in real life (such as pedophilia and rape). Take, for instance, one of the most challenging stories in *Delta of Venus,* "The Hungarian Adventurer," whose protagonist, the Baron, characterized as possessing "astonishing beauty, infallible charm, grace, the powers of a trained actor, culture, knowledge of many tongues, [and] aristocratic manners," first plays in bed with two girls (ten and twelve years old) until "[h]is penis, hidden in the thick quilt, rose over and over again between the little legs, and it was like this that he came, with a strength he had rarely known, surrendering the battle, which the girls had won in a manner they never suspected," and he then rapes his own daughters and son.[15] Nin definitely pushed the boundaries of sexual explorations, yet this was rarely acknowledged. Evaluators of the volume preferred to focus on less contentious fragments and presented the erotica as a revolution in the portrayal of female sexuality.

Nevertheless, Nin's erotic writings did become entangled in the debate on pornography taking place in the 1980s. As Rosemarie Tong demonstrates, divergent attitudes toward pornography well illustrate the difference of opinions on sexuality among various factions of feminism: antipornographers, usually a group of radical feminists who argue about harmful effects of pornography; and anti-antipornographers, a group of more liberally oriented feminists who defend freedom of expression and argue that deciding which representations of sexuality are detrimental for women and society is difficult. The former group was represented by Andrea Dworkin—a leader of the antipornography movement—who, alongside Catherine MacKinnon, spoke about the harmful impact of pornography on women. In 1985, the *Chicago Tribune* reported on Andrea Dworkin's speech at the American Bar Association. Dworkin was quoted as saying, "[W]e don't want even Anaïs Nin to be a vehicle of our oppression. . . . Because lots of art is pornography, and this pornography is used in hurting people." Dworkin therefore considered Nin's erotica on an equal footing with pornography.[16]

However, while some condemned Nin's erotica, others adapted it for either stage or screen. For instance, the *Chicago Tribune* reported on two theatrical adaptations, both by Karen Goodman. In 1987, Prop Theatre offered an adaptation of *Delta of Venus*. The reviews of the play stated that Nin offered the exploration of the erotic from a female perspective and that it explored "Nin's delicate, fascinating emotions." In 1991, another theatre company adapted *Little Birds*. Later, Zalman King, the director of *9½ Weeks,* made an erotic film titled *Delta of Venus* (1995) that was very loosely based on both Nin's erotic writings and her life.[17]

Above all, Nin's erotica proved to be popular among general readers. The collection appeared on the *New York Times* Best Seller List for thirty-six weeks when it was first published. But although it sold well, it did not receive the same attention from academia. Most of Nin's critics chose to ignore it. Writing about the reception of Nin's work in academia, Philip Jason observes that the two volumes of erotica "add little to Nin's stature." From the publication of *Delta* in 1977 through 1993, according to Jason, there were only five critical articles devoted to Nin's erotic stories, as well as a chapter in the revised edition of Sharon Spencer's study

Collage of Dreams (1981). This situation improved a little after 1993 (for instance, Helen Tookey devotes some space to discussing it), but as the contents of two journals devoted to Nin's scholarship (*Anaïs: An International Journal* [1993–97] and *A Café in Space: The Anaïs Nin Literary Journal* [2004–present]) indicate, Nin's critics still prefer to comment on her diaries and novels rather than on her erotica.[18]

There is, therefore, a disparity between the popular and the academic Nin: while the public has favored erotica, the scholars have largely ignored it. But precisely because the erotica enjoyed popular success, its release was an important step in amending Nin's image. The publication of erotica was the first point that sparked the process of eroticization of Nin, simply by connecting Nin with the sexual. Nin became a self-proclaimed (as she wrote in the preface to *Delta*) "madam of this snobbish literary house of prostitution." But while in *Delta of Venus* Nin figured just as an author of erotic fantasies, in the first unexpurgated diary, *Henry and June* (published in 1986), she became the prime star of sexual adventures.[19]

Henry and June—*the Diary, 1986*

Although Nin's partner Rupert Pole, who until his death in 2006 served as the head of her Trust, is listed as the official editor of *Henry and June,* the main editorial decisions were made again by John Ferrone, the editor of the erotica. Well aware of the publishing trends, Ferrone knew that the market was saturated with Nin's diary writing, and he voiced his opinion clearly in a letter to Pole dated 5 March 1985: "I feel that there is no way that we can start a third diary series. People are confused enough with two. Also, apart from dedicated readers, people in the publishing industry are tired of the never-ending diary; I'm talking about buyers, bookstore chains, sales reps; and it has become increasingly difficult to get review space. We've gotten a handful of reviews, at best, for the last two volumes" (referring to *The Early Diary*, volumes 3 and 4). Ferrone's words serve as a potent reminder that book publishing is a commercial venture and books are products to be sold. And what sells is an interesting story.[20]

What Ferrone considered interesting was a "very intense, concentrated" account of Nin's relationship with the Millers and an omission of Nin's reflections, which he termed "philosophizing." As the correspondence between him and Pole reveals, Ferrone was extremely hardnosed about the editing process. He had a very strong and uncompromising vision of *Henry and June.* In the introduction to the correspondence between himself and Pole, Ferrone explains how he went about the editing of this unexpurgated volume: "I saw as a model Anaïs's well-manicured editing of the first diary. . . . Anaïs had not hesitated to cut, add, refine, and possibly invent." Ferrone hence was ruthless with the material. After five months of editing the volume, he wrote to Pole on 11 November 1985, "I went through it six times, each time carving away a little more, until I thought we were down to the essential story. So don't tell me your favorite line is missing. . . . You and Gunther may both disagree with my handling of the material here and there, but editing is a very subjective process. Every editor would do it in a different way." Again, Ferrone's words are illuminating, for they reveal a great extent of editing and confirm that Nin's original diary was pared down until only "the essential story" was left.[21]

Ferrone's editing consisted not only of narrowing the focus of the diary but also of rewriting the original entries, even the ones that had already been rewritten by Nin. Chapter 2 of this book quotes Nin's description of meeting Henry Miller from both the original diary and the first published diary, *Diary 1*. I refer readers to these fragments (found on pp. 51–52) to compare them to the following unexpurgated version: "I've met Henry Miller. He came to lunch with Richard Osborn, a lawyer I had to consult on the contract for my D. H. Lawrence book. When he first stepped out of the car and walked towards the door where I stood waiting, I saw a man I liked. In his writing he is flamboyant, virile, animal, magnificent. He's a man whom life makes drunk, I thought. He is like me." So neither of the published versions corresponds to the original entry of Nin's diary. *Henry and June,* which claims to be unexpurgated, is so in the sense that it contains an abundance of new material about Nin, but it preserves neither the structure nor the style of Nin's original diary.[22]

Consequently, rather than being unexpurgated, *Henry and June* is differently expurgated, and its role in conveying the "truthful" (truthful to the original diary rather than truthful to how things really were in real life) story of Anaïs Nin's life is therefore rather ambiguous. Commenting on *Henry and June* and comparing it to the first expurgated volume of the *Diary,* which covers roughly the same years, Philip Jason notes, "[R]eading the volumes consecutively or even side-by-side, weaving back and forth between entries written about the same time, does not give readers the texture of the source or of the evolving Anaïs we are always seeking."[23]

Acknowledging Ferrone's/Pole's editing of *Henry and June* is important because their contribution complicated the authorship of the *Diary* and because their editing shaped Nin's persona. Although Nin allegedly intended to publish an uncensored version of the diary, we can only speculate how she would have gone about it. As Ferrone states, "[E]very editor would tackle this ms. in his own way."[24] We can never know whether she would have been content with Ferrone's/Pole's editing of *Henry and June.* By rewriting her diary without her input, Ferrone and Pole became coauthors of *Henry and June.* They, especially Ferrone, were the ones who decided what out of a vast quantity of original material would get published. They determined what shape and form the new volume would take, and as a result they significantly modified Nin's self-portrait.

By concentrating exclusively on Nin's sexual awakening and relationship with her husband Hugo, her lover Henry Miller, and his wife, June, Ferrone dramatically changed Nin's self-presentation. As chapter 2 demonstrates, Nin introduced herself in *Diary 1* predominantly as a budding writer. The first pages of *Henry and June* present a different Nin, a Nin who is virtually absent from the first seven volumes—the Nin preoccupied with sexuality. Because even if Nin does talk about sex in the first series, she does so rather vaguely and frequently writes from the position of an observer rather than a participant in sexual exploits. *Henry and June,* in contrast, is saturated with sexual connotations. A new vocabulary enters this purportedly unexpurgated diary. Nin fucks, masturbates, swallows sperm, and experiences orgasms (*HAJ,* 71). She describes "hours and hours of coition" (*HAJ,* 82) mainly with Miller but also with her husband Hugo and, later in the book, with her psychoanalyst Allendy.

Whereas *Diary 1* opens with a description of Louveciennes and Nin's house, *Henry and June* begins with description of Nin's husband Hugo and her own reflections on marriage, love, desire, and sex. Nin confesses that both she and her husband long for more stimulating sexual experiences, such as orgies, yet at the same time she fears that such cravings, if fulfilled, will destroy their intimacy and ultimately their relationship. And while both Nin from *Diary 1* and Nin from *Henry and June* crave to expand, develop, and lead an intense life, in the case of the former Nin it means to devote all her energies to writing, whereas in the case of the latter it signifies the need for "an older mind, a father, a man stronger than me, a lover who will lead me in love" (*HAJ,* 1). This statement becomes a guiding light for the *Henry and June* Nin, whose principal objective is the search for sexual fulfillment. Therefore, instead of a writer in search of appropriate modes of expression, there is a woman in search of a suitable man and exciting sexual experiences.

As early as page 9 of the book, there is a very visual description of failed oral sex with Lawrence Drake (an assistant to Edward Titus, who published Nin's book on D. H. Lawrence):

> My curiosity for sensuality is stirred. I have always been tempted by unknown pleasures. He has, like me, a sense of smell. I let him inhale me, then I slip away. Finally I lie still on the couch, but when his desire grows, I try to escape. Too late. Then I tell him the truth: woman's trouble. That does not seem to deter him. "You don't think I want that mechanical way—there are other ways." He sits up and uncovers his

> penis. I don't understand what he wants. He makes me get down on my knees. He offers it to my mouth. I get up as if struck by a whip.

This is just one of many descriptions of sexual acts that fill the volume. This is not to argue that the focus of *Henry and June* on the sexual makes for bad reading. On the contrary, the book provides a very insightful exploration of ambiguous human emotions. It captures the contradictory feelings experienced by a couple: on the one hand, there is a desire to maintain the illusion of pure and eternal love; on the other hand, there is a craving for more varied sexual experience. The volume explores the feelings of hate and love directed toward the same person, the simultaneous need to belong and to be free.

At the same time, however, it does present Nin in a very narrow way: Nin is almost exclusively preoccupied with sex and love. Just as Janet Malcolm criticized Plath's mother for publishing their correspondence, claiming that she handed Sylvia Plath over "to posterity in . . . [a] stained bathrobe and unwashed face,"[25] Ferrone can be criticized for handing over Nin in her underwear (and frequently without it). Following the success of *Delta of Venus,* Ferrone, rather than making available to the public Nin's diary in its original form, released another volume of erotica, this time involving the real personages. Because *Henry and June* was released twenty years after the first volume, it reached not only Nin's devoted audience but also a new generation of possible readers and presented them with a brand-new portrait of Nin. *Henry and June* is still incredibly popular today—as the website goodreads.com indicates—being the second most widely read and reviewed work by Nin, after *Delta of Venus*. Most of Nin's new readers get acquainted with the sexual Nin first.

The press, which during Nin's lifetime treated her mainly as a writer, after the release of *Henry and June* became interested in Nin the passionate lover. For example, the caption to Nin's picture that accompanied the review of *Henry and June* in the *Los Angeles Times* read, "Anaïs Nin (about 1929): Lover of Henry Miller and others."[26] Nin was no longer celebrated for her struggles as a woman artist. Instead, her sexual adventures were under the spotlight. The publication of *Henry and June* was very important to Nin's posthumous reputation. For existing Nin's fans, her carefully coined image collapsed and caused a lot of unease and disappointment with which her readers had to come to terms. For those who joined Nin's fandom with the release of *Henry and June,* Nin became mainly known as a sexual libertine and Miller's collaborator. The subsequent three volumes of unexpurgated diaries—*Incest* (1992), *Fire* (1995), and *Nearer the Moon* (1996)—also largely focused on the erotic.

Henry & June—*the Film, 1990*

The importance of *Henry and June* to Nin's afterlife lies also in the fact that this volume was adapted for the screen, thus introducing Nin, a very specific Nin, to an even broader audience. The film *Henry & June* was made by a well-known director, was distributed by a major studio, and starred then recognizable and today famous actors. Directed by Philip Kaufman and distributed by Universal Pictures, it starred Maria de Medeiros as Anaïs Nin, Uma Thurman as June Miller, Fred Ward as Henry Miller, Richard E. Grant as Nin's husband Hugh Guiler, and Kevin Spacey as Miller's friend Richard Osborne. Released in 1990, *Henry & June* earned \$1,032,492 during the first screening weekend and \$11,567,449 in total (according to IMDb, the Internet Movie Database), which is a respectable sum of money, especially for an NC-17 rated film. As Jody Pennington notes, *Henry & June* and *Showgirls* (1995) were the only NC-17 rated movies that grossed over \$10 million.[27]

Henry & June initially received the feared X rating, which usually meant a commercial death for a film, as movie theatres refused to screen X-rated films and newspapers refused to advertise them. However, the Motion Picture Association of America (MPAA), which is responsible for the movie rating system in the United States, modified the rating system a few weeks before the planned release of *Henry & June.* The MPAA replaced the X rating with a new NC-17 category, and *Henry & June* was its first recipient. This modification came down to a change of the category label, as both categories stood for exactly the same thing: no one under 17 was admitted to the screening. Nonetheless, the new rating was expected to help remove the stigma of the X, which had become associated with the pornography industry. The initial branding of *Henry & June* with the X rating and then the transformation of the X to an NC-17 rating were hotly debated in the press, and as a result the film received extra publicity and became the face of the change.

Consequently, Kaufman's film, which received enormous attention in the media upon its release because of a coincidental change of the rating system, introduced Nin to new audiences. It is highly probable that many people back then, and perhaps even nowadays, saw Nin before they read her. Paul Herron, the editor of the journal devoted to Nin *A Café in Space: The Anaïs Nin Literary Journal,* became familiar with Nin and Miller through the movie. In the introduction to *Anaïs Nin: A Book of Mirrors,* which he edited and self-published, Herron thus relates the beginning of his acquaintance with both writers: "As the credits rolled, I discovered that this Henry Miller and Anaïs Nin weren't fictional characters—*they were real people who had written books about what we'd just seen!* . . . I was chomping at the bit—I had to buy this *Tropic of Cancer* and the *Diary,* and there wasn't a moment to lose!" The film, therefore, had the potential to revive Nin and bring her to the attention of a new group of readers.[28]

In their study *Bond and Beyond: The Political Career of a Popular Hero,* Tony Bennett and Janet Woollacott demonstrate how film adaptations of Bond affect the novels. They claim, "The Bond novels . . . reach us already humming with the meanings established by the films and, as a consequence, have been hooked into orders of inter-textuality to which, initially, they were not connected."[29] The same can be said about Nin and the film *Henry & June:* the film will forever constitute an intertextual reference to Nin and her works. So what sort of Nin does Kaufman offer to his viewers?

Kaufman tried to re-create as faithfully as possible Nin from the 1930s. His film is rich in intertextual references. Thanks to the audiovisual possibilities of the movie, viewers can hear and see what can only be imagined when reading Nin's journal. For instance, Kaufman included many music pieces dating back to the beginning of the twentieth century, many of which were written by Nin's favorite composers, such as Claude Debussy, Erik Satie, and Frédéric Chopin, whom she often praised in the pages of her diary.[30] Apart from exposing viewers to music from the 1930s, Kaufman re-created an atmosphere of Paris by incorporating original photographs by Brassaï and fragments of films that Nin mentioned in her diary, such as *La Passion de Jeanne D'Arc* (1928) and *Un Chien Andalou* (1929). He also included a glimpse of Nin's original childhood journal and a picture of the adolescent Nin. Above all, Maria de Medeiros, the film's Anaïs Nin, as reviewers of *Henry & June* stated repeatedly, bore a striking resemblance to the character she played.

However, viewers should not be misled by this apparent authenticity, because Kaufman's film, just like the diary on which it is based, presents only a very narrow part of Nin's life, and as a result, it presents Nin to the film audience, and to Nin's potential readers, in a very particular way. It fossilizes Nin in a forever young and sexually adventurous pose, as the main concern of the film is Nin's sexual awakening. *Henry & June,* being a Hollywood production, follows certain classical rules of Hollywood narrative style, according to which a plot of the film should have "a clear forward direction" and should concentrate on a small number of characters whose goals should be established at the beginning of the film and achieved at the end of it.[31] In an attempt to produce a coherent film narrative, Kaufman condensed further the already condensed diary. Thus, the first scenes of the film establish Nin as a sexually curious yet not very experienced person. After meeting Henry and June, she begins to explore the realm of sexuality. The movie ends with Nin's splitting from June and Henry. Kaufman got rid of, for instance, Nin's psychoanalysis and her affair with Allendy, and, most important, he stripped Nin of many dilemmas regarding her affairs.

He did so by transforming many prose fragments of Nin's diary into dialogues. Although Nin's diary is full of quoted conversations, Kaufman took some of the reflective passages, not addressed to anyone, and changed them into dialogue. For instance, both in the *Diary* and in the movie the following line appears: "I have three desires now, to eat, to sleep and to fuck" (although in the film Nin does not actually say "fuck," both the way she pauses and the following scene of lovemaking clearly suggests what she was about to say). While in the book Nin does not address anyone in particular, in the film Nin says it to Miller. In the diary, Nin simply expresses her craving for more experience and a more intense existence, and she actually identifies Miller as someone unable to meet these desires. She writes, "I want to bite into life, and to be torn by it. Henry does not give me all this" (*HAJ,* 179). Therefore, the same sentence appears in totally different contexts.

The way Kaufman portrays Nin shapes what viewers, especially those who have never heard about Nin, find out about her. Let us consider the first few scenes and how they introduce Nin. The film opens with a scene at a publisher's office. Nin discusses her book on D. H. Lawrence. However, the publisher is more interested in Nin herself rather than her book. He is curious how she came to know so much about sex, because, as he asserts, "You write about sex with such an authority." Nin replies that she got her information from literature and from the erotic pictures she discovered in her new apartment. She sounds very naïve talking about her discovery with a childish enthusiasm. This sequence is a series of shots and reverse shots (showing first Nin and then the publisher) and a series of flashbacks to the discovery of the pictures, narrated as a voice-over. In the final shot of this sequence, the publisher enters the frame from the left, bends over, and starts to kiss the rather confused Nin. It is a very unexpected turn of events, both for Nin and for the viewer (although Nin did have an affair with her publisher's assistant, in the diary the romance is built up gradually).

In the third sequence, Nin writes in bed by her sleeping husband. She wears a white, fluffy nightgown. The light is soft and reddish, and the scene is built up mostly from closeups of Nin, which creates a sense of intimacy. While Nin writes in her diary, her voice-over simultaneously narrates what she records, which is the story of what really happened at the publisher's office. She relates how the man not only kissed her but also caressed her body, including her "most secret, sensitive part." Then Nin lifts her eyes from the diary, looks into the camera, and says from the voice-over, "I tell Hugo only part of the story." The scene slowly fades out.

The film therefore introduces Nin as a writer, but at the same time, her writing is from the very start closely connected with sexuality. At the publisher's office she is not treated as a partner in business but as a sexual object. It is her body, and not her creation, that is desired. In the third scene, and throughout the rest of the movie, Nin is established as a sort of "boudoir" or "leisure" writer, since apart from one scene, close to the beginning, in which Nin is seen at the typewriter, most of her writing takes place in bed. Kaufman's representation of Nin's writing as a leisure activity in the film becomes particularly evident when contrasted with his presentation of Miller's writing. When Nin writes, she does so in bed, and the voice-over makes her thoughts audible, which creates intimacy and provides spectators with an insight into her secrets. This is due to the fact that Nin is pictured writing a diary and not fiction. When Miller writes, he does so at the typewriter, in an artistic frenzy, smoking cigarettes, and sometimes writing continuously for a few days. The audience does not get to hear his thoughts; the only sound accompanying him is the clicking of the typewriter. However, the viewers can see the results of his labor—the mounting pile of typewritten pages. What is more, most scenes in Miller's house take place around his workplace: his desk with the typewriter and various notes pinned to the wall. At Nin's house, most of the action and writing are confined to the bedroom. Although Kaufman does present Nin as a writer, her writing and the progress of her ideas become secondary.

What is more, because of the specificity of film as a genre, Kaufman shapes Nin's character not only through its content (such as actions she performs, words she utters, and gestures she makes) but also through its visual presentation (such as how she looks, dresses, and poses). Nin is strongly eroticized through the costumes she wears and the poses she assumes in the film. Whenever Nin is shown writing, she wears some kind of negligee. In one scene she is stark naked. She lies passively on her back, looking into the camera; her open diary lies beside her. Only her bent knee prevents us from seeing, as Nin would put it, "her most secret, sensitive part."

This scene is framed like a picture: there is no movement, and only Nin's voice-over, narrating what she writes down in her diary, is audible. As Laura Mulvey explains, cinema offers numerous pleasures, one of which is scopophilia—pleasure in looking. According to Mulvey, in a patriarchal society, "pleasure in looking has been split between active/male and passive/female. . . . In their traditional exhibitionist role women are simultaneously looked at and displayed with their appearance coded for strong visual and erotic impact so that they can be said to connote *to-be-looked-at-ness*." Thus exposed, Nin is here clearly to satisfy viewers' pleasure. Kaufman's film and his portrayal of Nin support the conventional hegemonic position by which women function as the object and not the subject of the gaze.[32]

The film also contains several scenes of a fully dressed man and a skimpily dressed Nin. One such scene takes place at the beginning of the movie, when Nin, wearing just a slip, talks to her fully clad cousin Eduardo. Another one, probably more significant, occurs halfway through the movie, when Miller visits Nin upon completing his book *Tropic of Cancer*. He comes into Nin's room, eyes her up and down (and so does the camera), takes out his manuscript, puts it on the shelf, and says, "Finished." He then goes toward Nin, who is dressed in a long, black lace, see-through negligee, and they start kissing passionately. The sequence preceding this one shows Miller as an inspired artist with a cigarette dangling from his mouth as he frantically types. Continuous fade-ins and fade-outs suggest the passage of time. There is no indication as to what Nin does with her time when Miller works. But the movie suggests that she has not done much, since she does not have any writing of her own to show him. She just seems to be waiting for her man, looking impeccable in her sexy outfit and carefully applied makeup.

The film presents a highly sexualized image of Nin, thus diminishing her role as a writer. This eroticized image of Nin clashes with the image she created for herself during her lifetime by carefully editing her *Diaries,* in which she presented herself mainly as an artist. The film therefore contributes to the process of eroticization of Nin that began with the publication of her erotica and was reinforced by the first unexpurgated diary, *Henry and June.* Since then, there has been a great emphasis on Nin's sexual affairs rather than on her literary achievement. Not long after the release of the movie, the first biographical accounts of Nin were published, both under very suggestive titles: *Anaïs Nin: Naked under the Mask* and *The Erotic Life of Anaïs Nin.*

Anaïs Nin: Naked under the Mask, *1992*

The title of this fictionalized biography written by Elizabeth Barillé is supposed to connote uncovering the real Nin. But it also, more literally, brings to mind a naked Anaïs Nin. Barillé's story of Nin's life follows a chronology and is interspersed with short, usually one page long, vignettes that cover a given subject. The titles of these vignettes are written in capital letters, which makes them stand out in the table of contents. While some of these titles, such as ANAÏS, JOURNAL, FOOD, JAZZ, DJUNA, UCLA, and MUSIC, are quite neutral, others are typical watchwords that became associated with Nin after her death, including BEAUTY, COSTUME, LIAR, ORGASM, LESBIANISM, and INCEST.

Barillé (re)creates Nin's story, imitating Nin's voice as well as voices of her family members and friends. For example, the choice of Nin's name is told from the perspective of Nin's mother: "In desperation, I asked [Nin's father] to choose a first name for the baby. 'Anaïs,' he said. I shuddered.... It was the name the Ancient Persians had given to Venus; its ambiguity rang like a perverse incantation in my ears. What sort of future was he imposing on his daughter by giving her the name of a temple prostitute?"[33] Barillé's linking of Nin's name with "a temple prostitute" is just one account of the origins of the name Anaïs, however; Fitch proposes another. According to Fitch, the name Anaïs derives from a Syrian war goddess.[34] Moreover, Barillé implies that Nin's mother did not like the name, which is unlikely, as her own mother and one of her sisters bore the name. By suggesting that Nin's promiscuity was cast on her like a spell, she implies that Nin was destined to become a prostitute of the literary world.

The description of Nin's childhood games is also full of double entendres. Barillé writes, "She soon revealed herself as a rebel, having no friends but her brothers whom she dominated; she was mistress of all their games. She covered a table with a fringed cloth and made herself a tepee; and with a sheet and two chairs a stage set where she was a princess, or a courtesan. I nicknamed her Sarah Bernhardt" (10). The words Barillé uses—*mistress, princess, courtesan*—are again erotically tinged. However, despite its suggestive title, double meanings, and sexual connotations, Barillé's fictionalized biography does not entirely capitalize on sex. In fact, descriptions of sexual acts are not the focus of her narrative, which makes her account quite balanced in comparison to Fitch's biography.

Anaïs: The Erotic Life of Anaïs Nin, *1993*

From the very introduction, Fitch keeps the promise suggested by the title of her biography, *Anaïs: The Erotic Life of Anaïs Nin,* and concentrates chiefly on Nin's erotic encounters and controversial elements of her life. She highlights the love affairs, infidelities, and romances of the writer. Fitch's introduction opens, as every chapter in the book does, with a quotation. "I am a writer. I would rather have been a courtesan" (3), reads the motto for the introduction. This fragment, taken from Nin's diary, serves its purpose well, as it gives readers a foretaste of Fitch's attitude toward her subject. Fitch's biography is written to shock by focusing on the sexual. Out of the immense sea of Nin's possible words, Fitch picks up those in which Nin expresses her desire to be a harlot rather than a writer. Fitch's choice of the quotation justifies her search for the erotic Nin.

In the introduction, which serves as a condensed portrait of Nin, there is hardly a paragraph in which Nin is not described in erotic terms. Both quoting others and being herself creative with names, Fitch calls Nin "a Donna Juana," "Madonna of St. Clitoris," "Venus with an over-bite," "a diva . . . with a shy, virginal side," "a courtesan in Paris," and "an American Eve after the Fall" (4–7). In addition to these direct labels, Fitch builds an erotic portrait of Anaïs Nin in more nuanced ways. Her text overflows with erotic wordings, as, for instance, when she refers to Nin's writing as "the literary disrobing in her diary" (3) and as "literary striptease" (5). She also compares Nin to Madonna, the pop icon known for bold sexual performances. Most likely alluding to a documentary film titled *Madonna: Truth or Dare*, released in 1991, she writes, "While asserting that the ultimate dare is to tell the truth, they both conceal themselves" (5). By drawing this comparison, she reinforces an already existing image of the controversial and erotic Nin but also modernizes Nin for her readers who might not know much about Nin but surely know a lot about Madonna.

The tone set up in the introduction is followed in the rest of the book. Fitch's language is saturated with eroticism, and the life of Fitch's Nin orbits largely around the sexual. Nin is filled with either sexual longings, sexual energy, erotic dreams of orgies, or sexual frustrations. Reporting on the periods covered in the unexpurgated diaries, Fitch provides very elaborate descriptions of Nin's sexual encounters with various people. Her narrative technique consists mainly of rewriting Nin's own accounts. This is evident, for example, in the portrayal of a sexual act involving Nin and Drake (see pp. 153–154):

> Finally, she allows herself to be placed on the couch, yet lies very still. She lets him inhale her perfume,

> pleased that they share a sense of smell, but then panics again, trying to deter him with "woman's trouble." He declares that there are other, less routine, ways. She is confused about the situation. He unbuttons his fly and tells her to get on her knees, which she does. When he offers his penis to her mouth, she stumbles to her feet as if whipped. (101)

Fitch therefore follows Nin's diaries very closely, simply rephrasing Nin's utterances. She creates very vivid erotic scenes, unraveling them slowly and garnishing them with spicy details. The present tense of Fitch's writing gives her biography the air of a novel. Events unfold before the reader's eyes, and the biographer seems to be absent from the story. (The use of the present tense was one of the main accusations made against Fitch's biography in the reviews: critics claimed that it did not allow for enough biographical distance.)

While narrating periods of Nin's life that are not covered in the unexpurgated diaries, Fitch does not provide as many details, because of the lack of access to the Nin archive, but she does her best to keep the list of Nin's lovers updated by painstakingly investigating men who slept with Nin. She is also one of the Nin critics who are keen on demonstrating parallels between Nin's life and her fiction. Therefore, not only does she provide names and details of Nin's lovers but she also indicates their fictional equivalents.

Because Fitch's biography of Nin, like many biographies, traverses the academic and the popular, it contributes significantly to strengthening the image of Nin as a sexpot that has been developed systematically since 1977. Consequently, by 1993, with *Delta of Venus, Henry and June* (both the diary and the film), and *Anaïs: The Erotic Life of Anaïs Nin* available in the marketplace, the erotic Nin had become iconic.

NIN THE SEDUCTRESS

The title of Margot Duxler's book—*Seduction: A Portrait of Anaïs Nin*—is worth some attention, as it consolidates seduction as a recurrent theme associated with Nin that underpins her erotic portrait. Seduction is one of the most frequent images employed in descriptions of Nin. Writing about modern stardom, Stephen Hinerman claims that the circulation of popular, recognizable images plays a crucial part in constituting the celebrity. He states that "one way that stars are made in the twentieth century is through consistent patterns of visualization constructed in various (often analogous) narrative settings, which are then repeated until recognized by audiences as being associated with a particular star. In addition, certain verbal descriptors attach to the stars of pop culture. Written accounts of those stars will often employ these predictable descriptors." Seduction is used to describe either Nin herself, her behavior, her writings, or even her relationships with her readers. Nin is portrayed as a seductress or Donna Juana by reviewers, her writing is conceptualized in terms of seduction by her critics, and her life is fitted into a pattern of seduction by her biographers.[35]

The image of seduction was initiated by Nin herself, as she frequently referred to herself as a seductress, and the word *seduction* appears frequently on the pages of her diary. The concept of seduction entered Nin's diary with Dr. Allendy's analysis. Allendy told Nin that as a child she wanted unconsciously to seduce her father, and when she failed, she started behaving and dressing in a seductive way. For Allendy, her seductive manner was a clear indication of her lack of confidence.[36] Nin soon used the seduction metaphor to describe herself and to understand her own behavior. For instance, after showing her breasts to Allendy (because she considered them too small and wanted a reassurance of her femininity), she questioned, "Did I have to show him my breasts? Did I want to test my charm on him?" (*Diary 1*, 92). Allendy gave her, therefore, new means to express herself, which would influence her self-understanding and later encouraged critics to employ freely the image of seduction.

One of the first critics to use the image of seduction with respect to Nin's writing is Lynn Luria-Sukenick. In a 1976 article for *Shenandoah,* she describes Nin's diaries as "seductive rather than confessional, extending to the reader a subliminal invitation to fall in love—with her, *and* the world—and she instinctively knows, having been traditionally feminine in many respects, the importance of concealment to the arousal of desire." Another academic employing the seduction image is Nancy Scholar. Like Luria-Sukenick, she conceptualizes Nin's diary as a tool that helps her to seduce readers by giving them a false impression of authenticity. According to Scholar, Nin seduces her readers with a mixture of candor and mystery. As an example, she quotes the above-mentioned passage of the diary in which Nin shows her breasts to her psychoanalyst. The reader, Scholar says, becomes an additional witness in this unexpected gesture of exhibitionism. "This is autobiography as seduction: the writer invites and excites her readers with intimate suggestions, and then vanishes behind her mask," she states.[37]

Fitch in her biography also frequently uses the image of seduction. She presents Nin as a seductress and regards even such an innocent endeavor of an eleven-year old as starting a diary as a way "to convince—to charm and seduce—her father to rejoin them" (4). She explains that this description of the origin of the diary is Nin's own, and to prove it she refers readers to a footnote where she quotes Nin's actual account of the conception of the diary, born out of her "desire to keep a channel of communication with the lost father" (421). While Nin's explanation sounds perfectly normal—she wanted to keep in touch with her father after he abandoned the family—Fitch's erotically tinged wording implies controversy and odd behavior: in her account Nin becomes a Lolita who wants to win over her father.

The theme of seduction is also prominent in Barillé's narrative. In one of her short vignettes, entitled "Beauty," she states that "at an age when most little girls are playing with dolls, Anaïs was already cultivating the art of seduction" (29). In another fragment, this time imitating Nin's own voice, she writes, "In order to please, I had to please everybody. I had to seduce everybody" (38). And then in her own voice, the voice of a narrator, Barillé states, "Seduction, for Anaïs, was a way of freeing herself from the previous lover" (134).

Duxler in her psychological study, suggestively titled *Seduction: A Portrait of Anaïs Nin,* also makes seduction the main theme of Nin's work and life. Duxler, Nin's friend and a professional psychologist, offers an intimate portrait of Nin and a psychological interpretation of her personality. She believes that Nin's unhappy childhood, particularly the loss of the father, had tremendous repercussions throughout her life. According to her, "Anaïs's childhood left her with tremendous doubts about her intrinsic value and lovability." To deal with anxiety, fear of rejection, and lack of confidence, Nin made herself lovable by pleasing and seducing others. Duxler explains, "Seduction is an important defensive strategy. It is designed to protect an individual from the overwhelming trauma of disconnection from, or loss of, a crucially important relationship." Duxler writes about different manifestations of seduction. She regards Nin's multiple sexual relationships as one, and her creation of a perfect self that "would be adored by all, rejected by none, and triumph over loss and abandonment" as another. Not only does Duxler deem Nin's relationships as an act of seduction but also she interprets Nin's whole existence in these terms. Duxler's interpretation differs little from the one Dr. Allendy provided for Nin a few decades before.[38]

Thus, the word *seductress* has become one of the most frequently used watchwords referring to Anaïs Nin and one that contributes significantly to the construction of her erotic image. While Nin's critics and biographers use mainly the image of seduction, reviewers invent secondary watchwords such as *Donna Juana, temptress, femme fatale, courtesan,* and *playgirl of the Western world* to spice up their evaluations of both unexpurgated diaries and biographies in the 1990s.

NIN AS HENRY MILLER'S MISTRESS AND COLLABORATOR

Another significant posthumous portrait of Nin that emphasizes the erotic is that of Nin in relation to Henry Miller. As the previous chapters demonstrate, Miller was crucial to launching Nin's career, to the point that her agent feared that Nin was treated as "a package with Miller." Nin eventually managed to escape being packaged with Miller, and after the publication of the diaries she became known as a writer in her own right. Even Kate Millett—the most famous feminist to reclaim Nin, by praising her and calling Nin "the mother of us all"—who heavily criticized Miller's writings in her *Sexual Politics,* seemed to forgive Nin her involvement with the author of *Tropic of Cancer.* And Nin herself (as the collection of her lectures, *A Woman Speaks,* proves) talked increasingly about women, rather than men, who fascinated or influenced her. However, the release of *Henry and June* in 1986 reestablished the Nin-Miller association. By narrowly focusing *Henry and June* on Nin's relationship with the Millers, Ferrone, the editor, brought Nin's relationship with Henry Miller to public attention.

A year after the release of *Henry and June,* the volume *A Literate Passion: Letters of Anaïs Nin and Henry Miller* was published, expanding further on the relationship between Nin and Henry Miller. (One side of their correspondence—Miller's letters to Nin—was published twenty-two years earlier, in 1965.) *A Literate Passion* focused mainly on their personal relationship. In the words of the editor of the Miller-Nin correspondence, Gunther Stuhlmann, "Space limitations . . . made it necessary to eliminate material peripheral to the personal story—lengthy discussions of Dostoevsky, Proust, Joyce, D. H. Lawrence; detailed critiques of one another's work-in-progress; ruminations on films, books, and so on."[39] Again, the focus of the correspondence was on the personal aspect of the Nin-Miller relationship rather than on their professional development. Undoubtedly, this publication was possible because of the earlier release of *Henry and June,* which generated interest in the Nin-Miller relationship.

The story of Nin, Miller, and his wife, June, gripped the imagination of the public so powerfully that most plays about Nin refer to her years spent in Paris and recount the adventures of this ménage à trois. For instance, out of three plays staged after Nin's death that were reviewed in the *New York Times,* two were devoted to the Parisian period: *Anaïs*

Nin: The Paris Years (1986) and *Anaïs Nin: One of Her Lives* (2006). The release of the film *Henry & June* in 1990 tied Nin even more strongly to Henry Miller. The story of Miller and Nin is appealing for at least two reasons: first, it involves *two* well-known authors; and second, these two celebrities are entangled in a love triangle. The story of Nin and the Millers therefore satisfied the appetites of the audience at the turn of the twenty-first century who were hungry for tales about celebrities, love, and scandal. This trend is evident in a growing number of films devoted to the lives of famous writers, many of which focus on their love lives. By repeating similar scenarios, however, texts such as *Henry and June* reduce Nin's life to the time she spent in Paris and freeze Nin in a relationship with Henry Miller. Consequently, her relationship with Miller became one of the most recognizable characteristics of Nin.

This association is not necessarily beneficial to Nin, however, as sometimes she is pushed into the background and the focus is on Miller, who is regarded by many as the more famous of the duo. For instance, as discussed earlier in this chapter, the release of the film *Henry & June,* which coincided with the change of the movie rating system in the United States, was accompanied by a large number of press articles. The American press relating the change of the rating system often included and discussed *Henry & June* as the first recipient of the new rating. Reading these articles, one can easily get the impression that *Henry & June* is a film about Henry Miller rather than Anaïs Nin. Despite the facts that the movie was based on Nin's book and Kaufman's intention was to portray Nin's sexual awakening, the press gave a greater prominence to Henry Miller.

Nin's name did not appear in a single headline the way Miller's name did. For instance, the *Los Angeles Times* announced, "Henry Miller Meets the MPAA Movies: Philip Kaufman's very adult 'Henry and June,' a tale of the controversial author's days in Paris, apparently is the latest recipient of the dreaded X rating. Its U.S. release is in limbo." Similarly, the *San Francisco Chronicle* implied that Miller is the main protagonist of the film, entitling its article "Henry Miller—On Trial Again?" And while some of these articles gave equal importance to Nin in the main text, others persisted in eliding her. For example, for Hal Hinson from the *Washington Post,* the movie was about "the American writer Henry Miller . . . and his wife, June[,] . . . and their friend and lover, Anaïs Nin." Hinson did not even acknowledge that the film was based on Nin's work. In fact, not a single review discussed how faithful (or not) the film is to Nin's book, which usually takes place when adaptations of literary works are evaluated.[40]

However, even though Nin is sometimes regarded as the lesser writer of the two, the dyad Anaïs Nin–Henry Miller has joined the pantheon of iconic literary collaborations, such as Simone de Beauvoir–Jean-Paul Sartre and Sylvia Plath–Ted Hughes. The Nin-Miller literary partnership is discussed in a recent popular publication originally titled *Between the Sheets: The Famous Literary Liaisons of Nine 20th Century Women Writers* by Leslie McDowell, as well as the more academically oriented *Significant Others: Creativity and Intimate Partnership* (1993) edited by Whitney Chadwick and Isabelle de Courtivron, to which Noël Riley Fitch contributed a chapter; *Creative Collaboration* (2000) by Vera John-Steiner; and *Literary Liaisons: Auto/biographical Appropriations in Modernist Women's Fiction* (2002) by Lynnette Felber.[41]

In Leslie McDowell's *Between the Sheets,* Nin is one of nine women writers—along with Katherine Mansfield, H. D., Rebecca West, Jean Rhys, Simone de Beauvoir, Martha Gellhorn, Elizabeth Smart, and Sylvia Plath—whose love and literary life is examined. McDowell writes from the women writers' point of view, wondering how well or badly these female authors would have fared without their partners. She usually comes to the conclusion that they would not have been who they were without their companions. The table of contents to her book displays designations (allegedly ironic, according to McDowell) that are supposed to characterize each writer in relation to her male writing partner. Thus, for instance, de Beauvoir is labeled the "long termer," Plath the "wife," and Nin the "mistress," which is definitely the most sexually loaded descriptor on the list.

Upon opening the chapter on Nin, one first notices the photographs of Nin and Miller. The picture of Nin shows her in a transparent veil, which draws attention to her eyes and bare shoulders, thus emphasizing Nin's mysteriousness, exoticism, and sex appeal. The account that follows, however, is fairly balanced, as it pays equal attention to Nin's emotional and professional relationship with Miller. McDowell claims to present a new perspective on Nin's relationship with Henry Miller, refusing to treat Nin as a victim of Miller's recklessness. Although McDowell admits that Nin made great sacrifices for Miller and claims that no other relationship discussed in the volume "poses quite such a literary threat as Miller does to Nin," she also shows how Nin benefited from their cooperation, "gaining entry to the literary world she was desperate to join," and if she did suffer because of Miller, she did so knowingly, for the sake of her art. McDowell empowers Nin the mistress, highlighting the double meaning of the word—a woman who has a sexual affair with a married man but also "a woman in authority over others"—and pointing out the ironic fact that it was Nin who paid for Miller's expenses and showered him with gifts, thus subverting the traditional role of a mistress. She also regards Nin's numerous affairs as "one more subversive tactic Nin employed to overturn the traditionally subservient aspect of the role." This sexual empowerment, however, is dubious, as it reflects the postfeminist tendencies to empower women through their sexuality. In the postfeminist era, Nin's juggling of lovers can be read as a sign of power.[42]

John-Steiner in her book *Creative Collaboration* aims at demolishing the myth of individual creation. She believes that a creative activity, whether scientific or artistic, is a social rather than individual process, and she highlights the significance of collaboration to both scientists and artists. The discussion of the Nin-Miller dyad receives a limited treatment, both in number of pages and in complexity. Dealing with Nin and Miller, John-Steiner glosses over many painful experiences and presents their liaison as an exemplar of a supportive partnership.[43]

This continual focus on Nin's liaison with Miller gives us a skewed vision of reality. Although Miller was undoubtedly a very important person in her life, he was not the only one. He was not the only famous writer with whom she collaborated, either. In fact, their affair and literary partnership, very intense in the 1930s, gradually cooled off after they moved to the United States at the beginning of World War II. Their correspondence became less and less frequent, and they ceased seeing each other for well over a decade. But because so many cultural products concentrated on their relationship, the Nin-Miller dyad became iconic. Each of those products—whether a play, a film, or a critical study—strengthened the bond linking this duo.

THE ETERNALLY FEMININE AND EXOTIC NIN

Nin's eroticism is also conveyed through the portrayal of her persona as feminine and exotic. Erica Jong opens an article on Nin's unexpurgated diaries with such a remark: "Anaïs Nin: the very name conjures exoticism and eroticism."[44] As the analysis of Nin's portraits in the previous chapter shows, Nin was frequently constructed as both the essence of femininity and an extraordinary person during her lifetime. The association of Nin with femininity was reinforced after her death by, for example, the creation of the perfume called Anaïs Anaïs.

In the preface to her biography of Nin, Fitch writes that Nin inspired the Cacharel perfume Anaïs Anaïs, which was released in 1978. She quotes a letter from Lawrence Durrell to Henry Miller in which the former announces, "It will please you to know that the new Cacharel scent named after Anaïs ('Anaïs-anaïs') is a great success." Fitch also mentions that Cacharel used a phrase from Nin's diary, "A silky fragment of woman," as its slogan. When asked in a private correspondence about how she knew that the perfume was inspired by Nin and not simply by the name Anaïs, Fitch replied that Rupert Pole, Nin's partner and at that time executor of her estate, in a private conversation with her confirmed that

Cacharel asked for his permission to use Nin's name. Unfortunately, Fitch was unable to provide further details of this arrangement, and neither was the Anaïs Nin Trust. The particulars of this deal may remain forever unknown. Nonetheless, it is highly probable that Nin inspired and posthumously endorsed one of the first celebrity perfumes.[45]

The perfume, still very popular today, stands for femininity. The Cacharel official website advertises the fragrance as "delicate and ultra-feminine."[46] The perfume container, in white and soft pink colors, is adorned with pink lilies. While white lilies commonly symbolize innocence and purity, the addition of pink makes them look more sensual, and the open petals of the pictured lily may suggest labia. The early advertisements for the perfume used Sara Moon's drawing of very feminine women among flower petals. The advertisement consists of soft shades and is done in soft focus. The perfume therefore promotes a specific kind of femininity—soft, delicate, and sensual. Although very few people outside the Nin circle today recognize Anaïs Nin as an inspiration of this perfume (and it is impossible to state whether, and how many, people in the late 1970s made the link between the perfume and her persona), the fact that she did influence the creation of this ultrafeminine fragrance certifies that at a certain moment in time Nin stood for femininity in one of its most traditional guises—voluptuous, fragile, graceful, elusive.

People who buy Anaïs Anaïs may be oblivious to the fact that it was named after Anaïs Nin, but those who know Anaïs Nin are very likely to associate her name with the perfume. This is because people such as Noël Fitch and Judy Chicago remind the public of this fact. The opening and closing lines of Fitch's introduction to *The Erotic Life of Anaïs Nin,* for example, acknowledge that Nin's name was used by Cacharel. The opening remark reads thus: "Anaïs, Ah-nah-ees. Her name has inspired numerous legends of love and literature and a perfume by the French house of Cacharel." The closing statement reiterates these words and sums up Nin as "a key figure in illuminating the Age of Aquarius. . . . A dozen parodies. . . . Six books of criticism. Two dozen university dissertations. A

French perfume. A legend." Judy Chicago, a feminist artist, begins her Internet essay, tellingly titled "Anaïs Nin: Writer or Perfume?" by saying, "History has not been kind to Anaïs Nin. Within a year of her death, Cacharel produced a perfume called 'Anaïs Anaïs,' as if all that was left of her life and her work was the exotic odor of a memory."[47]

Another space that highlights Nin's femininity and creates her as an exotic individual are two biographies of Henry Miller: *Always Merry and Bright: The Life of Henry Miller* by Jay Martin and *The Happiest Man Alive: A Biography of Henry Miller* by Mary V. Dearborn. In both narratives Nin is introduced as a mythical woman. Because Miller perceived Nin as an exotic and mysterious woman, she is so (re)constructed by his biographers. Commenting on Miller's description of Anaïs in a letter to his friend Emil Schnellock, Dearborn explains, "What he wanted to convey to Schnellock was Nin's total exoticism, what [Miller] saw as her 'Oriental' mystery." Following this thread, Dearborn describes Nin's background as being "as exotic as her clothes and her home." In a similar vein, Martin writes, "The more he knew her, the more mythical, ever-changing, did Anaïs seem. He called her *Schneewitchen,* Snow-white, but he also detected Moorish, Jewish and African forebears in her. Like Ayesha, she had to be obeyed—but she demanded nothing but his good."[48]

Nin's extraordinariness is partly expressed through their depictions of her house. Writing about Miller's first visit to Louveciennes, Martin states, "Everything seemed slightly touched by the extraordinary and mythical." Both biographers make Louveciennes attractive, and both mention the fact that Nin's house was situated on the estate that once belonged to Madame du Barry, Louis XV's legendary mistress. Additionally, Martin paints an idyllic village scene: "The Watteau-like Louveciennes scene, the green pastures dotted with cows, the trees moving in the clear breezes, the whole quiet pastoral atmosphere came to have a healing effect upon [Henry]." Louveciennes is not so enchanting in the accounts of Nin's biographer. In Bair's narrative, Louveciennes is an "unfashionable tumbledown village."[49]

As for Nin's house, both Dearborn and Martin describe it in detail, and both note its peculiarity. Dearborn portrays it as an "enchanted cottage, filled with color, bright accents, and curiosities from other lands." For Martin, it has a Moorish atmosphere. Both biographers mention the Arabian lamp lighting the entrance. In general, they build up the picture of an extraordinary, bewitching place. Additionally, for Martin, Nin and her house symbolize stability. He likens Nin's home to the old civilizations, "China or Egypt or Araby, where everything had long ago arrived at its final determinations, and against the background of which the individual could confidently stand." Nin is therefore portrayed as a solid rock on which Henry can rely. Her surroundings are described as having calming effects on Henry. Bair again demystifies the charm of Nin's abode. While she acknowledges Nin's own portrayal of her charming house, she corrects her idealized version: "Actually, the house was dilapidated and impossible to heat." All in all, by adhering to Miller's accounts of Nin, Miller's biographers perpetuate the myth of her persona as exotic and mystifying. Fans of Miller will, therefore, long associate Nin with mystery and extraordinariness.[50]

The exotic and feminine Nin is also reiterated in various memoirs of Nin. People (such as friend and author Valerie Harms) comment on her exotic name; on her unusual clothes, which for some (such as Rochelle Lynn Holt) are elegant, while others (such as writer William Claire and Nin's niece, Gayle Nin Rosenkrantz, who recalls her as "an exotic looking, strangely dressed woman") deem them bizarre; on her distinctive appearance: for some attractive (Nin's critic, Duane Schneider, describes Nin as "a beautiful woman" and "extremely attractive"), for some enchanting (critic Suzette Henke describes her as "a princess out of a fairy tale"), for others artificial (psychotherapist and teacher Shirley Ariker writes, "Everything about her was false. Her face was like a mask" and her black hair "made her face all the more unreal").[51]

These four interrelated portraits—the erotic Nin, Nin the seductress, Nin in relation to Henry Miller, and the feminine and exotic Nin—being continuously reiterated and reconstructed in various times and places, contributed significantly to the fall of Nin as a women's liberation icon.

NIN THE (FALLEN) WOMEN'S LIBERATION ICON

After Nin's death and before the first unexpurgated diary, *Henry and June,* appeared in 1986, the seventh and final volume of the first series of *Diaries* was released, in 1980. It opens in the summer of 1966, after the publication of the first *Diary,* when Nin became a widely recognized writer. The form of this diary differs from the previous six volumes, partly because Nin's diary keeping decreased over the years and partly because its editing was taken over by Rupert Pole. *Diary 7* is largely devoid of inner monologues and consists primarily of Nin's descriptions of her journeys, lectures, and interviews, occasionally interspersed with her comments and observations. She reports visits to Bali, Cambodia, Hong Kong, Japan, Malaysia, Mexico, Morocco, the Philippines, Singapore, Tahiti, and Thailand and describes in great detail places, houses, people, and local customs.

As demonstrated in the previous chapter, during her most prolific years, Nin acquired a new identity—that of a women's representative. *Diary 7,* published posthumously in 1980, reinforces this portrait of Nin and summarizes her stance on feminism. In its pages, Nin comments frequently on the women's movement and her contribution to it. She refuses to align herself with any social movements, and feminism is no exception. Although she states a few times in the seventh volume that she supports women's liberation, she has her own understanding of what this liberation should involve. Her answer to feminists' demands is, as usual, an individual fight and an inner change. She writes, "Liberation is a work of one's own. Political problems can be solved only when we are ready from within, well oriented and self-respecting" (*Diary 7,* 187). Nin believes that the women's movement is not clearly defined, and she opposes its militant dimension. She bemoans the fact that there is too much hostility toward men and that women, instead of reading women writers, waste their energies on criticizing men writers, such as

Norman Mailer and Henry Miller (158). She disapproves of "the men haters, the artificial lesbians, the vociferous, bitter, violent women who achieve nothing" (283).

As a result, there is animosity between Nin and feminists, instances of which Nin recounts in *Diary 7*, even mentioning a few lectures during which she was booed. Feminists criticize her for her lack of involvement in political and social issues, for her promotion of male artists, for the way she dresses, and for her soft manner of speaking (*Diary 7*, 248). Nonetheless, despite her ambivalent position in the women's movement, Nin portrays herself as a representative of women. She writes, "Everyone knows now that I have at least half of the feminist women behind me, and many more who are not feminists but consider me a pioneer in independence, a heroine, a legend, a model, etc." (222). To support this view, Nin and her editors devote five pages of *Diary 7* to presenting excerpts from readers' letters (200–205). These quotations, which are from one sentence to seven sentences long, are interesting not only because they cast light on what the readers found interesting about Nin but also, first and foremost, because they reveal what Nin and the editors considered important to quote (it must be also remembered that the letters were chosen out of thousands of others and not a single letter of critique was included in the *Diary*).

From these five pages, Nin emerges as an inspiration for women, arousing in them various desires, such as to rediscover their lost, forgotten, and/or neglected self, to become a writer, to be independent, to accept themselves for who they are, or simply to pursue their dreams. Nin's readers strongly identify with her, her struggles, and her sensibility, and lines such as the following abound in these pages: "I know that you have been through everything I go through in my own struggle to find my full humanity" (201); "You describe so clearly what I feel every second of my waking and dream existence" (203); "You are writing my life also" (203); "In your Diaries I see the person I am and the person I want to be" (204). Two fragments relate Nin to the feminist movement yet see her as being different from it. "After a long period when I read only feminist propaganda and fiction," reads one of the passages, "it was a clear day and cool air to read your Diary" (201). The other praises her personal and intimate manner of dealing with problems that touch contemporary women: "There are women who roar and demand to be heard. You are so much more effective because you whisper in our ears and by so doing touch our very souls" (202). Thus, Nin's portrait is drawn indirectly, with readers' words. Because the selected fragments are very short, specific, taken out of their original context, and, most significantly, very admiring, they reconfirm her portrait as a women's representative. This portrait is given extra authority when it is confirmed by others.

The seventh volume met with harsh criticism, however. Assessing it for the *New York Times,* Katha Pollitt asserts that Nin's "distinctive blend of vanity and hypersensitivity has never been so galling." She accuses Nin of keeping secret the essential facts of her life, such as her partners and the source of her financing, considers Nin as a construct and "*the* quintessential male-directed woman," and decries anyone who has ever considered Nin's work as "unvarnished self-revelation." Labelling Nin's fans as "Ninians," she states that volume 7 "may make even devoted Ninians blush for their heroine." A similar label appears in James Wolcott's review for the *New York Review of Books,* in which he calls Nin's admirers "Ninnies." In these two reviews not only is Nin under attack but so are her readers. The ridiculing of Nin's fans, called dismissively Ninnies, Ninians, and Ninophiles, reflects the tendency to appraise women writers and their readers negatively. Writing about the reception of women authors, Carolyn Heilbrun notes that "either a woman author isn't studied, or studying her is reduced to an act of misplaced religious fanaticism." In his scornful review, Wolcott also deems Nin's career "a masterpiece of self-promotion" and states that "the hilariously vain *apercus* [glance, view, perception, insight] of Volume Seven will do more damage to her reputation than the cruelest slice from villainous Vidal," referring here to Vidal's review of 1971 (analyzed in the previous chapter).[52]

That volume 7 contributed to tarnishing Nin's reputation is unlikely, but a critical interest in Nin's writings did diminish between 1980 and 1992, if we take as our measure the number of book-length studies devoted to her; during those years, only one monograph on Nin was published, *Anaïs Nin* by Nancy Scholar. This lack of interest is quite surprising, especially considering the fact that in the 1980s "women fully joined the literary juries of the United States, as writers, critics, reviewers, publishers, anthologists, and historians, contributing to the verdicts, and challenging the laws."[53] Feminist literary theory blossomed in the 1980s and so did women's studies. So why was Nin pushed to the margins? There is no easy answer, but there are a few plausible reasons for this critical neglect of Nin.

First of all, Nin's extremely cautious version of feminism did not correspond with the needs of any faction of the feminist thought prevailing in the 1980s. For example, it may seem that feminists of a radical orientation, such as Mary Daly, the author of *Gyn/Ecology: The Metaethics of Radical Feminism* (1978), shared with Nin an enthusiasm for "revaluing the Feminine"; however, Nin's claims were not far-reaching enough. Nin certainly stood for the feminine, but rather than being one of Daly's "wild females," she would have been classified as Daly's "painted bird." "For Daly," as Tong explains, "painted birds are those women who permit 'daddy' to deck them out in splendor, to 'cosmeticize' and perfume them, to girdle and corset them." Nin's focus on her appearance, the flattering photographic portraits included in her *Diary* and the press, the posthumous release of the perfume Anaïs Anaïs that was inspired by her name, and the publication of *Henry and June,* which revealed her great dependence on men, made Nin into one of Daly's "mutant fembirds."[54]

The decade of the 1980s also saw the expansion of another faction of feminism, referred to by Chris Beasley as REI feminism (where REI stands for race, ethnicity, and imperialism). In the 1980s, as Elaine Showalter indicates, "the notion of a universal womanhood or sisterhood, unmarked by differences of race, religion, age, region, sexual orientation, and political affiliation, seemed like an outdated utopian fantasy." At a time when women were recognizing and confronting their differences, Nin's self-presentation as a spokesperson for all women lost its currency. It became evident that Nin spoke from a position of a white, middle-class, privileged woman, and her solutions to social problems were frequently naïve. For instance, shortly after Nin's death, Alice Walker, the author of the acclaimed *The Color Purple* (1983), wrote a very sympathetic obituary in *Ms.* that nonetheless pointed out Nin's limitations. "Anaïs's apolitical nature," Walker declared, "was self-indulgent and escapist; her analysis of poverty, struggle, and political realities, mere romantic constructions useful to very few (ghetto children, she is reported to have said, should 'write' as she had done, thus escaping their wretched existence)."[55]

Another probable explanation of why critics steered clear of Nin in the second half of the 1980s lies in the publication of her erotica collections, *Delta of Venus* and *Little Birds,* given the pornography debate that raged for most of the decade. On whichever side of the pornography debate women were, more and more of them realized that a woman's perspective on the erotic did not necessarily equate with a feminist one.

And finally, the lack of criticism on Nin can be also attributed to disappointment with Nin after the publication of *Henry and June,* a so-called unexpurgated diary that adjusted many of Nin's self-portraits. This portion of the diary was a serious blow to Nin's reputation as a women's representative, as many memoirs on Nin testify. One example of disillusionment with Nin is expressed in *Seduction: A Portrait of Anaïs Nin.* The author of the book, Margot Duxler, Nin's admirer and friend, is among those who became disillusioned with Nin. In the first chapter of *Seduction,* Duxler introduces herself, provides her family background, and situates herself in relation to Nin. Brought up by very strict and religious Jewish parents, Duxler admits to feelings of alienation from her family and a lack of understanding between herself and her mother, for whom marriage was the ultimate goal of a woman's life. Duxler then describes how upon discovering Nin, she felt that she had found herself a mentor. For her, Nin embodied freedom, sensuality, and creativity—everything that Duxler's parents despised, and everything that Duxler believed in. Duxler therefore identified with Nin and found her persona very inspirational. She was not the only one. Two collections of memoirs, *Recollections of Anaïs Nin by Her Contemporaries* and *Anaïs Nin: A Book of Mirrors,* are filled with confessions of women who found Nin inspiring. Suzette Henke, for instance, writes, "At the outset of the women's movement, Nin cast an aura around many of us hungry for independent role models."[56]

Duxler then recounts the circumstances of meeting Nin and describes their acquaintance that formed over time. Finally, she relates the sense of betrayal and sorrow she experienced once the uncensored diaries were published and she discovered the truth about Nin's life. She writes, "As the books were published . . . I finished reading each one with increasing distress and confusion, distraught to discover that the idealized maternal figure I had wanted and needed Anaïs to be, and whom she presented herself to be, was not, in fact, who she was." Duxler's story is symptomatic of what other Nin readers, who initially trusted Nin and treated her as their representative, felt once the so-called truth about their heroine was revealed.[57]

Barbara Kraft, another of Nin's fans and a friend, recounts a similar disenchantment. In her essay about Nin included in *Recollections of Anaïs Nin by Her Contemporaries*, she reports how upon meeting Nin, she "was captivated by Anaïs who inspired intense feelings in everyone she came in contact with." A friendship developed. Kraft, then the wife of a prominent member of the Los Angeles Philharmonic Orchestra, was persuaded by Nin to publish her diary. Although she had her doubts about the whole project, she decided to go ahead with the publication, a decision that cost her dearly. Kraft recalls, "Had I known the consequences of my 'truth,' I would have had second thoughts about publishing my diary; one of them would have concerned the repercussions the book would have on my daughter and our subsequent relationship. The repercussions to my own life were harsh. . . . Overnight I became a pariah in the world where I had lived for sixteen years, someone who could not be trusted." Kraft then describes a great sense of disappointment and betrayal experienced once Nin's unexpurgated diaries were published and it turned out that Nin, who encouraged her so strongly to release the diary in its original form (Kraft considered publishing under a pseudonym or turning her diary into a work of fiction), herself concealed many facts about her private life. The discovery that Nin had lied in her diaries caused a great deal of distress among Nin's enthusiasts, especially those who were acquainted with her.[58]

Two revelations were particularly upsetting for Nin's readers: Nin's sexual permissiveness and her dependence on men, and the fact that a poignantly described stillbirth in the first-ever published *Diary* was really a late-term abortion, as revealed in the second unexpurgated diary, *Incest*. However, not everyone felt betrayed by Nin. Some, like Erica Jong, still insisted on treating Nin as a feminist heroine. This battle over whether Nin is relevant, and to what extent, to feminism demonstrates cracks and divisions in feminist thought.

Feminists have always been divided on the issue of sexuality. Assessing Nin's attitude toward sexuality, some critics, such as Sharon Spencer and Erica Jong, regard Nin's views and behaviors as an expression of freedom, while others, like Barbara Kraft, consider them as a chain to patriarchy. The literary scholar Sharon Spencer sees Nin as "a woman who dared to fulfill herself erotically, an aspiration that in a century of acclaimed 'women's liberation' has brought her more severe condemnation than praise—and by whom: other women!" Similarly, for Erica Jong—the novelist whose *Fear of Flying* (1973) triggered at least as much debate about female sexuality as did the revelations about Nin's erotic life—Nin embodies psychological, sexual, and artistic freedom. Jong believes that those who denigrate Nin are afraid of expressing their own sexuality. In contrast, for Barbara Kraft, Nin was far from liberated, either sexually or psychologically. Kraft maintains, "Women who seek freedom through sexuality and define freedom as sexual promiscuity remain forever in shackles. If Anaïs's life teaches us anything, it should teach us this."[59]

This argument over whether Nin should be considered a sexually liberated heroine or a dupe of patriarchy reflects a bigger cultural debate about sexuality. While at the beginning of the women's movement many women embraced sexual permissiveness as an expression of liberation from patriarchal rule, with time, critics began to regard it as a new means of oppressing women. Similar tendencies can be observed nowadays: women are led to believe by various media that promiscuity is a newly gained freedom, a feminist achievement, whereas feminist critics such as Angela McRobbie warn against this postfeminist promotion of unbridled sexuality.

Another area contested among feminists is motherhood and a controversial issue related to it, namely, abortion. Many Nin's readers were upset by the fact that Nin had had an abortion that she described as a stillbirth at the end of *Diary 1*. The revelation of Nin's pregnancy in the first volume emerges rather unexpectedly. At the end of one entry, she announces simply that she saw a doctor who told her that she was too small to bear a child in a natural way and would need a Caesarean section. The next entry opens with the phrase "several months later" and information that she is pregnant (*Diary 1,* 338). Nin begins this passage—which ends with the delivery of a stillborn baby girl—with an invocation to an unborn child. Recalling her own abandonment by her father, Nin says that "it would be better to die than to be abandoned, for you would spend your life haunting the world for this lost father" (339). At no point does she disclose the identity of the father of her child. Instead, she provides many rather negative thoughts on fatherhood. She believes that men are too irresponsible and too selfish to care for a child, and she concludes that "there is no father on earth. . . . It would be better if you died inside of me, quietly, in the warmth and in the darkness" (339–40).

She then moves on to a very dramatic and detailed description of the delivery. She begins by saying that she had to be rushed to the clinic, as the doctor did not hear the breathing of her six-month-old fetus. She recounts hours of labor—cracking bones, swollen veins, heavy legs, ripping flesh, blood, pain, and never-ending pushing—and this dramatic account is interspersed with such touching comments as "[a] part of me lay passive, did not want to push out anyone, not even this dead fragment of myself, out in the cold, outside of me" (341). In this overall poignant depiction of birth, she does not, however, fail to mention that before she went into labor, she "combed [her] hair, . . . powdered and perfumed [herself], painted [her] eyelashes" (341). She ends her account by describing a dead baby and concluding that she "was designed for other forms of creation. Nature connived to keep me a man's woman, and not a mother; not a mother to children but to men" (346). The next day, weak but refreshed, after a "[m]orning toilette" that included "[p]erfume and powder," Nin entertains her visitors (346).

In 1992, the second volume of the unexpurgated series, *Incest,* was published. *Incest,* which continues the story began in *Henry and June,* made public other sexual affairs of the writer and disclosed probably the most controversial details of Nin's life: the incestuous relationship with her father that she engaged in as an adult and the fact that what she presented in the first volume of the first series as a stillbirth was really a late-term abortion. The account of the delivery published in *Incest,* apart from a few sentences, is the same as in *Diary 1.* What therefore shocked Nin's readers was not the description itself but the fact that it was a late-term abortion and not, as Nin claimed in *Diary 1,* a stillbirth. *Incest* revealed that upon finding out that she was pregnant, Nin was determined to get rid of the child; she first arranged a visit to a "sage-femme" who was supposed to help her abort the baby. Only when she was six months into her pregnancy did a doctor discover that the abortion attempts had failed. This fact did not change her mind, and she persisted in her decision to terminate the pregnancy.

When this new version of the putative childbirth emerged, critics who earlier had tended to focus on the moving parts of

Nin's accounts began to highlight Nin's selfishness and vanity. Particularly critical of this revelation were feminist critics. For Katha Pollitt, this disclosure demonstrates clearly that Nin never was "the bold truth-teller of women's secret experiences that she claimed to be." Furthermore, Pollitt regards Nin's failure to declare her abortion back in the 1960s (although Nin did sign *Ms.*'s petition "We Have Had Abortions") as a wasted opportunity on Nin's part to contribute to a fight for the legalization of abortion. Pollitt therefore does not criticize Nin so much for the abortion or the actual description of it but for the fact that she concealed it as a stillbirth.[60]

Another critic shocked by Nin's treatment of the abortion was Claudia Roth Pierpont, a contributor to the *New Yorker* who wrote several profiles of famous women writers, which were then brought together in a book entitled *Passionate Minds: Women Rewriting the World*. Pierpont disagrees with Pollitt that Nin's divulging the abortion back in the 1960s would have helped the feminist cause. According to her, this "horrifying scene" would have done more damage than good. Aghast, she asks rhetorically, "Is it imaginable that so brutal and frivolously self-serving an account could have contributed to the argument for abortion rights?" For Pierpont the answer is clear, and she concludes, "In this instance, rewriting her story was probably Nin's best deed for the feminist cause."[61]

Deirdre Bair, Nin's biographer, was also deeply appalled by Nin's description of the abortion. Bair, who tries to maintain an objective distance toward her subject throughout the biography, becomes one of Nin's harshest judges when dealing with this particular event. After giving details of Nin's pregnancy and her attempts to terminate it, Bair declares, "The account of the birth in the diary almost defies interpretation. It is a portrait of monstrous egotism and selfishness, horrifying in its callous indifference."[62]

The publication of *Incest* alienated many of Nin's readers, and Nin's image acquired a monstrous dimension. The previous chapter demonstrates that a famous person has to be, as

Leo Braudy observes, "different enough to be interesting, yet similar enough not to be threatening or destructive." During her prolific years, Nin managed to manipulate her image in such a way as to appeal to her audience. The details of her life that started to emerge after her death upset the balance she had striven to maintain. The fact that it was an abortion, rather than her affair with her father, that was responsible for most of the controversy seems to back up what Linda Wagner-Martin claims about biographies of women. According to Wagner-Martin, women are often judged in terms of what kind of mothers, wives, or daughters they were. She demonstrates this assertion with the example of Sylvia Plath, who was harshly criticized for abandoning her children when she committed suicide. Nin, too, is condemned for her failed motherhood, labeled by many as an act of ultimate selfishness.[63]

It seems that the only way to excuse Nin's deed is to treat her as a psychological case study, as Suzette Henke does. Henke's critical framework allows her to look sympathetically on Nin's account of abortion. She believes that the loss of Nin's father made Nin dread maternity. She explains, "Anaïs has identified so completely with the father who abandoned her that she herself must reject the potential daughter/son in order to avoid betrayal by an egotistical lover." According to Henke, Nin was afraid that she would experience a fate similar to that of her mother, who had been abandoned and left on her own with three children to care for. This tendency to psychoanalyze Nin, or even to pathologize her, emerges particularly clearly from the analysis of Nin's relationship with her father and the way in which Nin critics have dealt with it.[64]

NIN AS A TRAUMA SURVIVOR

Apart from revealing the truth about Nin's abortion, *Incest* also exposed the affair with her father. The release of *Incest* reflects a cultural phenomenon that most likely made the publication of the book possible: the incest recovery movement. Critics usually attribute the beginnings of this movement to the publication of *The Courage to Heal: A Guide for Women Survivors of Child Sexual Abuse* in 1988. The authors of this self-help book, Ellen Bass and Laura Davis, maintain that many of the people who were abused in their childhood do not have conscious memories of the abuse. *The Courage to Heal* was soon followed by similar publications, such as *Adult Children of Abusive Parents* (1989) by Steven Farmer, *Secret Survivors: Uncovering Incest and Its Aftereffects on Women* (1990) by E. Sue Blume, and *Reclaiming Our Lives: Hope for Adult Survivors of Incest* (1990) by Carol Poston and Karen Lison. What these books have in common, as Elizabeth Loftus and Katherine Ketcham explain, is a specific vision of memory as a storage box or a video recorder, and a belief in repression—the power of the mind to remove disturbing experiences from conscious awareness.[65]

Repression supporters claimed that traumatic experiences might leave the sufferer without any conscious memories but that these could be recovered during therapy because memory is like a box that can be explored at any point. They strongly encouraged therapy as a means of delving into the past because they believed "that even while the traumatic memories are safely buried, the emotions entombed with them seep into our conscious lives, poisoning our relationships and undermining our sense of self." For this reason, the supporters of the recovered memory theory were prone to attribute depression, panic attacks, eating disorders, and relationship difficulties to childhood sexual abuse. People sharing such beliefs belonged to one camp of what Roger Luckhurst terms "the Memory War," which, as its name suggests, is a heated debate about the nature of memory.[66]

The opponent camp consisted of people who were suspicious about the idea that one would be able to completely suppress memories from one's consciousness. Shortly after the search for repressed memories began, it met with a backlash. A counterargument was proposed, namely, that recovered memories were in fact false memories, frequently planted in patients' heads by eager therapists. An alternative model of memory was proposed: memory as a space of reconstruction where facts mingle with fiction. In 1992, The False Memory Syndrome Foundation was established; its aim was to find reasons for the spread of False Memory Syndrome (FMS), to help those who were affected by it, and to find ways to prevent it (according to the official website). In a counterattack, the advocates of FMS were accused by the supporters of repressed memories of being antiwoman, antichild, and antivictim and of wishing to destroy the gains of the feminist movement.[67]

The Memory War, as Luckhurst illustrates, was reflected in cultural narratives, such as novels, memoirs, and films throughout the 1990s. For instance, Jane Smiley in her novel *A Thousand Acres* (1991) featured the model of recovered memory, while Nicci French in *The Memory Game* (1997) investigated the possibility of implanting false memories. Also, some personal accounts exploring the recovered memories of sexual abuse in the family were published, such as Sylvia Fraser's *My Father's House* (1989).[68]

Nin's *Incest,* with its revelation of Nin's affair with her father, appeared when incest and sexual abuse were hotly debated, the Memory War was at its peak, and memoirs that discussed incest and sexual abuse flooded the market. *Incest* can be therefore considered as a product of its time—the product, as Luckhurst explains, "of a shift in awareness about the prevalence of sexual abuse and admission of its primary location: inside the family." *Incest* was soon followed by critical assessments of Nin's relationship with her father. Nin scholarship in the 1990s was characterized by the growing use of psychoanalytical and psychological theories. More and more frequently, Nin was treated as a victim of childhood abuse. The only way to come to terms with Nin's conscious involvement in a sexual relationship with her father in her adulthood, or with "the ultimate transgression," as the back cover of *Incest* labeled it, seems to have been to regard her as a troubled and wounded individual or, alternatively, to dismiss the story as an instance of confabulation.[69]

Fitch is one of the first of Nin's critics to concentrate on the relationship with her father. In the introduction and the first chapter of the biography *Anaïs: The Erotic Life of Anaïs Nin,* Fitch insists that Nin's life was determined by her absent father. As early as the second paragraph of the introduction, she confronts readers with a scandalous piece of information regarding Nin—her incestuous relationship with her father. She further implies that Nin was seduced and abused by her father as a child and that this resulted in her affair with him in her adult life. Although Fitch admits that "this fact is impossible to prove conclusively," she builds the whole account of Nin's life around this assumption, maintaining that "the pattern of seduction seems evident from her life and art, even without her verbal clues."[70]

To support her hypothesis, Fitch uses a variety of methods. She quotes critics such as Alice Miller, a psychologist who pioneered work on parental child abuse with her first book, *The Drama of a Gifted Child* (1979). In *Thou Shalt Not Be Aware* (1981), to which Fitch constantly refers, Miller attacked psychoanalysis because she believed that Freudian theories "helped to conceal the fact that sexual abuse of children occurs frequently and results in later emotional disturbances in the victims of such abuse." Fitch also reads Nin's fiction as an expression of painful events that allegedly took place in her formative years, as in the following fragment: "Much later, in her creation of Djuna, her strongest fictional alter ego, she presents a child with 'enormous fairy-tale' eyes who is sexually violated by the watchman at the orphanage where she lives." Fitch therefore implies that Nin expressed in her fiction what she was unable to confess in her diary, and she tends to select quotes from Nin's friends that prove her theory. She notes, for instance, "As Henry Miller will observe years later, she never spoke of her childhood experiences or friends, it was like a 'lack or a gap.'"[71]

Commenting on biography in an article titled "Shaping the Truth," Miranda Seymour writes, "Life in the raw is often shapeless: the biographer must create their persuasive narrative by inserting a connecting thread. Subjectivity inevitably comes into play in this manufactured coherence." It is hard to avoid an impression that Fitch is determined to fit various aspects of Nin's life into a coherent jigsaw puzzle. Her focus on discovering Nin's psychological problems is her way of creating a consistent and attention-grabbing narrative. In the preface alone, Fitch mentions nymphomania, neurosis, and childhood trauma as possible psychological disorders plaguing Nin. This confirms Hermione Lee's claim that "[w]omen writers whose lives involved abuse, mental illness, self-harm, [and] suicide have often been treated, biographically, as victims or psychological case-histories first and as professional writers second."[72]

In *Biography: A Very Short Introduction,* Hermione Lee states that in the post-Freudian era even biographers skeptical about psychoanalysis were obliged to write about their subject's infancy, sexuality, illnesses, and dreams; otherwise their accounts were regarded as incomplete. Lee also demonstrates that despite the fact that psycho-biography is rarely practiced in its full form, many contemporary biographers are influenced by psychoanalytical lingo.[73] And so is Fitch. Her application of Alice Miller's works allows her to concentrate on Nin's childhood as a source of her future problems because although Miller rejects Freud's theories, she does focus on childhood as a crucial stage of personal development and blames abusive parents for neuroses afflicting their adult children.

Malcolm Bowie explains perfectly why the recourse to childhood and psychoanalysis is so alluring and useful for biographers:

> An adult life is such a tangled affair, with so many disparate strands running through it, that almost any simplifying mechanism will be welcome.... Through the thicket of the adult subject's professional and personal lives, through the jungle of affective, economic, and socio-political forces in which his [sic] individuality is forged and modified, the Freud-inspired biographer can travel with a reliable navigational aid. The early configurations of the individual's libido as contained or discharged within the family group hold the key to his later erotic career.... If we add to these intellectual benefits the spectacle of the young child as the hero of the Oedipal drama and therefore as a

creature of intense and conflicting passions, the charm of psychoanalysis as a biographical aid will begin to seem irresistible. It will be both a scientific procedure and a dramaturgical device. It will allow us to construct hypotheses and theorems that are intellectually convincing but at the same time dark, fearful, and incest-fringed.[74]

Providing a psychoanalytical or psychological interpretation of the subject's life is especially tempting in the case of Nin because of her lifelong involvement in psychoanalysis and her great confidence in it. For Nin, psychoanalysis was a narrative tool with the help of which she attempted to understand herself. Elizabeth Podnieks thus summarizes Freud's influence on Nin's sense of self: "His division of the mind into the conscious and the unconscious and later into the ego, superego, and id would be reflected in her own sense of self as fractured and in her Freudian drive to recover by means of analysis full self-knowledge."[75]

Fitch's role in her biography of Nin can be likened to that of an analyst during a psychoanalytic session. She assumes that Nin could not remember some of her childhood experiences, and Fitch offers an interpretation of these allegedly buried memories. Fitch's biography therefore reflects the search for repressed memories that was characteristic of the last decade of the twentieth century. She states, for instance, that Nin "does not have a childhood, in part because of a loss of memory and in part because of her isolated dreaming." On another occasion, when she tries to find reasons why Nin engaged in an incestuous relationship with her father, she points to "unacknowledged childhood sexual memory against which she is powerless." And while describing Nin's sessions with Allendy, Fitch concludes that "[a] psychoanalyst today with the same information—a description of a violent, patriarchal father, a lifetime of seductive behavior, and dreams of prostitution in a patient who is nonorgasmic, passive, masochistic yet fearful of pain, and sickened by her own sexual aggressiveness—would look for childhood sexual experiences in the patient. But . . . [Allendy] does not." Fitch is probably right: had Nin found herself in the therapist office in the 1990s, she might have been encouraged to uncover her "buried" memories.[76]

Writing about modern psychotherapy, Loftus and Ketcham note that the central question "Who am I?" was reduced at the end of the twentieth century to "How did I get this way?" They explain, "To understand who we are and why we are the way we are, many therapists encourage us to go back to our childhoods and find out what happened to us there. If we are in pain, we are told there must be a cause; if we cannot locate the cause, we have not looked deep enough." Fitch's biography reflects this phenomenon—it reconstructs Nin's traumatic childhood to cast light on Nin's adult behavior, especially some of her actions, such as the affair with her father, that seem to escape any understanding.[77]

Two critical studies of Nin's writings—Diane Richard-Allerdyce's *Anaïs Nin and the Remaking of Self: Gender, Modernism and Narrative Identity* and a chapter devoted to Nin in Suzette A. Henke's *Shattered Subjects: Trauma and Testimony in Women's Life-Writing*—also reflect the Memory War phenomenon. Both critics regard Nin's early childhood as the scene of traumatic events (the loss of the father and the alleged [sexual] abuse). Both employ the concept of "narrative recovery" to understand Nin's works, and both claim that writing served Nin as a means of ordering the chaotic events of her life, thus giving her mastery over them. Henke argues that autobiography, which she defines broadly as encompassing diaries, journals, and confessions, has the potential to be a form of scriptotherapy—"the process of writing out and writing through traumatic experience in the mode of therapeutic reenactment." She regards writing as an incredibly useful tool that can help victims of trauma recover and one that serves a similar purpose to that of psychoanalysis. Henke explains, "Autobiography could so effectively mimic the scene of psychoanalysis that life-writing might provide a therapeutic alternative for victims of severe anxiety and, more seriously, of post-traumatic stress disorder." According to her, Nin's fragmented persona revealed in the unexpurgated diaries is re-created and perfected in the edited version. While Henke concentrates on Nin's diaries, Richard-Allerdyce gives prominence to Nin's fiction, considering it an effective means of "mourning the past."[78]

What is more, both Henke's and Richard-Allerdyce's studies fit into the paradigm of sexual abuse. Although neither of them overtly pronounces Nin a victim of sexual abuse, it is implied in some of their utterances. Richard-Allerdyce explains that "Nin herself believed, I think rightly, that her non-diary writings would provide the distance she needed to deal with some of the psychological damage she suffered during childhood—whether as the result of her father's abandonment of his family when Anaïs was a child, or (as Fitch has argued and Nin later believed . . .) as the result of early sexual violation." The possibility of sexual abuse lurks also in Henke's phrases and sentences, such as this one: "Anaïs's girlish self-image is constructed in the paedophilic gaze of the artist-father who admires her slender, nubile body." Henke refers here to photos taken by Joaquin Nin of his toddler daughter, which she regards as "pornographic photo sessions." Linde Salber, the German biographer of Nin, offers a different perspective on these photographic endeavors. She explains that at the beginning of the twentieth century, photography was a popular pastime of the middle class, and she does not see anything deviant about Nin's father's photographic interests. A similar explanation was given by Nin's brother Joaquín Nin-Culmell, who protested against interpreting the father-daughter photo sessions as an abnormal activity. Henke acknowledges his opinion in a footnote, but this does not stop her from insinuating that the behavior of Nin's father went beyond the norms of decent conduct.[79]

In both Richard-Allerdyce's and Henke's studies, there are also overtones of a discourse of repressed memories. Richard-Allerdyce, for example, quotes Alice Miller—the psychologist also quoted by Fitch—saying that "the works of writers, poets, and painters tell the encoded story of childhood traumas no longer consciously remembered in adulthood," and she adds that "Nin's work resonates with her unsayable response to early paternal abuse (whether sexual or otherwise psychological and physical) and the 'earth-shattering' effects of that violation on her later life." Throughout her book, she interprets Nin's writing with the help of such concepts as suppressed memory, lapse of memory, denial, and repression. Similarly, Henke notes, "A sixteen-year-old Anaïs seems thoroughly to have repressed negative memories of her father and can only nod weakly in assent to her mother's promptings." She refers here to a conversation Nin had with her mother in 1919 regarding the circumstances of her father's abandonment. Her mother "reminded" her that her father had always been very brutal and that it was he who had deserted them and not the other way round. For Henke, this is a case of repressed memories. However, an alternative interpretation can be provided: The participation of Nin's mother in a recovery process may be regarded as a case of planting memories in Nin. Perhaps Nin, who revered her father, as her early diary suggests, did not discover the "true" face of her father but re-created him according to her mother's stories.[80]

Another psychological analysis of Nin is offered by Margot Beth Duxler in her *Seduction: A Portrait of Anaïs Nin*. Like Fitch, Richard-Allerdyce, and Henke, Duxler too treats Nin as a traumatized child. Duxler explains metaphorically, "Like a tree that has survived a blight and grown around an infestation in its roots, so did Anaïs survive, with the scars of her childhood invisible but powerfully affecting her later development." Nin once again becomes a psychological case study. Duxler assumes that because of the early trauma, Nin developed "a false self," a seductive self, and lived most of her life under its guise. Only the diary was a haven where Nin felt safe enough to expose her real self.[81]

This psychological approach to Nin's life helped Duxler deal with her own disappointment with Nin after she discovered that "in many ways *she was not who she had seemed to be*," and ultimately to reclaim Nin. Although the "unedited" diaries created a sense of betrayal among Nin readers, they simultaneously gave them new means to defend her—Nin's outrageous behavior recorded in the diaries could be treated as a serious psychological disturbance. Nin can be exonerated, but only if enough evidence is brought forward to demonstrate that she was a particularly disturbed individual. Such an interpretation of Nin's conduct allows Duxler to resist, for example, one of the most common accusations against Nin, namely, that Nin was narcissistic. Duxler explains, "If Anaïs appears to be self-obsessed, narcissistic, or indulgent, as some critics have claimed, it is because the development of her spontaneous and authentic self was damaged and inhibited by the nature of the early trauma she endured."[82]

However, the portrayal of Nin as a victim is double-edged, as it also allows Duxler to discount and reinterpret many of Nin's statements. She writes, for example, "Anaïs often remarked that she needed numerous partners because she could not be all of herself with any one individual, but the compulsive quality of her multiple relationships indicates more of a pathological symptom than an expression of free will." Nin's sexual behavior is therefore explicable only if dealt with as a psychological abnormality. It seems that little has changed in the treatment of sexually liberated women since the nineteenth century, when, as Elaine Showalter explains, "uncontrolled sexuality seemed the major, almost defining symptom of insanity in women." Duxler's statement practically echoes the opinions of Victorian doctors. She too implies, although in more politically correct wording, that Nin's compulsive sexuality is a symptom of mental disturbance. Nin therefore can be saved, but only if she is locked in a metaphorical lunatic asylum. The only way to deal with her is to treat her as a seriously troubled and wounded person, a victim of childhood abuse. This psychological treatment of Nin speaks volumes of our relationship to incest as the ultimate "unsayable." The only way to justify Nin's complicity in the affair with her father in adulthood is to treat her as a victim in childhood. To think of their affair as the affair of two consenting adults would mean to think through the unthinkable.[83]

NIN THE LIAR

In reviewing *Incest* for the *New York Times,* Katha Pollitt was among those critics who questioned the reliability of the unexpurgated volumes because, as she explained, while the first series of the diaries was being published, people were led to believe that they too included honest confessions. She states, "For the real Anais Nin, and the real story told in the diary, we'll have to wait for her biography." Pollitt's comment on biography as an honest record of a person's life confirms what Linda Wagner-Martin writes about this form of narrative. Wagner-Martin thus describes the common preconception about biography: "[D]espite today's greater cultural awareness of how complicated the shaping of identity is, biography is still thought to be an art dependent on fact. The premise is that if enough letters and manuscript materials are available, if enough photos are scrutinized, if enough people are interviewed, somehow objective truth about the subject will surface."[84]

Pollitt's article generated two responses in the *New York Times*. One was from Rupert Pole, Nin's partner and a literary executor of the Nin estate at the time, who denied any major interference with the material.[85] The other was from Sally Duros, presumably a Nin fan, who attacked Pollitt for suggesting that a future biography would be more trustworthy than Nin's own records. Duros argued that Nin had written the diaries for herself alone and because of that they could be trusted.[86] This comment repeats one of many myths circulating about Nin's diaries: Duros believes that because Nin kept her diaries locked in vaults, they must have been secret and private. It is a good illustration of how Nin's readers, who possess different levels of knowledge about Nin, create their own Nin. This exchange of letters also reflects a wider debate about the nature of autobiographical writings. Which genre is the most trustworthy? Is it diary, autobiography, or biography? For many readers, it still appears to be biography, as Nin's own accounts of her life were invalidated once two biographies of her were published. In reviews of both Fitch's *The Erotic*

Life of Anaïs Nin and Bair's *Anaïs Nin: A Biography,* Nin was established as a liar.

Many reviewers of Fitch's and Bair's books took an opportunity to evaluate Nin rather than the two biographies in question. They focused on detailing and judging Nin's life. As many of the titles and subtitles of the reviews suggest, reviews concentrate on the sensational, and they pronounce Nin a liar. Miranda Seymour's review of Fitch's biography for the *New York Times,* for example, is titled, "Truth Wasn't Sexy Enough: Anaïs Nin's Diaries Were a Fraud and Even Her Marriages Were Lies," while Carol Anshaw's review in the *Chicago Tribune* bears the title, "Anaïs Nin: Many Words, Many Lovers and a Host of Lies." In the cases when the title of the review does not refer to Nin's lies, the opening lines usually do, as in the *Palm Beach Post*'s review, which begins thus: "Forget what you've read in the diaries . . . [as] they were doctored before publication. . . . Nin lied all the time." Several reviews of Bair's biography echo that response. In the review titled "Lies and Whispers," the *Maclean's* review declares Nin a "tormented author . . . addicted to sex and deceit." The *Chicago Tribune*'s reviewer opened her review with the following depiction of Nin: "A compulsive liar, a legendary beauty, the author of diaries fascinating in their erotic candor and monotonous in their narcissism." The *Philadelphia Inquirer* review begins in a similar way: "Anaïs Nin lied and fornicated the way the rest of us breathe."[87]

Although the publication of the unexpurgated diaries revealed that Nin concealed a lot of details regarding her life, the reviews of them did not proclaim Nin a liar the way the reviews of biographies did. This can be at least partly explained by the fact that the unexpurgated diaries were advertised as a revelation of truth about Nin's life, and such negative words as *liar* were nowhere to be found, while the biographies were spiced up with many negatively tinged epithets, one of which was *liar*. In the dramatic introduction to her biography, Fitch asks, "Why does a writer who kept a diary all her life need a biographer?" and she answers immediately: "*Because her diary is itself a work of fiction,* an act of self-invention. Untrue confessions." Bair too highlights Nin's lies. Despite being more cautious and subtle than Fitch when it comes to introducing Nin, Bair does mention the fact that Nin's diary is regarded by many as a "liary." Although she is not the one who passes the judgment (she lets others speak instead), by simply mentioning this label, Bair makes it more and more attached to Nin's name. Moreover, describing Nin as a liar gave both biographers a chance to establish themselves as necessary to the process of exposing the truth about Nin's life. "Literary biographies," as Joe Moran declares, "often sell themselves through the promise of 'revelations' about their subject." *Sell* is a key word here, as biographies of such figures as Nin thrive on scandal and controversy. Fitch, Bair, and those who reviewed their biographies played a major role in creating another posthumous portrait of Nin—Nin as a compulsive liar.[88]

FROM A FAMOUS WRITER TO A MAJOR MINOR ONE

The eroticization and pathologization of Nin, made evident above, deflected attention from Nin the writer. *Diary 7* was the last volume that followed the pattern set up by Nin during her lifetime and gave prominence to her as a writer, despite the fact that it was published posthumously in 1980. In the seventh installment, Nin recounts her success and comments on her new status—that of a celebrated person. At the beginning of her success Nin reacts very positively to it. She is glad to be finally appreciated. She notes, "I face the love, tributes I receive with pleasure. I am like a new woman, born with the publication of the Diary" (*Diary 7,* 35).

Nin is depicted as an extremely busy public person. She reports on her eventful schedule, enumerates the places where she has lectured, and provides accounts of her interviews, book-signing tours, and appearances on television shows. She mentions good reviews and colleges where her books are taught. She emphasizes her lack of time in several letters to her friends that are included in *Diary 7*. In one of them, Nin apologizes for not replying and explains, "As a writer you sing your ballad, and suddenly when the world answers, it overwhelms you! I lecture and the students treat me like the Beatles! I am swamped in correspondence" (71). While commenting on her trip to Germany, she relates a very positive experience of being treated like a celebrity: "How they treat their writers! Like movie stars. My hand has been kissed to shreds. Flowers in the room" (118).

The initial enthusiasm, however, quickly wears off, and Nin becomes tired of public life. "The lectures are frustrating," she notes later in the volume, adding, "They are the opposite of personal and intimate friendship" (126). Eventually, she describes her popularity as a snare. She writes in a letter to a friend, "Recognition has come this year with a tidal wave of letters, lectures, work. I work from seven a.m. to midnight! A new kind of trap—fame!" (*Diary 7*, 167). She becomes troubled by her popularity. Fame, and the new duties it brings, overwhelms her. At the same time, Nin expresses a wish to be recognized not only by ordinary readers but also by her peers. In a letter to Harry Moore, she remarks, "It seems to me I have done enough work [as a writer], yet I have nothing to show for it. At sixty-seven should I not be considered by the National Institute of Arts?" (quoted in *Diary 7,* 159). She therefore craves a more prestigious form of acknowledgment.

Diary 7 was the last publication coming from the Nin estate that focused on Nin the writer rather than on her private life. The seventh volume continued the portrait of Nin that she highlighted during her lifetime and represented her mainly as a writer—a writer who after long years of obscurity became renowned. With the publication of the unexpurgated series, this focus shifted toward Nin's personal life. This, in turn, made Nin into a controversial figure, as Fitch's and Bair's introductions attest. Both biographers describe mixed reactions brought by the mention of Nin's name among people interviewed during their research. Fitch writes, "Much like her first liberator, D. H. Lawrence, she inspires extremes of attack and adoration. . . . For every acquaintance who called her calculating, dishonest, humorless, and narcissistic, there are two who testify to her charm, wit and unselfishness." In a similar vein, Bair observes, "I tried to talk to the many persons who figured throughout her life, and I was astonished at the range of their responses, especially how, in so many cases, the mere mention of her name provoked vehemence and outrage."[89]

Bair also mentions the fact that during the writing process many of the encountered people expressed the opinion that Nin did not deserve a biography. Giving reasons why she found Nin worthwhile, she writes, "The twentieth century will be remembered for many concepts that brought sweeping societal change, and Anaïs Nin was among the pioneers who explored three of the most important: sex, the self, and psychoanalysis. When future generations seek to understand how these evolved in our time, Anaïs Nin will be the major minor writer whose work they must consult." So, within two decades, Nin turned from a successful writer into a "major minor writer" whose works are worthwhile only as a reflection of their times. This view is later reiterated by Podnieks, who, in comparing Nin to Woolf, regards these authors as the opposite ends of the spectrum: while "Woolf is one of the most well respected writers, and probably the most well respected female writer, of the twentieth-century English literature.... Nin is a minor one."[90]

As a result, some critics taking on Nin's output as a subject of their analyses distance themselves from Nin. This can be seen in a statement made by Wendy DuBow in a collection of memoirs edited by Paul Herron, titled *Anaïs Nin: A Book of Mirrors*. Wendy DuBow, who wrote a doctoral dissertation on Nin and edited a collection of interviews with her, makes sure that she is not mistaken for a Nin admirer: "For me, working on Nin wasn't a question of love, or even like, after the first month; it was about intellectual challenge.... I'm fascinated by the thoughts her writing prompts for me. But mostly she embarrasses me. I feel for her at times like I do for bad comedians: they seem like nice enough people but I cringe watching them bomb onstage." This need to establish herself as a nonfan of Nin may stem from her desire to construct herself as a professional and rational academic who displays a necessary detachment and is devoid of any emotional investment in her subject of study. Such a need is even more understandable when we take into consideration the fact that in the early 1990s the view of fans as passive cultural dupes began to be challenged by studies such as Henry Jenkins's *Textual Poachers*. Prior to the publication of Jenkins's work, fans were often treated dismissively in academia. In his study, considered seminal by many media scholars, Jenkins rejected the tradition of a distanced observation and attacked the dominant view of fans as "brainless consumers," "social misfits," and "infantile, emotionally and intellectually immature" individuals who "are unable to separate fantasy from reality."[91]

This apprehension of being mistaken for a Nin fan may be further deepened by the fact that Nin always had a small circle of critics, with many of whom she also developed some sort of personal acquaintance. Nin scholars were therefore more than "acafans" or "scholar-fans"—academics who are also fans. Her academic scholarship was maintained for a long time by "acafriends"—scholars who knew her personally. The volume *Recollections of Anaïs Nin by Her Contemporaries* contains personal essays about Nin by such top Nin scholars as Bettina Knapp, Benjamin Franklin V, Duane Schneider, Sharon Spencer, Philip K. Jason, and Suzette Henke, all of whom knew Nin personally.

But even today, as many of these critics retire from academia, Nin scholarship still inhabits the intersection of fandom and academia. It is best exemplified by *A Café in Space: The Anaïs Nin Literary Journal,* which, although not a peer-reviewed journal, is a respected (and the sole) source of contemporary scholarship on Nin. The journal includes substantial articles on Nin and writers associated with her (such as Henry Miller, Lawrence Durrell, and Gore Vidal), penned by both burgeoning and established scholars, as well as fragments of her earlier unpublished works while simultaneously not shying away from publishing more "fannish" pieces, such as reports on journeys to places connected with Nin and poems dedicated to her. *A Café in Space* therefore brings together the much-contested terrains of fandom and academia. In dealing with Nin, one risks being accused of not only being a Nin fan but also of being a coterie critic, and perhaps that is what DuBow tried to avoid.

DuBow's anxiety, however, seems to be as much connected with her struggle to separate her fan and academic identities as with her desire to distance herself specifically from Nin. Commenting on DuBow's account, Nancy Gobatto rightly observes, "DuBow's stance on Nin reveals the current academic bias against studying Anaïs Nin and her work. . . . If an academic feminist who has dedicated a significant amount of her career studying Nin still feels she must qualify this decision, one can imagine what the non-Nin scholars have to say about Nin as the focus of academic inquiry."[92] Some of Nin's critics appear to be worried about their own academic reputation if they decide to analyze her output. Anxiety about being a Nin scholar is also expressed by Ruth Charnock, who, after having completed her PhD, decided to stop working on Nin for a while because she "started to feel uncomfortable about working on a writer who seemed to command so little critical respect in academic fora." Charnock elaborates:

> Faced with [negative] reactions [to Nin at academic conferences], wanting to be a serious academic myself, I began to dislike Anaïs Nin and dislike having to talk about her in public. Whereas I had long-believed Nin was a dangerous woman for all the right reasons—she was fearless, she went into the stuffiest, most patriarchal-seeming spaces, such as the psychoanalyst's office, and shook them up, she believed, to the last, in her own artistry despite constant disbelief from others—it began to seem as if Nin was going to be dangerous for my career, dangerous for me in all the wrong ways.[93]

Negative responses to Nin the writer, varying from outright disparagement to allegedly harmless classification of her as a "major minor writer," must have made scholars, especially budding ones, afraid to undertake the study of Nin's works for fear of being ridiculed.

Nonetheless, there are critics who have not been discouraged by Nin's minor status and have given her works the consideration they deserve (in fact, the above-mentioned scholar Ruth Charnock has recently undertaken another project on Nin). Two other recent examples are apparent in the analyses of Elizabeth Podnieks and Helen Tookey: Podnieks positions Nin as a major diarist, while Tookey regards Nin's works as central to the cultural and literary landscape of the twentieth century, and they both do their best to reassert Nin's rightful place in modernist scholarship, as Nin was largely forgotten even by those whose aim was to salvage and reexamine previously marginalized figures. Classic texts on neglected female modernists such as Shari Benstock's *Women of the Left Bank: Paris, 1900–1940* (1986) and Bonnie Kime Scott's *The Gender of Modernism* (1990) either include only a brief section on Nin's works (the former) or altogether fail to acknowledge Nin's contribution to and affiliation with the modernist movement (the latter). As Tookey rightly observes, "[I]f Nin was 'rescued,' alongside other modernist women, by Benstock, she was more or less 'lost' again afterwards, making fleeting appearances in introductions and conclusions . . . , but never quite appearing in the main text of feminist-modernist criticism." Podnieks and Tookey demonstrate that Nin's works have many parallels with works of other modernist writers, and they encourage focusing on such apparently marginal figures as Nin because they could enrich our understanding of our cultures and literary histories.[94]

After Nin's death, her self-presentation was to a large extent overridden by a set of new portraits. While the seven original volumes of the *Diary* developed a set of very controlled images of Nin and presented her mainly as a writer, over the whole series of the published *Diaries,* including the unexpurgated ones, her images start to spill out, giving rise to a multiplicity of Nins. Nin became a polysemic figure, capable of producing multiple meanings and signifying different things for different people. The reviews of biographies alone reveal the multiplicity of images of Nin circulating in our culture. Depending on which Nin a reviewer decides to highlight in his or her review, there is Nin as "a compulsive liar, a legendary beauty, the author of the diaries"; Nin, a "courtesan" and "eccentric Donna Juana"; Nin, "the former feminist icon"; Nin, "a poignantly bewitching female"; Nin, "the Samuel Pepys of the 20th century"; Nin, "[m]odern letters' most famous diarist . . . a monster of self-absorption, power seduction, larcenous deception both petty and grand"; Nin, "the famous femme fatale," "a writer of erotica," and "the ultimate 20th-century diarist." Nonetheless, the ever-growing eroticization and the focus (and cashing in) on the scandalous aspects of Nin's life made her either a curiosity or a psychological case study, and as a result, Nin the writer became of secondary importance.[95]

Conclusion

Anaïs Nin in the Twenty-First Century

Whereas the end of the twentieth century witnessed a revival of interest in Anaïs Nin, triggered by the publication of the so-called unexpurgated diaries and manifested in biographies of Nin, the film *Henry & June,* and new critical studies of Nin's works, the first decade of the twenty-first century saw a waning in Nin's popularity. At the beginning of the twenty-first century, there was not a single event that would have the significance and scope of Kaufman's film or Bair's biography. However, Nin did not disappear completely from public consciousness or academic debates, and with the recent Ohio University Press reprint of her most distinguished pieces of fiction as well as the publication of new portions of the unexpurgated *Diary* (*Mirages* in 2013 and *Trapeze* in 2017), it is likely that we will hear more of Anaïs Nin.

As far as Nin's presence in popular culture is concerned, she continues to inspire various projects, but in the twenty-first century she has not yet made it to the headlines. The ventures inspired by Nin are rather small-scale, and one has to look for Nin in order to encounter her. Among the projects influenced by Nin there is one by Judy Chicago—the feminist artist and Nin's former acquaintance, famous for her installation *The Dinner Party*. In 2004 Chicago released *Fragments from the Delta of Venus*—a collection of sensuous watercolors that are matched with quotations from Nin's erotic stories. The product description on the Amazon website presents Nin as Chicago's mentor, an "iconic erotic writer," and "a feminist of the first wave."[1] In 2010, songwriter Pam

Shaffer released her debut album *As We Are* containing lyrics inspired by Nin's *Diary*.

Theater seemed especially willing to appropriate Nin, as several plays about her were staged throughout America in the "noughties." In the summer of 2006, Wendy Beckett's *Anaïs Nin: One of Her Lives* ran in New York. As Kaufman did in *Henry & June*, Beckett concentrated on Nin's life in Paris in the early 1930s and on the famous love triangle between Anaïs and Henry and June Miller. In 2008, *Anaïs Nin Goes to Hell*, a comedy written by David Stallings, was performed to great acclaim at the New York Fringe Festival. The play, despite what its title might suggest, is not about Nin scorching in hell repenting her felonies but about her trip to the inferno in the role of an adviser on men to other well-known women. The official advertisement for the play announces, "Imagine an island in hell where Cleopatra, Joan of Arc, and Queen Victoria . . . wait for their men. What happens when women's lib icon Anaïs Nin arrives to turn their afterlife upside down?"[2] Calling Nin a "women's lib icon" in this context—when Nin's main role is to advise on men—points to a certain derailment of the term, as it is equated here overtly with expertise on men and covertly with sexual promiscuity. In another theatrical production, a musical revue titled *The Mistress Cycle* (2009), Nin is presented as one of five "notorious mistresses" along with "Tess Walker, a contemporary Manhattan photographer[;] . . . Diane de Poitiers, the mistress of King Henri II of 16th century France; Lulu White, a turn-of-the-century New Orleans bordello Madame; and Ching, a 14-year-old concubine in 12th century China."[3] Once again Nin's wantonness is emphasized. So Nin appears under a variety of already familiar guises in popular culture—as a feminist, a writer of erotica, an expert on men, a mistress, and Miller's partner.

There has recently appeared, however, a new portrait of Nin. It is the helpless and dying Nin presented in Barbara Kraft's memoir, *Anaïs Nin: The Last Days*. Nin's published *Diary* ends in 1974, three years before her death in 1977, so until the release of Kraft's memoir in 2011, readers knew little about Nin's everyday existence during the final three years of her life; most of that information came from Nin's biographies. Kraft, who had met Nin at a creative writing workshop, became Nin's devoted supporter during a long and difficult fight with cancer. Her memoir tells the story of Nin's final days. In the pages of Kraft's narrative, Nin—"a myth, a muse, a goddess, a literary legend"[4]—turns into a frail, vulnerable, suffering, frightened, elderly woman struggling with a terminal illness that leaves her joined to a forever leaking colostomy bag.

Yet the memoir is not altogether devoid of more familiar Nins. There is the Nin celebrated by women when Kraft recounts how thousands of female volunteers answered Nin's call for a blood donation. Kraft reconstructs the conversation she had with a nurse who supposedly commented, "I've never seen a turnout like this before for anyone and I have been a nurse for fifteen years, ten in this hospital, and we get a lot of celebrities here."[5] There is the Nin preoccupied with looks, struggling to be elegant in the least glorious of situations (which brings to mind Nin's account of childbirth recounted in *Diary 1*). There is the determined Nin, this time not to be published but to survive, whose "I have a great deal to live for" reappears like a refrain throughout Kraft's book.

Kraft's memoir can be classified as an example of pathography—"a form of autobiography or biography that describes personal experiences of illness, treatment, and sometimes death," which, as Anne Hawkins asserts, almost did not exist before 1950 but has become increasingly popular ever since, reaching the peak of popularity in the 1980s and the 1990s. While Ann Jurecic does not entirely agree with Hawkins's dating—her study clearly demonstrates that by the mid-twentieth century accounts of people suffering from tuberculosis and polio were published—they both seem to agree on the point that "by the late twentieth century illness and disability narratives were established as literary genres."[6]

Accounting for the popularity of pathographies, Hawkins explains, "Pathographies are compelling because they describe dramatic human experience of real crisis: they appeal to us because they give shape to our deepest hopes and fears about such crises, and in doing so, they often draw upon profound archetypal dimensions of human experience." She also observes that despite the fact that these stories are personalized, they recycle the same themes and the same metaphorical paradigms, such as the image of illness as battle, an image that is also perceptible in Kraft's account. Jurecic, in turn, attributes the proliferation of such narratives to historical, cultural, political, and medical changes, such as the paperback revolution of the 1940s that enabled the cheap production of books, thus expanding the range of genres that were published; the growing institutionalization and specialization of the medical profession, which brought an increased efficacy but also a loss of intimacy between doctors and patients, which in turn stimulated patients to voice their dissatisfaction with the way they were being treated; and in the 1980s, the rapid increase of AIDS, whose victims "used writing as a weapon in a cultural battle against homophobia, the disdain of the medical establishment, and the indifference of the government."[7]

During the past three decades, hundreds of memoirs on AIDS, cancer, and mental and eating disorders, among other illnesses, flooded the market. Some—such as Susanna Kaysen's *Girl, Interrupted* (1993), Elizabeth Wurtzel's *Prozac Nation* (1994), and Jean Dominique-Bauby's *The Diving Bell and the Butterfly* (1997)—elicited a tidal wave of media coverage and enjoyed significant popularity. Kraft's account was therefore born as much of her desire to share the story of Nin's last days as of the times that allowed this story to be told. Its publication was possible thanks to a widespread popular fascination with grim details of other people's lives and a public appetite for stories about suffering, terminal illness, and the process of dying.

Joyce Carol Oates, an American novelist, is highly critical of the genre and considers pathography to be "hagiography's diminished and often prurient twin." While hagiographies, which originally depicted the life of saints, tend to idealize their subjects, pathographies have a tendency to emphasize the inglorious details of people's lives to catch readers' attention. In reviewing David Roberts's biography *Jean Stafford,* Oates accuses him of paying too much attention to Stafford's debilitating illnesses and not enough to her body of works, and Oates vents her frustration with biographies that "so mercilessly expose their subjects, so relentlessly catalogue their most private, vulnerable and least illuminating moments, as to divest them of all mystery save the crucial and unexplained: How did a distinguished body of work emerge from so undistinguished a life?"[8] Kraft's memoir likewise capitalizes on dissecting Nin's private life and is devoid of any discussions of Nin's literary legacy. It pictures Nin in her most vulnerable state.

Although Kraft claims that Nin wanted the story of her illness to be told and that she specifically appointed Kraft to do so, we have nothing but Kraft's word for it. And just as Kraft doubts Pole's declaration that Nin wanted the publication of her unexpurgated diaries, so too may we doubt hers. Questioning Kraft's motives for writing this memoir seems justified when we take into consideration her disillusionment with Nin's failure to reveal the truth in her *Diaries*. As mentioned in the previous chapter, Kraft was encouraged by Nin to share her life story, which she did in 1976 by publishing *The Restless Spirit: Journal of a Gemini*. Because the consequences of this publication were disastrous to Kraft's life, she was deeply disappointed to find out that Nin's life narrative was heavily edited. As a result, Kraft's *Anaïs Nin: The Last Days* is to an extent an attempt to deal with her own disappointment with Nin. The narrative of Nin's declining health is interspersed with Kraft's reflections on Nin and their relationship. In one fragment, Kraft confesses, "Now, all these years later, my thinking less of you was finally gone, over with."[9] Her confession has a chance to be known publicly only because of Nin's name on the cover. There is a possibility that readers are not interested in Kraft's memoir for Kraft's sake but because they want to know more about the final years of Nin's life. It is Kraft, however, who reaps the benefits.

Another powerful development in the twenty-first century involves changes not so much in Nin's image as in the way it has been distributed—Nin has gone digital. Nin's books are available on Kindle; she can be glimpsed in various video clips on YouTube; one of 'her' Facebook pages has garnered over ninety thousand "likes"; there are a couple of people tweeting as "Anaïs Nin"; and Nin has her own blog. The digital revolution has had and will continue to have profound implications on how Nin's posthumous existence will unfold in the future. There are three major changes connected with the developments of new media: information on Nin is more easily available, there is a bigger involvement of ordinary people in creating Nin's image, and Nin's portraits are marked by a new kind of temporariness.

If one wanted to find out something about the author prior to the nascence of the Internet, one had to consult the encyclopedia, a biography, or one of the critical works on a particular writer. Of course, the bits and pieces of information about the author circulated in the media—one could come across the author in the press, on the radio, or on television, but such encounters were rather accidental. Today one simply needs to type the writer's name into a search engine to get an abundance of details. I would guess that more people have consulted the *Wikipedia* entry for Anaïs Nin than all of critical works (including biographies) devoted to her. *Wikipedia* page-view statistics show that the Anaïs Nin page is accessed on average 20,000 times a month. Despite warnings by professors that *Wikipedia* is not a reliable source of information, for many it is the first introduction to a new subject, in this case to Anaïs Nin.

What is more, whereas previously knowledge about the author was provided by experts, today it can be constructed by anyone (*Wikipedia* being the best example). The power of making Nin's image is therefore shifting. New media, especially the Internet, are characterized by a bigger participation of the audience in the creation of content, which, as P. David Marshall points out, leads to "democratization of cultural production."[10] In the second chapter, I demonstrate the importance of institutional readers to the construction of Nin's image. It is hard to imagine that in the twenty-first century, institutional readers—reviewers, journalists, and academics—will continue to hold the same prestige and significance that they did forty years ago. Take, for instance, reviews of books, once solely provided by journalists, academics, writers, or, informally, by one's friends. Today books are widely reviewed by ordinary readers on the Internet, and one can easily subscribe to the reviews of someone who has reading preferences similar to ours.

The Internet, as P. David Marshall observes, has challenged the social category of audience. And as Marshall explains, "Several writers have tried to define this subjectivity with neologisms such as the pro-sumer..., where the idea of the producer and the consumer are wedded together, or the prod-user, where the user and producer are merged." The Internet undeniably encourages a bigger participation of the audience. And while "in some instances," as Marshall notes, "that action of producing is quite limited to just moving from website to website in a particularly individual and idiosyncratic way; in other cases, the user is actively transforming content for redistribution."[11]

Some Internet constructions of Nin's image provide interesting examples of posthumous collaboration. Such is the case of Nin's Facebook page, maintained by Hazal Tuncer, where Nin seems to exist as herself. The page contains several pictures of Nin, and posts are mainly made up of Nin quotations. As a result, Nin "speaks" in her own voice, but ultimately she has no control over which of her statements are posted. This might be regarded as a new form of impersonation. Whereas previously fans dressed up and made up as their favorite stars, the Internet gives them new opportunities for taking on the star's identity.

Another implication of new media is the transience of representations. Over the years, different images of Nin have been highlighted, but with the advent of the Internet, her portraits have acquired a new kind of temporariness. Whereas published books can usually be consulted even after many years and newspaper articles can be dug out of archives, that is not always the case with Internet images, because some websites are taken down, others go dead, and even existing websites may pile up so much information that mining a website's abundance proves impossible. This temporariness is best exemplified by Helen Tookey's study, *Anaïs Nin, Fictionality and Femininity*. In analyzing some websites devoted to Anaïs Nin, Tookey examined how Nin's fans perceived her at the end of the twentieth century. Tookey demonstrated that although most of Nin's fans were aware of the problematic nature of revelations uncovered in the unexpurgated *Diaries* and biographies, they were not bothered by them the way some intellectuals and academics were, and they treated Nin as an inspirational figure. Tookey came to the conclusion that "rather than simply being duped by Nin, they collude[d] with her in producing and playing with particular fantasies of femininity." Tookey in a way immortalized these comments in her book, because websites she analyzed no longer exist. One of them, as she acknowledged, was even taken down between the time she subjected it to examination and the time when her study was published.[12]

Because of this temporariness and the plethora of websites devoted to Nin, there is no way of summarizing Nin's cyber existence. Predicting which Nin the Internet users encounter most frequently is also difficult. I would guess that first-timers looking for some facts about Nin tend to consult the *Wikipedia* entry and perhaps other search results coming up on the first Google web page, while more-established fans are familiar with websites devoted specifically to Nin, such as *The Anaïs Nin Official Blog,* founded and maintained by Paul Herron. Predicting how Nin's afterlife will unfold in the future is also impossible: Will she remain "a major minor writer"? Will she become a heroine of some movement yet to come? Will there one day be a renewed appreciation of Nin and her works? Or will she sink into complete oblivion? It remains to be seen. What is certain is that these potential rises and falls of Nin will greatly depend on forthcoming cultural developments and debates as well as on technological advances in the way information is circulated.

Notes

INTRODUCTION: ANAÏS NIN AND HER DIARY

1. Elizabeth Mehren, "Pages: No Monopoly for Madonna," *Los Angeles Times,* 13 Nov. 1992, http://articles.latimes.com/1992-11-13/news/vw-339_1_anais-nin (emphasis in the original).

2. bell hooks, "Power to the Pussy: We Don't Wannabe Dicks in Drag," in *Madonnarama: Essays on Sex and Popular Culture,* ed. Lisa Frank and Paul Smith (Pittsburgh: Cleis Press, 1993), 67.

3. Helen Tookey's monograph, *Anaïs Nin, Fictionality and Femininity: Playing a Thousand Roles* (Oxford: Clarendon Press, 2003), deals with various "versionings" of Nin (Tookey uses Brenda Silver's concept of versioning introduced in *Virginia Woolf Icon* [Chicago: University of Chicago Press, 1999]), but only a part of Tookey's last chapter focuses on the reception of Nin in popular culture. Besides examining a response to Nin in the British press and on the Internet, Tookey does not focus on any particular context, whereas I concentrate on the making of Anaïs Nin's public persona in the United States, strongly believing that nowhere else was Nin's stardom so prominent.

4. Deirdre Bair, introduction to *Anaïs Nin: A Biography* (New York: G. P. Putnam's Sons, 1995), xviii.

5. The following brief biography of Nin is based on Deirdre Bair's *Anaïs Nin: A Biography.*

6. Philip K. Jason, *Anaïs Nin and Her Critics* (Columbia, SC: Camden House, 1993), 27.

7. Ibid., 38.

8. Bair, *Anaïs Nin,* 300.

9. Ibid., 257.

10. The edition of *Winter of Artifice* published by Gemor Press differed from the version published in France. The most obvious change was in the title, from which the article *The* was dropped. For a detailed discussion of changes to the collection, see Jason, *Anaïs Nin,* 39.

11. Edmund Wilson, review of *Under a Glass Bell*, by Anaïs Nin, in *The Critical Response to Anaïs Nin*, ed. Philip K. Jason (Westport, CT: Greenwood Press, 1996), 75, previously published in *New Directions* 7 (1942): 429–39.

12. Paul Herron, "Anaïs Nin's *A Spy in the House of Love*," *Anaïs Nin Blog*, 29 Mar. 2010, http://anaisninblog.skybluepress.com/2010/03/anais-nins-a-spy-in-the-house-of-love/.

13. *The Diary of Anaïs Nin, 1955–1966*, vol. 6, ed. and with a preface by Gunther Stuhlmann (New York: Harcourt Brace Jovanovich, 1976), 116 (hereafter cited as *Diary 6*). In the United States, Nin's diaries were released as *The Diary of Anaïs Nin*, while in the United Kingdom they were published as *The Journals of Anaïs Nin*. The two versions are almost identical, except for the titles. The volume numbers were added to the titles for the American and British paperback editions.

In the present volume, I use *diary* and *journal* interchangeably, which is a common practice in academia: "These terms are often interchangeable, despite attempts by various writers to make specific claims for each one." Elizabeth Podnieks, *Daily Modernism: The Literary Diaries of Virginia Woolf, Antonia White, Elizabeth Smart, and Anaïs Nin* (Montreal: McGill-Queen's University Press, 2000), 13–14.

14. Podnieks, *Daily Modernism*, 284 (emphasis added). The story of the inception of the diary is the one given by Anaïs Nin herself; her brother claims that their mother was the one who encouraged Anaïs to begin the journal aboard the ship, to keep Anaïs busy. Joaquín Nin-Culmell, "Anaïs, My Sister," in *Anaïs Nin: Literary Perspectives*, ed. Suzanne Nalbantian (New York: St. Martin's Press, 1997), 24.

15. Bair, *Anaïs Nin*, 511.

16. Ibid., 378.

17. Podnieks, *Daily Modernism*, 285.

CHAPTER 1: LITERARY CELEBRITY,
THE MODERNIST MARKETPLACE, AND MARKETING THE DIARY

1. *The Early Diary of Anaïs Nin, 1920–1923*, vol. 2, edited by Rupert Pole, with a preface by Joaquin Nin-Culmell (New York: Harcourt Brace Jovanovich, 1982), 313.

2. Joe Moran, *Star Authors: Literary Celebrity in America* (London: Pluto Press, 2000), 58. Loren Glass, *Authors Inc.: Literary Celebrity in the Modern United States, 1880–1980* (New York: New York University Press, 2004), 5. Since the 1990s, there have been several movie productions that adapted, or imagined, life stories of

popular writers for the screen. Thus, we could follow the lives of Anaïs Nin and Henry Miller in *Henry & June* (1990), George Sand in *Impromptu* (1991), C. S. Lewis in *Shadowlands* (1993), Dorothy Parker in *Mrs. Parker and the Vicious Circle* (1994), Arthur Rimbaud in *Total Eclipse* (1995), Oscar Wilde in *Wilde* (1997), William Shakespeare in *Shakespeare in Love* (1998), James Joyce in *Nora* (2000), Iris Murdoch in *Iris* (2001), Sylvia Plath in *Sylvia* (2003), James Matthew Barrie in *Finding Neverland* (2004), Truman Capote in *Capote* (2005), Beatrix Potter in *Miss Potter* (2006), Jane Austen in *Becoming Jane* (2007), John Keats in *Bright Star* (2009), Ernest Hemingway and Martha Gellhorn in *Hemingway and Gellhorn* (2012), and Charles Bukowski in *Bukowski* (2013). The list is not exhaustive. Some of these movies might be regarded as biopics; however, most of them are either semifictional or fictional.

3. Glass, *Authors Inc.,* 2; Moran, *Star Authors,* 6; Rose Marie Cutting, introduction to *Anaïs Nin: A Reference Guide* (Boston: G. K. Hall, 1978), xix. Barry Siegel "500 Attend Ceremony for Times Women of the Year," *Los Angeles* Times, 25 March 1976, OC_A1; In *Esquire,* Nin was described as a "[b]abysitter to big boys of American literature. Her diaries outshine, and out-scandalize, them all" ("The 75 Greatest Women of All Time," *Esquire,* 19 Apr. 2010, www.esquire.com).

4. Jeffrey J. Williams, "Academostars: Name Recognition," in *The Celebrity Culture Reader,* ed. P. David Marshall (London: Routledge, 2006), 373, 376.

5. Moran, *Star Authors,* 4.

6. Ibid., 10. The ability to coproduce fame and a star's image is not limited to literary celebrities, however. For instance, several essays in *Madonna Connection* (1993) indicate that Madonna's success stems from her ability to manipulate her image.

7. Richard Dyer, *Heavenly Bodies: Film Stars and Society* (London: BFI Macmillan, 1986), 2–3; P. David Marshall, introduction to *The Celebrity Culture Reader,* ed. P. David Marshall (London: Routledge, 2006), 9.

8. Richard Dyer, *Stars,* rev. ed. (London: British Film Institute, 1998), 60, 61; Moran, *Star Authors,* 41.

9. Joanna Russ, *How to Suppress Women's Writing* (Austin: University of Texas Press, 1983), 27; Charlotte Templin, *Feminism and the Politics of Literary Reputation: The Example of Erica Jong* (Lawrence: University Press of Kansas, 1995), 4.

10. Toril Moi, *Simone de Beauvoir: The Making of an Intellectual Woman* (Oxford: Blackwell, 1994), 73–74, 78, 80.

11. Brenda Silver, *Virginia Woolf Icon* (Chicago: University of

Chicago Press, 1999), 11. According to Silver, gender constantly intersects with cultural class. She also states that the extent to which Woolf's representations come to normalize our understanding of gender or class depends on a particular context. Ibid., 86.

12. Helen Tookey, *Anaïs Nin, Fictionality and Femininity: Playing a Thousand Roles* (Oxford: Clarendon Press, 2003), 2.

13. Kevin J. H. Dettmar, introduction to *A Companion to Modernist Literature and Culture,* ed. David Bradshaw and Kevin J. H. Dettmar (Malden, MA: Blackwell Publishing, 2006), 4.

14. Aaron Jaffe, *Modernism and the Culture of Celebrity* (Cambridge: Cambridge University Press, 2006), 56, 165.

15. *The Early Diary of Anaïs Nin, 1923–1927,* vol. 3 *(Journal of a Wife),* edited by Rupert Pole, with a preface by Joaquin Nin-Culmell (New York: Harcourt Brace Jovanovich, 1983), 237 (hereafter cited parenthetically in the text as *ED 3*); *The Early Diary of Anaïs Nin, 1927–1931,* vol. 4, edited by Rupert Pole, with a preface by Joaquin Nin-Culmell (New York: Harcourt Brace Jovanovich, 1985), 80 (hereafter cited parenthetically in the text as *ED 4*).

16. Mark S. Morrisson, "Nationalism and the Modern American Canon," in *The Cambridge Companion to American Modernism,* ed. Walter Kalaidjian (Cambridge: Cambridge University Press, 2005), 20.

17. Diane Richard-Allerdyce, *Anaïs Nin and the Remaking of Self: Gender, Modernism, and Narrative Identity* (DeKalb: Northern Illinois University Press, 1998), 13–14, 8; Tookey, *Anaïs Nin,* 3.

18. Elizabeth Podnieks, *Daily Modernism: The Literary Diaries of Virginia Woolf, Antonia White, Elizabeth Smart, and Anaïs Nin* (Montreal: McGill-Queen's University Press, 2000), 71, 74.

19. Kevin J. H. Dettmar and Stephen Watt, introduction to *Marketing Modernisms: Self-Promotion, Canonization, Rereading,* ed. Kevin J. H. Dettmar and Stephen Watt (Ann Arbor: University of Michigan Press, 1996), 1; Andreas Huyssen, *After the Great Divide: Modernism, Mass Culture, Postmodernism* (Bloomington: Indiana University Press, 1986), vii.

20. Dettmar and Watt, introduction to *Marketing Modernisms,* 8.

21. Margo Culley, *A Day at a Time: The Diary Literature of American Women from 1764 to the Present* (New York: Feminist Press at City University of New York, 1985); Harriet Blodgett, *Centuries of Female Days: Englishwomen's Private Diaries* (New Brunswick, NJ: Rutgers University Press, 1988) and *Capacious Hold-All: Anthology of Englishwomen's Diary Writings* (Charlottesville: University Press of Virginia, 1992); Laura Marcus, *Auto/biographical Discourses: Criticism, Theory, Practice* (Manchester: Manchester University Press, 1994), 1.

22. Sidonie Smith, *Reading Autobiography: A Guide for Interpreting Life Narratives* (Minneapolis: University of Minnesota Press, 2001), 114, 114–15.

23. Ibid., 128.

24. Ibid., 137.

25. Suzanne L. Bunkers and Cynthia A. Huff, "Issues in Studying Women's Diaries: A Theoretical and Critical Introduction," in *Inscribing the Daily: Critical Essays on Women's Diaries*, ed. Suzanne L. Bunkers and Cynthia A. Huff (Amherst: University of Massachusetts Press, 1996), 1.

26. Elaine Showalter, introduction to *A Jury of Her Peers: American Women Writers from Anne Bradstreet to Annie Proulx* (London: Virago, 2009), xv.

27. Sharon Spencer, *Collage of Dreams: The Writings of Anaïs Nin* (Chicago: Swallow Press, 1977), 121.

28. Benjamin Franklin V and Duane Schneider, *Anaïs Nin: An Introduction* (Athens: Ohio University Press, 1979), 169, 172.

29. Nancy Scholar, *Anaïs Nin* (Boston: Twayne, 1984), 24; Lynn Z. Bloom and Orlee Holder, "Anaïs Nin's *Diary* in Context," *Mosaic* 11, no. 2 (1978): 191–202, quoted in Joan Bobbitt, "Truth and Artistry in the *Diary of Anaïs Nin*," in *The Critical Response to Anaïs Nin*, ed. Philip K. Jason (Westport, CT: Greenwood Press, 1996), 191; Marcus, *Auto/biographical Discourses*, 234.

30. Spencer, *Collage of Dreams*, 118.

31. Tookey, *Anaïs Nin*, 15; Podnieks, *Daily Modernism*, 284; Scholar, *Anaïs Nin*, 15.

32. Franklin and Schneider, *Anaïs Nin*, 176, 175; Scholar, *Anaïs Nin*, 21.

33. Paul John Eakin, *How Our Lives Become Stories: Making Selves* (Ithaca, NY: Cornell University Press, 1999), 123, 46; Podnieks, *Daily Modernism*, 42; Tookey, *Anaïs Nin*, 15.

34. Edmund Wilson, excerpt of the review of *Under a Glass Bell*, by Anaïs Nin, in Jason, *Critical Response*, 75; Karl Shapiro, "The Charmed Circle of Anaïs Nin," in Jason, *Critical Response*, 154. To present the history of Nin's revision and publication efforts, I drew on both the manuscript and the published version of the diary, as well as Bair's biography of Nin.

35. Gerald Kennedy, *Imagining Paris: Exile, Writing and American Identity* (New Haven, CT: Yale University Press, 1993), 14, 21.

36. David Burke, *Writers in Paris: Literary Lives in the City of Lights* (Berkeley, CA: Counterpoint, 2008), 3.

37. Anaïs Nin, Journal 32 (20 Oct. 1931–1 Feb. 1932), box 16, folder 1, Anaïs Nin Papers, Charles E. Young Research Library,

University of California, Los Angeles (hereafter cited as Nin Papers).

38. Henry Miller to Anaïs Nin, 12 Oct. 1933, in *A Literate Passion: Letters of Anaïs Nin and Henry Miller, 1932–1953,* ed. Gunther Stuhlmann (San Diego, CA: Harcourt Brace, 1987), 216 (emphasis in the original).

39. Bair, *Anaïs Nin,* 184.

40. *Incest: From "A Journal of Love," the Unexpurgated Diary of Anaïs Nin, 1932–1934* (New York: Harcourt Brace Jovanovich, 1992), 260, 265 (emphasis in the original).

41. Anaïs Nin, Journal 54 (July–Sept. 1937), box 19, folder 4, p. 1, Nin Papers. A similar fragment can also be found in *The Diary of Anaïs Nin, 1934–1939,* vol. 2, ed. and with a preface by Gunther Stuhlmann (New York: Swallow Press and Harcourt Brace, 1967), 208 (hereafter cited as *Diary 2*).

42. Anaïs Nin, Journal 55 (Sept.–Nov. 1937), box 19, folder 5, p. 125, Nin Papers. A similar description of the revision process also appears in her diary: "Rewriting volume forty-five (New York, Rank, Henry). There are in the diary so many flowers like the Japanese paper flowers which need to be placed in water to achieve their flowering. So I am putting all the closed buds in water." *Nearer the Moon: From "A Journal of Love," the Unexpurgated Diary of Anaïs Nin, 1937–1939* (New York: Harcourt Brace Jovanovich, 1996), 156.

43. Anaïs Nin to Jean Paulhan, Nov. 1937, letter copied and pasted to Journal 55 (Sept.–Nov. 1937), box 19, folder 5, p. 151, Nin Papers.

44. Otto Rank's preface can be found in *Anaïs: An International Journal* 2 (1984).

45. Bair, *Anaïs Nin,* 264.

46. *Mirages: The Unexpurgated Diary of Anaïs Nin, 1939–1947* (Athens: Swallow Press / Ohio University Press, published in association with Sky Blue Press, 2013), 101.

47. Robert Sickles, *American Popular Culture through History: The 1940s* (Westport, CT: Greenwood Press, 2004), 4.

48. Bair, *Anaïs Nin,* 279–80.

49. Anaïs Nin, Journal 63 (8 Dec. 1940–June 1941), box 21, folder 1, p. 127, Nin Papers.

50. Anaïs Nin, Journal 65 (4 Nov. 1941–24 Oct. 1942), box 21, folder 3, pp. 64, 69, 70, Nin Papers.

51. Nin, Journal 63, p. 352.

52. Philip K. Jason, "The Gemor Press," in *Anaïs: An International Journal* 2 (1984): 27, 28; Anaïs Nin to Caresse Crosby, fall 1944, in *Anaïs: An International Journal* 2 (1984): 47.

53. Henry Miller to Anaïs Nin, April 1944, in Stuhlmann, *Literate Passion,* 360.

54. Nin, *Mirages: Unexpurgated Diary, 1939–1947*, 215, 216.

55. *The Diary of Anaïs Nin, 1944–1947*, vol. 4, ed. and with a preface by Gunther Stuhlmann (New York: Harcourt Brace Jovanovich, 1971), 82 (hereafter cited as *Diary 4*).

56. Nin, *Mirages: Unexpurgated Diary, 1939–1947*, 219.

57. Philip K. Jason, *Anaïs Nin and Her Critics* (Columbia, SC: Camden House, 1993), 56.

58. Lawrence H. Schwartz, *Creating Faulkner's Reputation: The Politics of Modern Literary Criticism* (Knoxville: University of Tennessee Press, 1990), 204.

59. Bair, *Anaïs Nin*, 324.

60. Ibid., 379.

61. *The Diary of Anaïs Nin, 1947–1955*, vol. 5, ed. and with a preface by Gunther Stuhlmann (New York: Harcourt Brace Jovanovich, 1974), 237 (hereafter cited as *Diary 5*).

62. *Diary 6*, 253–54.

63. Bair, *Anaïs Nin*, 474.

64. Anaïs Nin to Hugh Guiler, 14 Nov. 1964, box 35, folder 7, Nin Papers.

65. Gunther Stuhlmann to Anaïs Nin, 6 Nov. 1964, box 35, folder 7, Nin Papers; Anaïs Nin to Gunther Stuhlmann, 9 Nov. 1964, box 35, folder 7, Nin Papers.

66. Anaïs Nin to Hugh Guiler, c. Jan. 1965, box 36, folder 2, Nin Papers.

67. Anaïs Nin to Hiram Haydn, 26 Sept. 1965, Paul Herron's archive.

68. Anaïs Nin to Alan Swallow, 16 Apr. 1965, box 36, folder 3, Nin Papers; Nona Balakian to Anaïs Nin, 16 June 1964, box 35, folder 4, Nin Papers.

69. Anaïs Nin to Lynne (last name unknown), 18 May 1965, box 36, folder 3, Nin Papers.

70. Gunther Stuhlmann to Anaïs Nin, 1 July 1965, box 36, folder 4, Nin Papers. Harcourt Brace and World, operating from 1970 until 2007 as Harcourt Brace Jovanovich, was the American publisher of Nin's diary. The company merged in 2007 with Houghton Mifflin and is currently known as Houghton Mifflin Harcourt.

71. Anaïs Nin to Hugh Guiler, 8 Dec. 1965, box 36, folder 3, Nin Papers.

CHAPTER 2: PUBLIC PROMOTION OF THE PRIVATE SELF

1. *The Diary of Anaïs Nin, 1966–1974*, vol. 7, ed. and with a preface by Gunther Stuhlmann (New York: Harcourt Brace Jovanovich, 1980), 109 (hereafter cited as *Diary 7*).

2. Anaïs Nin, Journal 54 (July–Sept. 1937), box 19, folder 4, Nin Papers. This fragment in a slightly changed form can be found in *Diary 2*, 223.

3. Margo Culley, "Introduction to *A Day at a Time: Diary Literature of American Women, from 1764 to 1895*" (1985) in *Women, Autobiography, Theory: A Reader*, ed. Sidonie Smith and Julia Watson (Madison: University of Wisconsin Press, 1998), 217, 218–19; Felicity A. Nussbaum, "The Ideology of Genre" (1989), in *Women, Autobiography, Theory: A Reader*, ed. Sidonie Smith and Julia Watson (Madison: University of Wisconsin Press, 1998), 165; Lynn Z. Bloom, "'I Write Myself for Strangers': Private Diaries as Public Documents," in *Inscribing the Daily: Critical Essays on Women's Diaries*, ed. Suzanne L. Bunkers and Cynthia A. Huff (Amherst: University of Massachusetts Press, 1996), 24.

4. Culley, "Introduction to *A Day*," 219; Helen Tookey, *Anaïs Nin, Fictionality and Femininity: Playing a Thousand Roles* (Oxford: Clarendon Press, 2003); Elizabeth Podnieks, *Daily Modernism: The Literary Diaries of Virginia Woolf, Antonia White, Elizabeth Smart, and Anaïs Nin* (Montreal: McGill-Queen's University Press, 2000), 284–85.

5. *Henry and June: From "A Journal of Love," the Unexpurgated Diary of Anaïs Nin, 1931–1932* (New York: Harcourt Brace Jovanovich, 1986), 12.

6. Culley, "Introduction to *A Day*," 218, 217.

7. I am indebted here to Peter Hamilton's concept of a double construction that he uses in reference to documentary photography. Hamilton describes the two-phase construction process that takes place before pictures reach the viewer: "First, the photographer is involved in a process of construction in choosing and framing his or her images as 'to make known, to confirm, to give testimony to others.'" Then a second process of construction takes place. In the case of documentary photography, it is a process of selection "out of their original ordering and narrative context to be placed alongside textual information and reports in a publication." Hamilton, "Representing the Social: France and Frenchness in Post-war Humanist Photography," in *Representation: Cultural Representation and Signifying Practices*, ed. Stuart Hall (London: Sage, 1997), 86.

8. *The Early Diary of Anaïs Nin, 1923–1927*, vol. 3 *(Journal of a Wife)*, edited by Rupert Pole, with a preface by Joaquin Nin-Culmell (New York: Harcourt Brace Jovanovich, 1983), 26.

9. Anaïs Nin, Journal 32 (20 Oct. 1931–1 Feb. 1932), box 16, folder 1, p. 77, Nin Papers (emphasis in the original).

10. *The Diary of Anaïs Nin, 1931–1934*, vol. 1, ed. and with an introduction by Gunther Stuhlmann (New York: Swallow Press and Harcourt, Brace & World, 1966), 8 (hereafter cited as *Diary 1*).

11. Anaïs Nin to Henry Miller, 9 March 1932, in *A Literate Passion: Letters of Anaïs Nin and Henry Miller, 1932–1953*, ed. Gunther Stuhlmann (San Diego, CA: Harcourt Brace, 1987), 21.

12. Anaïs Nin to Hiram Haydn, 7 Dec. 1965, *A Café in Space: The Anaïs Nin Literary Journal* 4 (2007): 133–34.

13. P. David Marshall, introduction to *Celebrity Culture Reader*, 6, 10.

14. Elyse Lamm Pineau, "A Mirror of Her Own: Anaïs Nin's Autobiographical Performances," in *The Critical Response to Anaïs Nin*, ed. Philip K. Jason (Westport, CT: Greenwood Press, 1996), 234, 233.

15. Helen Tookey, *Anaïs Nin, Fictionality and Femininity: Playing a Thousand Roles* (Oxford: Clarendon Press, 2003), 6–7; Arthur Marwick, *The Sixties: Cultural Revolution in Britain, France, Italy and the United States, c. 1958–c. 1974* (Oxford: Oxford University Press, 1998), 3; Elizabeth Wilson, *Bohemians: The Glamorous Outcasts* (London: I. B. Tauris Publishers, 2000), 115.

16. Lisa Rado, ed., *Modernism, Gender and Culture: A Cultural Studies Approaches* (New York: Garland, 1994), 7. In talking about the "sixties," I employ Arthur Marwick's classification and consider that the period is longer than just an actual decade starting in 1960. Explaining the span of his book, *The Sixties,* Marwick says that dividing historical movements into clear-cut decades is not viable; many of the ideas of the sixties draw on the "insignificant movements" in the fifties while inspiring people long after 1969. As a closing date, he proposes 1974, claiming that although both the international oil crisis, which led to a widespread recession, and the withdrawal of American troops from Vietnam took place in 1973, it was not until 1974 that ordinary people began to feel the consequences of these events. Such a periodization suits the purpose of this book, since 1974, which Marwick proposes as the closing year of the sixties, coincides with Nin's retirement from public life. Marwick, *The Sixties*, 7.

17. Nin to Haydn, 7 Dec. 1965, in *A Café in Space*, 134.

18. Mary Dearborn, Miller's biographer, claims that Miller wrote the preface and had Nin sign it. See Dearborn, *The Happiest Man Alive: A Biography of Henry Miller* (New York: Simon and Schuster, 1991), 171.

19. "The romantics," as Pericles Lewis states, "prefigured many aspects of modernism: the emphasis on the lone genius who follows his (or occasionally her) own inspiration and disregards the tenets and rules of art; a faith in the spiritual qualities of art understood as independent of organized religion; the basic hostility of the artist to

society and convention; and the efforts to create an art that speaks the language of the common people." Lewis, *The Cambridge Introduction to Modernism* (Cambridge: Cambridge University Press, 2007), 7. Although Nin's use of the generic *he* might suggest that she associated creativity with masculinity, it is more probable that she followed general trends in the use of the pronoun. The generic *he* remained unchallenged until the 1970s. Feminist linguists, politicians, and campaigners of the women's movement such as Dale Spender and Bella Abzug questioned the use of the generic *he* and other linguistic forms (e.g., *Mrs.* and *Miss*) that perpetuated the inferior status of women.

20. Philip K. Jason, "The Gemor Press," *Anaïs: An International Journal* 2 (1984): 25, 29. For the price of *Ulysses,* see Mark S. Morrisson, "Publishing," in *A Companion to Modernist Literature and Culture,* ed. David Bradshaw and Kevin J. H. Dettmar (Malden, MA: Blackwell Publishing, 2006), 141. The price of *This Hunger* is based on a listing of this book on the website www.abebook.com in July 2013.

21. Anaïs Nin, "The Story of My Printing Press," reprinted in *In Favor of the Sensitive Man and Other Essays* (San Diego, CA: Harcourt Brace, 1976), 67.

22. Morrisson, "Publishing," 135.

23. Mark S. Morrisson, "Nationalism and the Modern American Canon," in *The Cambridge Companion to American Modernism,* ed. Walter Kalaidjian (Cambridge: Cambridge University Press, 2006), 18.

24. Nin, "Story of My Printing Press," 68; Marwick, *The Sixties,* 490. For more on underground papers, see John McMillian, *Smoking Typewriters: The Sixties Underground Press and the Rise of Alternative Media in America* (Oxford: Oxford University Press, 2011).

25. Dearborn, *Happiest Man Alive,* 277, 279. Dearborn lists the following volumes with Miller's name in the title: *Letters from Your Capricorn Friend: Henry Miller and the* Stroker, *1978–1980,* by Henry Miller (New York: New Directions, 1984); *Letters from Henry Miller to Hoki Tokuda Miller,* ed. Joyce Howard (New York: Freundlich, 1986); *Dear, Dear Brenda: The Love Letters of Henry Miller to Brenda Venus,* ed. Gerald Seth Sindell (New York: Henry Holt, 1986); *A Literate Passion: Letters of Anaïs Nin and Henry Miller, 1932–1953,* ed. Gunther Stuhlmann (New York: Harcourt Brace, 1987); and *The Durrell-Miller Letters, 1935–1980,* ed. Ian MacNiven (New York: New Directions, 1988).

26. Joanna Pawlik, "Artaud in Performance: Dissident Surrealism and the Postwar American Literary Avant-garde," in *Papers of Surrealism,* no. 8 (2010): 1, www.surrealismcentre.ac.uk

/papersofsurrealism/journal8/acrobat%20files/Articles/Pawlik%20final%20version.pdf.

27. Shari Benstock, *Women of the Left Bank: Paris, 1900–1940* (Austin: University of Texas Press, 1986), 4.

28. Anaïs Nin to Caresse Crosby, 13 Aug. 1967; Caresse Crosby to Anaïs Nin, Aug. 1967. Both letters are quoted in *Anaïs: An International Journal* 2 (1984): 52, 53.

29. *Diary 6*, 319.

30. *Diary 4*, 88.

31. Edward J. Rielly, *American Popular Culture Through History: The 1960s* (Westport, CT: Greenwood, 2003), 23.

32. Wilson, *Bohemians*, 17–18.

33. Ibid., 3 (emphasis in the original).

34. Ibid., 102, 159, 161, 165.

35. Ibid., 52, 24.

36. Ibid., 24.

37. Determining why Nin rejected homosexual bonds is beyond the scope of this study, but the ideas about homosexuality circulating at the beginning of the twentieth century did not encourage one to take on the label. Although homosexuality stopped being viewed as a crime or a sin in the nineteenth century, many Victorian psychiatrists and sexologists began defining it as a pathology—a disease that could, and should, be treated. Moreover, Shari Benstock shows that most fictional representations of homosexuality (particularly of lesbianism) reflected "scientific thinking about homosexual behavior that cast lesbian women as sexual deviants—men trapped in women's bodies." Benstock, *Women of the Left Bank*, 59.

38. *Diary 5*, 260.

39. Marwick, *The Sixties*, 496; for the percentage of hippies in the population, see ibid., 480.

40. Wilson, *Bohemians*, 17.

41. Maurice Isserman and Michael Kazin, *America Divided: The Civil War of the 1960s* (Oxford: Oxford University Press, 2000), 73.

42. Rielly, *American Popular Culture*, 17.

43. *The Diary of Anaïs Nin, 1939–1944*, vol. 3, ed. and with a preface by Gunther Stuhlmann (New York: Swallow Press and Harcourt Brace, 1969), 50 (hereafter cited as *Diary 3*).

44. Sigmund Freud, "Some Psychological Consequences of the Anatomical Distinction between Sexes," in *The Masculinity Studies Reader*, ed. Rachel Adams and David Savran (Malden, MA: Blackwell Publishing, 2002), 19.

45. Calvin S. Hall, *A Primer of Freudian Psychology* (New York: Meridian, 1999), 17.

46. *The Early Diary of Anaïs Nin, 1927–1931*, vol. 4, edited by Rupert Pole, with a preface by Joaquin Nin-Culmell (New York: Harcourt Brace Jovanovich, 1985), 269.

47. Charles Darwin, *The Descent of Man and Selection in Relation to Sex* (New York: D. Appleton, 1896), 564; Nin, *Diary 1*, 276.

48. Benstock, *Women of the Left Bank*, 75–76.

49. For details, see chapters 6 and 7 of Wilson's *Bohemians*.

CHAPTER 3: PUBLIC RELATIONS OF THE SELF

1. *Diary 3*, 271.

2. Suzette Henke, "Suzette Henke," in *Recollections of Anaïs Nin by Her Contemporaries*, ed. Benjamin Franklin V (Athens: Ohio University Press, 1996), 119; Harriet Zinnes, "Harriet Zinnes," in ibid., 28; *Diary 7*, 3; Deirdre Bair, *Anaïs Nin: A Biography* (New York: G. P. Putnam's Sons, 1995), 451, 499; Linde Salber, *Tysiąc i jedna kobieta: Anaïs Nin i jej życie* [Thousand and one woman: The story of Anaïs Nin] (Gdynia, Poland: Uraeus, 1999), 409. Salber's biography appeared originally in German and was translated into Polish by M. Dutkiewicz.

3. Gunther Stuhlmann, preface to Nin, *Diary 7*, vii; Richard Centing, "Spying on the Doors," *Under the Sign of Pisces: Anaïs Nin and Her Circle* 1, no. 2 (Spring 1970): 11. See the opening lines of The Doors song "Spy," released in 1970.

4. Bair, *Anaïs Nin*, 503–4, 511; Richard Centing, "Teaching Anaïs Nin," *Under the Sign of Pisces: Anaïs Nin and Her Circle* 2, no. 3 (Summer 1971): 6–7. *Under the Sign of Pisces*, the first journal devoted to Nin, reported on the most interesting courses in which Nin was included: the *Diary* was part of the syllabus in courses organized at Yale University ("Images of Women in Literature" by Dianne Alstad), at San Diego College ("Women Writers" by Joyce Nower), at Douglass College ("The Literature of Women's Liberation" by Elaine Showalter), at the University of California–Santa Barbara ("Women and Literature" by Nancy Hoffman), and at Jersey City State College, where Nin's works were taught regularly by Sharon Spencer.

5. Anaïs Nin to Roger Boulogne, 10 Nov. 1969, quoted in Bair, *Anaïs Nin*, 490.

6. Charlotte Templin, *Feminism and the Politics of Literary Reputation: The Example of Erica Jong* (Lawrence: University Press of Kansas, 1995), 8.

7. Rose Marie Cutting, introduction to *Anaïs Nin: A Reference Guide* (Boston: G. K. Hall, 1978), xvi–xviii.

8. William Goyen, "Portrait of the Artist as a Diarist: The Diary of Anaïs Nin," review of *Diary of Anaïs Nin, 1947–1955*, vol. 5, *New York Times Book Review*, 14 Apr. 1974. Nancy Hoffman, "Serialized Life," review of *Diary of Anaïs Nin, 1947–1955*, vol. 5, *New Republic*, 15 June 1974, 31–32.

9. Robert Kirsch, "Journal of a Troubled Journey," review of *Diary of Anaïs Nin, 1931–1934*, vol. 1, *Los Angeles Times*, 17 Apr. 1966, B2; Karl Shapiro, "The Charmed Circle of Anaïs Nin," in *The Critical Response to Anaïs Nin*, ed. Philip K. Jason (Westport, CT: Greenwood Press, 1996), 157, 155 (emphasis in the original).

10. Duane Schneider, "Fusion of Two Worlds," review of *Diary of Anaïs Nin, 1934–1939*, vol. 2, *Kenyon Review* 30, no. 1 (1968): 137, 140; Daniel Stern, "Princess of the Underground," review of *Diary of Anaïs Nin, 1934–1939*, vol. 2, *Nation*, 4 Mar. 1968, 312; Daniel Stern, "The Novel of Her Life," review of *Diary of Anaïs Nin, 1944–1947*, vol. 4, *Nation*, 29 Nov. 1971, 571; Anna Balakian, review of *Diary of Anaïs Nin, 1944–1947*, vol. 4, *New York Times Book Review*, 16 Jan. 1972.

11. Henrietta Buckmaster, "What Is the Sum of Her Words," review of *Diary of Anaïs Nin, 1931–1934*, vol. 1, *Christian Science Monitor*, 16 June 1966, 5; Jocelyn Knowles, "Anaïs Nin Has Done It Again," review of *Diary of Anaïs Nin, 1934–1939*, vol. 2, *Los Angeles Times*, 25 June 1967, C39; Jean Garrigue, review of *Diary of Anaïs Nin, 1939–1944*, vol. 3, *New York Times Book Review*, 23 Nov. 1969; Laurie Stone, "Anaïs Nin: Is the Bloom off the Pose?," review of the *Diaries*, by Anaïs Nin, *Village Voice*, 26 July 1976, 43.

12. Templin, *Feminism*, 19 (emphasis in the original); Laura Marcus, *Auto/biographical Discourses: Criticism, Theory, Practice* (Manchester: Manchester University Press, 1994), 234; Kate Millett, "Anaïs—A Mother of Us All: The Birth of the Artist as Woman," *Anaïs: An International Journal* 9 (1991): 6.

13. Robert Mazzocco, "To Tell You the Truth," review of *The Paris Diary of Ned Rorem*, by Ned Rorem, *The Diary of Anaïs Nin, 1931–1934*, vol. 1, by Anaïs Nin, and *A Very Easy Death*, by Simone de Beauvoir, *New York Review of Books*, 8 Sept. 1966; Aldan Whitman, "Books of the Time," review of *Diary of Anaïs Nin, 1934–1939*, vol. 2, *New York Times*, 22 July 1967, 23; Anatole Broyard, "Of Art, Ecstasy and Water," review of *Diary of Anaïs Nin, 1944–1947*, vol. 4, *New York Times*, 26 Oct. 1971, 39.

14. Sidonie Smith, *Reading Autobiography: A Guide for Interpreting Life Narratives* (Minneapolis: University of Minnesota Press, 2001), 118.

15. Kirsch, "Journal of a Troubled Journey," B2; Harry T. Moore, "A Long-Awaited Diary," review of *Diary of Anaïs Nin, 1931–1934,* vol. 1, *St. Louis Dispatch,* 1 May 1966, B4; Saul Maloff, "The Seven Veils," review of *Diary of Anaïs Nin, 1934–1939,* vol. 2, *Newsweek,* 3 July 1967, 36.

16. Garrigue, review of *Diary of Anaïs Nin, 1939–1944,* vol. 3; Audrey C. Foote, "Her Own Best Work of Art," review of *Diary of Anaïs Nin, 1955–1966,* vol. 6, *Washington Post,* 29 Aug. 1976, M4; Knowles, "Anaïs Nin Has Done It Again," C39.

17. Chris Beasley, *Gender and Sexuality: Critical Theories, Critical Thinkers* (London: Sage, 2005), 19; Joanne Hollows, *Feminism, Femininity, and Popular Culture* (Manchester: Manchester University Press, 2000), 5, 2.

18. Hollows, *Feminism, Femininity,* 3.

19. Flora Davis, *Moving The Mountain: Women's Movement in America since 1960* (New York: Simon and Schuster, 1991), 87–88.

20. Gunther Stuhlmann, introduction to *Diary 1,* v.

21. Ibid.

22. Fanny Butcher, "A Long Awaited Literary Flight," review of *Diary of Anaïs Nin, 1931–1934,* vol. 1, *Chicago Tribune,* 22 May 1966, 7; Buckmaster, "Sum of Her Words?" 5; Thomas Bishop, "Pick of the Paperbacks," review of *Diary of Anaïs Nin, 1931–1934,* vol. 1, *Saturday Review,* 31 May 1969, 29.

23. Kirsch, "Journal of a Troubled Journey," B2; Mazzocco, "To Tell You the Truth"; Moore, "A Long-Awaited Diary," B4.

24. Moore, "A Long-Awaited Diary," B4; Butcher, "A Long Awaited Literary Flight," 7.

25. John Rodden, *George Orwell: The Politics of Literary Reputation* (London: Transaction Publishers, 2003), 66.

26. Ibid., 110.

27. Ibid., 117.

28. Henrietta Buckmaster, "Incantations: For the Initiated Only," review of *Diary of Anaïs Nin, 1944–1947,* vol. 4, *Christian Science Monitor,* 11 Nov. 1971, B7.

29. Joe Moran, *Star Authors: Literary Celebrity in America* (London: Pluto Press, 2000), 39–40; Richard Ohmann, "The Shaping of a Canon: U.S. Fiction, 1960–1975," *Critical Inquiry* 10, no. 1 (Sept. 1983): 203.

30. Ohmann, "Shaping of a Canon," 205, 204.

31. Ibid., 202; Jean Garrigue, "The Self behind the Selves," review of *Diary of Anaïs Nin, 1931–1934,* vol. 1, *New York Times Book Review,* 24 Apr. 1966, 1.

32. Templin, *Feminism,* 10, 32.

33. Henry Miller, "Un Etre Etoilique," in Jason, *Critical Response,* 147; Cutting, introduction to *Anaïs Nin,* ix.

34. Templin, *Feminism,* 22; Swallow quoted in Bair, *Anaïs Nin,* 470. Bair quotes Alan Swallow but does not provide the source of this quotation. Very likely it was a letter Nin received from Swallow.

35. Hugh Guiler to Anaïs Nin, 27 Jan. 1965, box 36, folder 2, Nin Papers. Andre Bay was an editor of Editions Stock in Paris, while Peter Owen was Nin's publisher in the UK.

36. Anaïs Nin to Hugh Guiler, c. Feb. 1965, box 36, folder 2, Nin Papers; Henry Miller, "Miller on Nin," *Village Voice,* 26 May 1966, 5; Miller's prologue quoted in Richard Centing, "The Henry Miller Odyssey," *Under the Sign of Pisces: Anaïs Nin and Her Circle* 1, no. 1 (Winter 1970): 4.

37. Gore Vidal, "Taking a Grand Tour of Anaïs Nin's High Bohemia via the Time Machine," review of *Diary of Anaïs Nin, 1944–1947,* vol. 4, *Los Angeles Times,* 26 Sept. 1971, S1; 5; 23.

38. Ibid., 23, 5, 5.

39. Ibid., 23.

40. Kim Krizan, "Gore Vidal's Life: How He Distorted His Relationship with Anaïs Nin," *A Café in Space: The Anaïs Nin Literary Journal* 10 (2013): 7.

41. Katha Pollitt, "Apologia Ended," review of *Diary of Anaïs Nin, 1966–1974,* vol. 7, *New York Times Book Review,* 13 July 1980, 24; Vidal, "Taking a Grand Tour," S1.

42. Bair, *Anaïs Nin,* 492.

43. Robert Kirsch to Anaïs Nin, 20 Nov. 1965, box 36, folder 6, Nin Papers; Anaïs Nin to Robert Kirsch, c. Nov. 1965, quoted in *Diary 7,* 122.

44. Bair, *Anaïs Nin,* 486; Anaïs Nin to Bettina Knapp, c. winter 1968–69, quoted in *Diary 7,* 73.

45. Anaïs Nin to Peter Owen, 11 May 1965, box 36, folder 3, Nin Papers.

46. Anaïs Nin to Oliver Evans, May 1965, box 36, folder 4, Nin Papers.

47. Anaïs Nin to Oliver Evans, 26 Oct. 1965, box 36, folder 4, Nin Papers; Oliver Evans to Anaïs Nin, n.d., box 36, folder 6, Nin Papers. For examples of Nin's opinion of critics, see her lectures gathered in *A Woman Speaks: The Lectures, Seminars, and Interviews of Anaïs Nin,* ed. Evelyn J. Hinz (London: Penguin Books, 1992), 98.

48. Aaron Jaffe, *Modernism and the Culture of Celebrity* (Cambridge: Cambridge University Press, 2005), 106; Leonard Diepeveen, "'I Can Have More Than Enough Power to Satisfy Me': T. S. Eliot's Construction of His Audience," in *Marketing Modernisms: Self-Promotion, Canonization, Rereading,* ed. Kevin J. H. Dettmar and Stephen Watt (Ann Arbor: University of Michigan Press, 1996), 52.

49. Templin, *Feminism*, 13.

50. Loren Glass, *Authors Inc.: Literary Celebrity in the Modern United States, 1880–1980* (New York: New York University Press, 2004),17.

51. Moran, *Star Authors,* 19. Not only were Nin's works discussed in the press, but also her public appearances were frequently reported in newspapers.

52. Bair, *Anaïs Nin,* 481; Evelyn J. Hinz, introduction to *A Woman Speaks,* xiii; Noël Riley Fitch, *Anaïs: The Erotic Life of Anaïs Nin* (London: Abacus, 1996), 388; Cutting, introduction to *Anaïs Nin,* xix; Wendy DuBow, introduction to *Conversations with Anaïs Nin,* ed. Wendy DuBow (Jackson: University Press of Mississippi, 1994), xi.

53. Estelle Jelinek, "Anaïs Nin: A Critical Evaluation," in Jason, *Critical Response,* 45–46. Jelinek's article appeared originally on 31 December 1974 in *off our backs: a women's newsjournal* under a different title: "Anaïs Reconsidered." It was later expanded and included in Jason's collection. All quotations from Jelinek's article are taken from Jason's *Critical Response.* Anaïs Nin to Bruce Harkness, 20 Nov. 1963, box 34, folder 8, Nin Papers; Jelinek, "Anaïs Nin," 53–54.

54. Salber, *Tysiąc i jedna kobieta,* 409; Anaïs Nin to Hugh Guiler, 9 Nov. 1963, box 34, folder 6, Nin Papers; Bair, *Anais Nin,* 499, 502.

55. Elyse Lamm Pineau, "A Mirror of Her Own: Anaïs Nin's Autobiographical Performances," in Jason, *Critical Response,* 234, 236.

56. Hinz, *Woman Speaks,* 175. Hinz earlier wrote a critical study on Nin's works, which Nin approved, and she was also appointed by Nin as her official biographer in 1974. Bair, *Anaïs Nin,* 518. Hinz never fulfilled her role, however.

57. Brenda R. Silver, *Virginia Woolf Icon* (Chicago: University of Chicago Press, 1999), 17.

58. My main source of interviews is a collection entitled *Conversations with Anaïs Nin* (1994), edited by Wendy M. DuBow. This book comprises twenty-four reprinted interviews, carried out originally between 1965 and 1976. I have excluded two interviews from my study because they were intended for an audience outside of the United States. Instead, I have included one interview from the *Village Voice* that was omitted from the collection. My analysis consists of twenty-three interviews, the majority of which—sixteen—were conducted in three years, from 1970 to 1972.

59. Barbara Freeman, "A Dialogue with Anaïs Nin," in *Conversations with Anaïs Nin,* ed. Wendy DuBow (Jackson: University Press of Mississippi, 1994), 186, previously published in *Chicago*

Review, no. 2 (1972); Susan Edmiston, "Portrait of Anaïs Nin," in ibid., 43, previously published in *Mademoiselle,* Oct. 1970.

60. Karla Jay, "Two Interviews with Anaïs Nin," in ibid., 133–36, previously published in *Everywoman,* 17 Dec. 1971; Jeffrey Bailey, "Link in the Chain of Feeling: An Interview with Anaïs Nin," in ibid., 235–49, previously published in *New Orleans Review* 5, no. 2 (1976).

61. Bailey, "Link in the Chain," 243. Nin was frequently accused of being self-obsessed, egocentric, and narcissistic.

62. Paul John Eakin, *How Our Lives Become Stories: Making Selves* (Ithaca, NY: Cornell University Press, 1999), 123.

63. Frank Roberts, "Writers at Work: Anaïs Nin Talks with Frank Roberts," transcribed in DuBow, *Conversations with Anaïs Nin,* 13, original broadcast, KPFK-FM, Los Angeles, 1965.

64. Ibid., 11–12.

65. Clare Loeb, "Anaïs Nin on Women's Liberation," transcribed in ibid., 27, original broadcast, KPFK-FM, Los Angeles, 1971.

66. Ibid., 34.

67. Ibid., 28.

68. Milton Hoffman, "An Interview with Anaïs Nin," transcribed in ibid., 144–45, original broadcast, WBAI, New York, 1971.

69. Nancy Williamson, Evelyn Clark, and Barbara Reyes, "A Conversation with Anaïs Nin," in ibid., 75, previously published in *Second Wave: A Magazine of the New Feminism* (Summer 1971).

70. Ibid., 90, 91.

71. Hinz, *Woman Speaks,* 33 (emphasis in the original).

72. Anaïs Nin, "Notes on Feminism," *Massachusetts Review* 13, no. 1–2 (Winter–Spring 1972): 25–28; "Liberation: A Simultaneous Happening," *New York Times,* 14 Jan. 1972, 33.

73. Jelinek, "Anaïs Nin," in Jason, *Critical Response,* 45–54.

74. Advertisement for *The Diary of Anaïs Nin, 1931–1934,* vol. 1, in the *New York Times,* 20 May 1966, 45.

75. Advertisement for *The Diary of Anaïs Nin, 1944–1947,* vol. 4, in the *New York Times,* 17 Oct. 1971, BR15.

76. Kevin Wallace, "The Diarist Who Sold Out the House," *San Francisco Chronicle,* 8 Apr. 1974, 2, microfilm, Anaïs Nin Papers, Charles E. Young Research Library, University of California, Los Angeles; Barry Siegel, "500 Attend the Ceremony for *Times* Women of the Year," *Los Angeles Times,* 25 Mar. 1976, OC_A1, 2; Digby Diehl, "*Times* Woman of the Year: Anaïs Nin, Feminism's Beacon," *Los Angeles Times,* 30 Mar. 1976, OC_C1; Bertha Harris, "Who Chose These Women, and Why?" *Village Voice,* 30 Sept. 1972, 71.

77. Jelinek, "Anaïs Nin," in Jason, *Critical Response*, 47, 48, 54.
78. Millett, "Anaïs," 4.
79. Marshall, introduction to *Celebrity Culture Reader*, 3.
80. Susan Edmiston, "Portrait of Anaïs Nin," in DuBow, *Conversations with Anaïs Nin*, 45, 50.
81. Susan Stocking, "Persona Unmasked with Visit Anaïs Nin," in ibid., 99, previously published in *Los Angeles Times*, 7 Nov. 1971.
82. Freeman, "Dialogue with Anaïs Nin," 186; Daniel Stern and Dominique Browning, "Anaïs Nin: An Interview," in DuBow, *Conversations with Anaïs Nin*, 212, previously published in *Helicon Nine: A Journal of Women's Arts and Letters* 1, no. 1 (1975).
83. Clark in Williamson et al., "Conversation with Anaïs Nin," 85; Keith Berwick, "A Conversation with Anaïs Nin," transcribed in DuBow, *Conversations with Anaïs Nin*, 59, originally broadcast on Channel 28, Los Angeles, 1970; Stocking, "Personas Unmasked," 98; Erica Jong quoted in William McBrien, "Anaïs Nin: An Interview," in DuBow, *Conversations with Anaïs Nin*, 209, previously published in *Twentieth Century Literature*, Oct. 1974.
84. Adapted from Baum by P. David Marshall in "Intimately Intertwined in the Most Public Way: Celebrity and Journalism," in *Celebrity Culture Reader*, ed. P. David Marshall (New York: Routledge, 2006), 320.
85. Carole Getzoff, "A Spy in the House of Nin," *Village Voice*, 6 Jan. 1975, 17.
86. Stocking, "Personas Unmasked," 98, 103.
87. Leo Braudy, *The Frenzy of Renown: Fame and Its History* (New York: Vintage Books, 1986), 8; Richard Dyer, *Stars*, rev. ed. (London: British Film Institute, 1998), 47.
88. Edmiston, "Portrait of Anaïs Nin," 43.
89. Fern Marja Eckman, "The Non-legend of Anaïs Nin," in DuBow, *Conversations with Anaïs Nin*, 172, previously published in *New York Post*, 19 Feb. 1972; Edmiston, "Portrait of Anaïs Nin," 47.
90. Hoffman, "Interview with Anaïs Nin," 143; Studs Terkel, "Interview with Anaïs Nin," in DuBow, *Conversations with Anaïs Nin*, 152, original broadcast, WFMT-FM, Chicago, 1972; Eckman, "Non-legend of Anaïs Nin," 172; Freeman, "A Dialogue with Anaïs Nin," 191.
91. Eckman, "Non-legend of Anaïs Nin," 172; Terkel, "Interview with Anaïs Nin," 152.
92. Elizabeth Wilson, *Bohemians: The Glamorous Outcasts* (London: I. B. Tauris Publishers, 2000), 6.
93. C. Gerald Fraser, "Anaïs Nin, Author Whose Diaries Depicted Intellectual Life, Dead," *New York Times*, 16 Jan. 1977; Celeste Durant, "Anaïs Nin Dies: Noted as Writer and Feminist," *Los*

Angeles Times, 16 Jan. 1977, 1; Martin Weil, "Author, Diarist, Dies at 73," *Washington Post,* 16 Jan. 1977.

CHAPTER 4: SUCCESS, SCANDAL, SEX,
AND THE SEARCH FOR THE "REAL" ANAÏS NIN

1. *Diary 7,* 107.

2. Anaïs Nin, fragment from the preface to Margo Moore's photographs included in *Diary 7,* 319.

3. According to Noël Riley Fitch, "Daisy Aldan and Renate Druks remain convinced to this day that publication of the erotica, as well as unexpurgated diaries, is in poor taste and not what Anaïs wanted. Others, including Henry Miller and Rupert Pole, are convinced that she died wanting everything published." Fitch, *Anaïs: The Erotic Life of Anaïs Nin* (London: Abacus, 1996), 408. Commenting on the publication of the unexpurgated journals, Barbara Kraft in her memoir makes a similar comment: "Perhaps Anaïs did want it all published, but I remain unconvinced, as did her brother Joaquin." Kraft, *Anaïs Nin: The Last Days, a Memoir* (Huntington Woods, MI: Sky Blue Press, 2011), 57.

4. Fitch occasionally refers to the unpublished journals but not to the extent that Bair does. Deirdre Bair, "The Making of *Anaïs Nin: A Biography,*" interview by Paul Herron, *A Café in Space: The Anaïs Nin Literary Journal* 7 (2010): 29.

5. The critical writings on Nin between 1985 and 1992 were sustained mainly by Gunther Stuhlmann—Nin's agent and editor—who began publishing *Anaïs: An International Journal* in 1983, an annual journal that, in addition to critical articles, included previously unpublished portions of the diary, Nin's correspondence, and recollections of Anaïs Nin by her friends. Sidonie Smith and Julia Watson, "Situating Subjectivity in Women's Autobiographical Practices," in *Women, Autobiography, Theory: A Reader,* ed. Sidonie Smith and Julia Watson (Madison: University of Wisconsin Press, 1998), 32, 39.

6. Diane Richard-Allerdyce, *Anaïs Nin and the Remaking of Self: Gender, Modernism, and Narrative Identity* (DeKalb: Northern Illinois University Press, 1998). Suzette Henke, *Shattered Subjects: Trauma and Testimony in Women's Life Writing* (Basingstoke, UK: Macmillan, 2000), 55–81 (chapter 3: "Anaïs Nin's Interior Cities: Incest, Anxiety, and Father-Daughter Loss").

7. Deirdre Bair, *Anaïs Nin: A Biography* (New York: G. P. Putnam's Sons, 1995), 515; John Ferrone, "The Making of *Delta of Venus,*" *A Café in Space: The Anaïs Nin Literary Journal* 7 (2010): 53, 55; Bair, *Anaïs Nin,* 515–16.

8. *Diary 3,* 58.

9. Anaïs Nin, preface to *Delta of Venus* (Orlando, FL: Harvest Books, 2004), xv.

10. Ferrone, "Making of *Delta,*" 57. Readers who mention the origins of Nin's erotica consistently tell the same story of a wealthy patron demanding for her to leave out poetry and concentrate on sex. They know the story from Nin's preface, which still opens most editions of the book. For instance, a user called Mish wrote on 6 March 2013, "Anais Nin and a few of her writer friends were asked by an anonymous wealthy collector to write a series of erotic short stories for $1.00 per page for his pleasure. However the collector was specific in the kind of erotica he wanted. Anaïs was to omit any warmth, emotion or poetry to her writing and only concentrate on the sex." Another, Astrid Reza, commenting on Nin's preface, declared, "How necessities create wonders to writers." www.goodreads.com/book/show/11041.Delta_of_Venus.

11. Ferrone, "Making of *Delta,*" 55, 56.

12. For Aubry's *Story of O* and further details on the sexual revolution, see David Allyn, *Make Love Not War: The Sexual Revolution; An Unfettered History* (Boston: Little, Brown, 2000), 65.

13. Harriet Zinnes, "Collector's Item," review of *Delta of Venus,* by Anaïs Nin, *New York Times Book Review,* 10 July 1977, 11; Michelle M. Leber, review of *Delta of Venus,* by Anaïs Nin, *Library Journal,* 1 May 1977, 1044.

14. Susan Wood, "Nin's 'Erotica'—Writings to Please a Wealthy Patron," review of *Delta of Venus,* by Anaïs Nin, *San Francisco Chronicle* magazine *This World,* 24 July 1977, 42, microfilm, Anaïs Nin Papers, Charles E. Young Research Library, University of California, Los Angeles; Charles McGrath, "The Delts of Venus," *New Yorker,* 5 June 1978, 33.

15. Anaïs Nin, "The Hungarian Adventurer," in *Delta of Venus* (Orlando, FL: Harvest Books, 2004), 1, 5.

16. Rosemarie Tong, *Feminist Thought: A Comprehensive Introduction* (London: Routledge, 1995), 112–23; Andrea Dworkin quoted in Dick Polman, "An Angry Voice Fights for Women's Dignity," *Chicago Tribune,* 31 July 1985, 1.

17. Lawrence Bommer, "A Woman's View of Erotica," *Chicago Tribune,* 6 Nov. 1987, 6; Sid Smith, "'Erotica' Is Racy Fun That Deserves a Salute," *Chicago Tribune,* 12 Nov. 1987, 23.

18. Ferrone, "Making of *Delta,*" 58; Philip K. Jason, *Anaïs Nin and Her Critics* (Columbia, SC: Camden House, 1993), 51–52.

19. Nin, preface to *Delta of Venus,* xii.

20. At that point, in 1985, two series of Nin's diaries were available—first the seven diaries (mostly published during Nin's lifetime)

and then the four volumes of the *Early Diaries,* published posthumously. John Ferrone to Rupert Pole, 5 Mar. 1985, in "The Making of *Henry and June,* the Book: Correspondence, 1985–1986," *A Café in Space: The Anaïs Nin Literary Journal* 4 (2007): 9.

21. Ferrone, "Making of *Henry,*" 8; John Ferrone to Rupert Pole, 11 Nov. 1985, in "Making of *Henry,*" 11.

22. Anaïs Nin, *Henry and June: From "A Journal of Love," the Unexpurgated Diary of Anaïs Nin, 1931–1932* (New York: Harcourt Brace Jovanovich, 1986), 5–6 (cited parenthetically in the text as *HAJ*).

23. Philip K. Jason, "Dropping Another Veil: Anaïs Nin's *Henry and June,*" in *The Critical Response to Anaïs Nin,* ed. Philip K. Jason (Westport, CT: Greenwood Press, 1996), 202.

24. John Ferrone to Rupert Pole, 5 Dec. 1985, in "Making of *Henry,*" 13.

25. Janet Malcolm, *The Silent Woman: Sylvia Plath and Ted Hughes* (London: Papermac, 1994), 34.

26. Carolyn See, "Anaïs Nin Trapped in a Web of Love," review of *Henry and June,* by Anaïs Nin, *Los Angeles Times Book Review,* 6 Oct. 1986.

27. Jody W. Pennington, *The History of Sex in American Film* (London: Praeger, 2007), 91. *Henry & June,* directed by Philip Kaufman (Universal Studios, 1990), DVD (cited parenthetically in the text as *H&J*).

28. Paul Herron, ed., introduction to *Anaïs Nin: A Book of Mirrors* (Huntington Woods, MI: Sky Blue Press, 1996), xxxiii (emphasis in the original). Brenda Silver demonstrates that many readers are more likely to associate Virginia Woolf with Edward Albee's play *Who's Afraid of Virginia Woolf?* than with Woolf's actual works. Silver, *Virginia Woolf Icon* (Chicago: University of Chicago Press, 1999), 102.

29. Tony Bennett and Janet Woollacott, *Bond and Beyond: The Political Career of a Popular Hero* (London: Palgrave Macmillan, 1987), quoted in John Storey, *Cultural Studies and the Study of Popular Culture,* 2nd ed. (Athens: University of Georgia Press, 2003), 56–57.

30. Kaufman even included a piece by Anaïs's brother Joaquín Nin-Culmell, who was a composer and pianist.

31. Peter Lehman and William Luhr, *Thinking about Movies: Watching, Questioning, Enjoying,* 2nd ed. (Oxford: Blackwell Publishing, 2003), 29.

32. Laura Mulvey, "Visual Pleasure and Narrative Cinema," in *The Norton Anthology of Theory and Criticism,* ed. Vincent B.

Leitch et al. (London: W. W. Norton, 2001), 2184, 2186 (emphasis in the original).

33. Elizabeth Barillé, *Anaïs Nin: Naked under the Mask*, trans. E. Powell (London: Lime Tree, 1992), 7 (hereafter cited parenthetically in the text).

34. Fitch, *Anaïs*, 18 (hereafter cited parenthetically in the text).

35. Stephen Hinerman, "(Don't) Leave Me Alone: Tabloid Narrative and the Michael Jackson Child-Abuse Scandal" (1999) in Marshall, *Celebrity Culture Reader*, 456.

36. *Diary 1*, 87.

37. Lynn Luria-Sukenick, "The Diaries of Anaïs Nin," in Jason, *Critical Response*, 176; Nancy Scholar, *Anaïs Nin* (Boston: Twayne, 1984), 38, 40.

38. Margot Beth Duxler, *Seduction: A Portrait of Anaïs Nin* (Boulder, CO: EdgeWorks, 2002), 104, 106, 107.

39. Gunther Stuhlmann, introduction to *A Literate Passion: Letters of Anaïs Nin and Henry Miller, 1932–1953*, ed. Stuhlmann (San Diego, CA: Harcourt Brace, 1987), xix.

40. Jack Mathews, "Henry Miller Meets the MPAA Movies," *Los Angeles Times*, 27 Aug. 1990, 1; Judy Stone, "Henry Miller on Trial Again? Kaufman's New Movie Unofficially Given an X Rating," *San Francisco Chronicle*, 27 Aug. 1990, F2; Hal Hinson, "*Henry and June*: Hot and Daring," *Washington Post*, 5 Oct. 1990, D1.

41. The subtitle of Leslie McDowell's book was changed for a later printing, as *Between the Sheets: Nine 20th Century Women Writers and Their Famous Literary Partnerships* (New York: Overlook Duckworth, 2012); Noël Riley Fitch, "The Literate Passion of Anaïs Nin and Henry Miller," in *Significant Others: Creativity and Intimate Partnership*, edited by Whitney Chadwick and Isabelle de Courtivron (London: Thames and Hudson, 1993), 155–72; Vera John-Steiner, *Creative Collaboration* (Oxford: Oxford University Press, 2000); Lynnette Felber, *Literary Liaisons: Auto/biographical Appropriations in Modernist Women's Fiction* (DeKalb: Northern Illinois University Press, 2002).

42. McDowell, *Between the Sheets*, 182, 164, 173, 174.

43. John-Steiner, *Creative Collaboration*, 76–78, 83–84.

44. Erica Jong, "A Story Never Told Before—Reading the New, Unexpurgated Diaries of Anaïs Nin," in Jason, *Critical Response*, 205.

45. Lawrence Durrell to Henry Miller, quoted in Fitch, *Anaïs*, 412; Fitch, *Anaïs*, 492; Noël Riley Fitch, e-mail message to the author, 4 Feb. 2011.

46. Advertisement for Anaïs Anaïs perfume, www.cacharel.com, 17 Jan. 2011.

47. Fitch, *Anaïs*, 3, 9; Judy Chicago, "Anaïs Nin: Writer or Perfume?," *Gadfly Online*, 30 July 2001, www.gadflyonline.com.

48. Mary V. Dearborn, *The Happiest Man Alive: A Biography of Henry Miller* (New York: Simon and Schuster, 1991), 141, 142; Jay Martin, *Always Merry and Bright: The Life of Henry Miller* (Santa Barbara, CA: Capra Press, 1978), 267.

49. Martin, *Always Merry and Bright*, 240, 266; Bair, *Anaïs Nin*, 103.

50. Dearborn, *Happiest Man Alive*, 142; Martin, *Always Merry and Bright*, 266; Bair, *Anaïs Nin*, 103.

51. Gayle Nin Rosenkratz, "Gayle Nin Rosenkratz," in *Recollections of Anaïs Nin by Her Contemporaries*, ed. Benjamin Franklin V (Athens: Ohio University Press, 1996), 1; Duane Schneider, "Duane Schneider," in Franklin, *Recollections*, 55; Suzette Henke, "Suzette Henke," in Franklin, *Recollections*, 120; Shirley Ariker, "Shirley Ariker," in Franklin, *Recollections*, 75.

52. Katha Pollitt, "Apologia Ended," review of *Diary of Anaïs Nin, 1966–1974*, vol. 7, *New York Times Book Review*, 13 July 1980, 7, 7 (emphasis in the original), 24, 24; Carolyn Heilbrun, "The Politics of the Mind: Women, Tradition, and the University," quoted in Silver, *Virginia Woolf Icon*, 149; James Wolcott, "Life among the Ninnies," *New York Review of Books*, 26 June 1980.

53. Elaine Showalter, *A Jury of Her Peers: American Women Writers from Anne Bradstreet to Annie Proulx* (London: Virago, 2009), 467.

54. Tong, *Feminist Thought*, 105.

55. Chris Beasley, *Gender and Sexuality: Critical Theories, Critical Thinkers* (London: Sage, 2005), 22; Showalter, *Jury of Her Peers*, 493; Alice Walker, "Anaïs Nin, 1903–1977," *Ms.*, April 1977, 46.

56. Henke, "Suzette Henke," in Franklin, *Recollections*, 119.

57. Duxler, *Seduction*, 13. The people I refer to here were either acquainted with Nin or were her critics. Confirming or refuting this assumption could be accomplished through research based on reader responses.

58. Barbara Kraft, "Barbara Kraft," in Franklin, *Recollections*, 141, 145–46.

59. Sharon Spencer, "Sharon Spencer," in Franklin, *Recollections*, 82; Jong, "Story Never Told Before," 203; Kraft, "Barbara Kraft," in Franklin, *Recollections*, 150.

60. Katha Pollitt, review of *Incest*, by Anaïs Nin, *New York Times Book Review*, 22 Nov. 1992, BR3.

61. Claudia Roth Pierpont, *Passionate Minds: Women Rewriting the World* (New York: Vintage Books, 2000), 78.

62. Bair, *Anaïs Nin*, 200.

63. Leo Braudy, *The Frenzy of Renown: Fame and Its History* (New York: Vintage Books, 1986), 8; Linda Wagner-Martin, *Telling Women's Lives: The New Biography* (New Brunswick, NJ: Rutgers University Press, 1994), 25.

64. Suzette Henke, *Shattered Subjects: Trauma and Testimony in Women's Life Writing* (Basingstoke, UK: Macmillan, 2000), 72.

65. See Roger Luckhurst, "Memory Recovered/Recovered Memory" in *Literature and the Contemporary: Fictions and Theories of the Present,* ed. Roger Luckhurst and Peter Marks (Harlow, UK: Pearson Education, 1999), 80–93; and Elizabeth Loftus and Katherine Ketcham, *The Myth of Repressed Memory: False Memories and Allegation of Sexual Abuse* (New York: St. Martin's Press, 1994).

66. Loftus and Ketcham, *Myth of Repressed Memory*, 7, 140.

67. Ibid., 5, 205–6.

68. Roger Luckhurst, *The Trauma Question* (London: Routledge, 2008), 122, 207–5.

69. Luckhurst writes, "The success of the genre of memoir was one of the most notable publishing phenomenon [sic] of the 1990s, and as Leigh Gilmore observed[,] 'the cultural awareness that something significant was happening around and through memoir crystallised in relation to the recognition of trauma's centrality to it.'" Luckhurst, *Trauma Question,* 117; Luckhurst, "Memory Recovered/ Recovered Memory," 85. An alternative interpretation of Nin's incest revelation that has appeared recently is to deny its existence. Such a stance is taken by Lesley McDowell, who suggests, "It's possible, too, that it's a fantastical account that bears no relation to reality, but is the result of her venture into psychoanalysis, as she attempted to understand its narrative theories by constructing a much more literal story of herself." McDowell, *Between the Sheets*, 165–66.

70. Fitch, *Anaïs*, 3, 4.

71. Alice Miller, "Child Abuse and Mistreatment," www.alice-miller.com/books_en.php?page=3; Fitch, *Anaïs*, 16–17.

72. Miranda Seymour, "Shaping the Truth," in *Mapping Lives: The Uses of Biography,* ed. Peter France and William St. Clair (Oxford: Oxford University Press, 2002), 264; Hermione Lee, *Biography: A Very Short Introduction* (Oxford: Oxford University Press, 2009), 128–29. We could add incest to Lee's list.

73. Lee, *Biography*, 109.

74. Malcolm Bowie, "Freud and the Art of Biography," in France and St. Clair, *Mapping Lives,* 179–80.

75. Elizabeth Podnieks, *Daily Modernism: The Literary Diaries of Virginia Woolf, Antonia White, Elizabeth Smart, and Anaïs Nin* (Montreal: McGill-Queen's University Press, 2000), 312.

76. Fitch, *Anaïs*, 16, 149, 127–28.
77. Loftus and Ketcham, *Myth of Repressed Memory*, 7.
78. Henke, introduction to *Shattered Subjects*, xii–xiii; Diane Richard-Allerdyce, *Anaïs Nin and the Remaking of Self: Gender, Modernism, and Narrative Identity* (DeKalb: Northern Illinois University Press, 1998), 8.
79. Richard-Allerdyce, *Anaïs Nin*, 8; Henke, *Shattered Subjects*, 59; Linde Salber, *Tysiąc i jedna kobieta: Anaïs Nin i jej życie* [Thousand and one woman: The story of Anaïs Nin] (Gdynia, Poland: Uraeus, 1999), 15. The biography appeared originally in German and was translated into Polish by M. Dutkiewicz. Joaquín Nin-Culmell, "Anaïs, My Sister," in *Anaïs Nin: Literary Perspectives*, ed. Suzanne Nalbantian (New York: St. Martin's Press, 1997), 23.
80. Richard-Allerdyce, *Anaïs Nin*, 7; Henke, *Shattered Subjects*, 57.
81. Duxler, *Seduction*, 104.
82. Ibid., back cover (emphasis added), 119.
83. Ibid., 129; Elaine Showalter, *The Female Malady: Women, Madness and English Culture, 1830–1980* (London: Virago Press, 1987), 74.
84. Pollitt, review of *Incest*, BR3; Wagner-Martin, *Telling Women's Lives*, 9.
85. The letters exchanged between Pole and Ferrone (discussed earlier) and Bair's biography proved otherwise.
86. Sally Duros, letter to the editor, *New York Times Book Review*, 3 Jan. 1993, BR12.
87. Miranda Seymour, "Truth Wasn't Sexy Enough: Anaïs Nin's Diaries Were a Fraud and Even Her Marriages Were Lies," *New York Times*, 17 Oct. 1993, BR18; Carol Anshaw, "Anaïs Nin: Many Words, Many Lovers and a Host of Lies," review of *Anaïs: The Erotic Life of Anaïs Nin*, by Noël Riley Fitch, *Chicago Tribune*, 24 Oct. 1993, 3; "Biography Explores Complex Life of Nin," review of *Anaïs: The Erotic Life of Anaïs Nin*, by Noël Riley Fitch, *Palm Beach Post*, 13 Mar. 1994, 6J; John Bemrose, "Lies and Whispers," review of *Anaïs Nin: A Biography*, by Deirdre Bair, *Maclean's*, 6 Mar. 1995, 85; Penelope Mesic, "Flings and Eros: Anaïs Nin and the Trials of Making Avant-Garde Whoopee," review of *Anaïs Nin: A Biography*, by Deirdre Bair, *Chicago Tribune*, 19 Mar. 1995, 5; Carlin Romano, "Anaïs Nin: The Diarist Who Would Be a Courtesan," review of *Anaïs Nin: A Biography*, by Deirdre Bair, *Philadelphia Inquirer*, 23 Apr. 1995, M01.
88. Fitch, *Anaïs*, 4 (emphasis in the original); Bair, introduction to *Anaïs Nin*, xvi; Joe Moran, *Star Authors: Literary Celebrity in America* (London: Pluto Press, 2000), 63.

89. Fitch, *Anaïs,* 5; Bair, introduction to *Anaïs Nin,* xv.

90. Bair, introduction to *Anaïs Nin,* xviii; Podnieks, *Daily Modernism,* 9.

91. Wendy DuBow, "Ninny or Not," in Herron, *Anaïs Nin,* 191; Henry Jenkins, *Textual Poachers: Television Fans and Participatory Culture* (New York: Routledge, 1992), 10.

92. Nancy Gobatto, "Anaïs Nin and Feminism: An Overview," *A Café in Space: The Anaïs Nin Literary Journal* 4 (2007): 53.

93. Ruth Charnock, "Shaming the Shameless: What Is Dangerous about Anaïs Nin?," *Dangerous Women Project,* 29 June 2016, http://dangerouswomenproject.org/2016/06/29/anais-nin/.

94. Helen Tookey, *Anaïs Nin, Fictionality and Femininity: Playing a Thousand Roles* (Oxford: Clarendon Press, 2003), 2.

95. Mesic, "Flings and Eros," 5; Romano, "Anaïs Nin," M01; "Bair, Deirdre," review of *Anaïs Nin: A Biography,* by Deirdre Bair, *Kirkus Reviews,* 15 Dec. 1994; Marie Arana-Ward, "Playgirl of the Western World," review of *Anaïs Nin: A Biography,* by Deirdre Bair, *Washington Post,* 16 Apr. 1995, X03; Delilah Jones, "Unfolding an Erotic Life," review of *Anaïs: The Erotic Life of Anaïs Nin,* by Noël Riley Fitch, *St. Petersburg Times,* 23 Jan. 1994, 4D; Anshaw, "Anaïs Nin: Many Words, Many Lovers and a Host of Lies," 3; Frances Katz, "In Search of the Real Anaïs Nin," review of *Anaïs: The Erotic Life of Anaïs Nin,* by Noël Riley Fitch, *Boston Herald,* 25 Nov. 1993, 60.

CONCLUSION: ANAÏS NIN IN THE TWENTY-FIRST CENTURY

1. Advertisement for *Fragments from the Delta of Venus,* www.amazon.com (accessed 12 June 2012).

2. Advertisement for *Anaïs Nin Goes to Hell,* www.theateronline.com (accessed 10 Nov. 2010).

3. *The Mistress Cycle,* www.kurtjohns.com (accessed 20 Aug. 2011).

4. Barbara Kraft, *Anaïs Nin: The Last Days, a Memoir* (Huntington Woods, MI: Sky Blue Press, 2011), 13.

5. Ibid., 14.

6. Anne Hunsaker Hawkins, *Reconstructing Illness: Studies in Pathography,* 2nd ed. (West Lafayette, IN: Purdue University Press, 1999), 1; Ann Jurecic, *Illness as Narrative* (Pittsburgh: University of Pittsburgh Press, 2012), 2.

7. Hawkins, *Reconstructing Illness,* 31; Jurecic, *Illness as Narrative,* 9, 6–10.

8. Joyce Carol Oates, "Adventures of Abandonment," review of *Jean Stafford: A Biography,* by David Roberts, *New York Times,* 28 Aug. 1988.

9. Kraft, *Anais Nin,* 67.

10. P. David Marshall, "New Media—New Self: The Changing Power of Celebrity," in *The Celebrity Culture Reader,* ed. P. David Marshall (London: Routledge, 2006), 638.

11. Ibid., 637–38.

12. Helen Tookey, *Anaïs Nin, Fictionality and Femininity: Playing a Thousand Roles* (Oxford: Clarendon Press, 2003), 200.

Bibliography

WRITINGS OF ANAÏS NIN
Published Diary

Linotte: The Early Diary of Anaïs Nin, 1914–1920. Vol. 1. Translated by Jean L. Sherman. Edited by John Ferrone. Preface by Joaquin Nin-Culmell. New York: Harcourt Brace Jovanovich, 1978.

The Early Diary of Anaïs Nin, 1920–1923. Vol. 2. Edited by Rupert Pole. Preface by Joaquin Nin-Culmell. New York: Harcourt Brace Jovanovich, 1982. UK reprint, London: Peter Owen, 1983.

The Early Diary of Anaïs Nin, 1923–1927. Vol. 3. Edited by Rupert Pole. Preface by Joaquin Nin-Culmell. New York: Harcourt Brace Jovanovich, 1983. UK reprint, with the added title *Journal of a Wife,* London: Peter Owen, 1984.

The Early Diary of Anaïs Nin, 1927–1931. Vol. 4. Edited by Rupert Pole. Preface by Joaquin Nin-Culmell. New York: Harcourt Brace Jovanovich, 1985. UK reprint, London: Peter Owen, 1994.

The Diary of Anaïs Nin, 1931–1934. Edited and with an introduction by Gunther Stuhlmann. New York: Swallow Press and Harcourt, Brace & World, 1966. UK reprint (as *Journals of Anaïs Nin, 1931–1934*), London: Peter Owen, 1966. Cited as *Diary 1.*

The Diary of Anaïs Nin, 1934–1939. Edited and with a preface by Gunther Stuhlmann. New York: Swallow Press and Harcourt Brace, 1967. UK reprint (as *Journals of Anaïs Nin, 1934–1939*), London: Peter Owen, 1967. Cited as *Diary 2.*

The Diary of Anaïs Nin, 1939–1944. Edited and with a preface by Gunther Stuhlmann. New York: Swallow Press and Harcourt Brace, 1969. UK reprint (as *Journals of Anaïs Nin, 1939–1944*), London: Peter Owen, 1970. Cited as *Diary 3.*

The Diary of Anaïs Nin, 1944–1947. Edited and with a preface by Gunther Stuhlmann. New York: Harcourt Brace Jovanovich, 1971. UK reprint (as *Journals of Anaïs Nin, 1944–1947*), London: Peter Owen, 1972. Cited as *Diary 4.*

The Diary of Anaïs Nin, 1947–1955. Edited and with a preface by Gunther Stuhlmann. New York: Harcourt Brace Jovanovich,

1974. UK reprint (as *Journals of Anaïs Nin, 1947–1955*), London: Peter Owen, 1974. Cited as *Diary 5*.

The Diary of Anaïs Nin, 1955–1966. Edited and with a preface by Gunther Stuhlmann. New York: Harcourt Brace Jovanovich, 1976. UK reprint (as *Journals of Anaïs Nin, 1955–1966*), London: Peter Owen, 1977. Cited as *Diary 6*.

The Diary of Anaïs Nin, 1966–1974. Edited and with a preface by Gunther Stuhlmann. New York: Harcourt Brace Jovanovich, 1980. UK reprint (as *Journals of Anaïs Nin, 1966–1974*), London: Peter Owen, 1980. Cited as *Diary 7*.

Henry and June: From "A Journal of Love," the Unexpurgated Diary of Anaïs Nin, 1931–1932. Introduction by Rupert Pole. Biographical notes by Gunther Stuhlmann. New York: Harcourt Brace Jovanovich, 1986. UK reprint, London: Peter Owen, 1986.

Incest: From "A Journal of Love," the Unexpurgated Diary of Anaïs Nin, 1932–1934. Introduction by Rupert Pole. Biographical notes by Gunther Stuhlmann. New York: Harcourt Brace Jovanovich, 1992. UK reprint, London: Peter Owen, 1993.

Fire: From "A Journal of Love," the Unexpurgated Diary of Anaïs Nin, 1934–1936. Preface by Rupert Pole. Biographical notes and annotations by Gunther Stuhlmann. New York: Harcourt Brace Jovanovich, 1995. UK reprint, London: Peter Owen, 1996.

Nearer the Moon: From "A Journal of Love," the Unexpurgated Diary of Anaïs Nin, 1937–1939. Preface by Rupert Pole. Biographical notes and annotations by Gunther Stuhlmann. New York: Harcourt Brace Jovanovich, 1996. UK reprint, London: Peter Owen, 1996.

Mirages: The Unexpurgated Diary of Anaïs Nin, 1939–1947. Edited by Paul Herron. Introduction by Kim Krizan. Athens, OH: Swallow Press, published in association with Sky Blue Press, 2013.

Trapeze: The Unexpurgated Diary of Anaïs Nin, 1947–1955. Edited by Paul Herron. Introduction by Benjamin Franklin V. Athens, OH: Swallow Press, published in association with Sky Blue Press, 2017.

Journal Manuscripts
(Anaïs Nin Papers, Charles E. Young Research Library, University of California, Los Angeles)

Journal 32. "Mon Journal and Note Book: Book II—June." 20 Oct. 1931–1 Feb. 1932. Box 16, folder 1.

Journal 54. "COSMIC: Consumation [sic], Collective, Self-Abnegation, Le Monde, Isolation Circles." July–Sept. 1937. Box 19, folder 4.

Journal 55. "Mon Journal and Note Book: Maya." Sept.–Nov. 1937. Box 19, folder 5.

Journal 63. "Mon Journal: House of Death and Escape." 8 Dec. 1940–June 1941. Box 21, folder 1.
Journal 65. "Birth of the Press." 4 Nov. 1941–24 Oct. 1942. Box 21, folder 3.
Journal 66. "Mon Journal: A la Recherche des Jeux Perdus with Martha Jaeger." 27 Oct. 1942–3 Oct. 1943. Box 21, folder 4.

Selected Articles and Reviews by Nin

"Novelist on Stage." Review of *The Complete Plays of D. H. Lawrence*, by D. H. Lawrence. *New York Times Book Review*, 10 Apr. 1966.
Review of *Diary of a Century*, by Henri Latrigue. *New York Times Book Review*, 21 Feb. 1971.
"Liberation: A Simultaneous Happening." *New York Times*, 14 Jan. 1972.
"Notes on Feminism." *Massachusetts Review* 13, nos. 1–2 (Winter–Spring 1972): 25–28.

Other Works by Nin Quoted

"The Story of My Printing Press." In *In Favor of the Sensitive Man and Other Essays*. San Diego, CA: Harcourt Brace, 1976.
A Woman Speaks: The Lectures, Seminars, and Interviews of Anaïs Nin. Edited by Evelyn Hinz. London: Penguin Books, 1992.
Delta of Venus. New York: Harcourt Brace Jovanovich, 1977. Paperback edition, Orlando, FL: Harvest Books, 2004.

INTERVIEWS WITH ANAÏS NIN

Bailey, Jeffrey. "Link in the Chain of Feeling: An Interview with Anaïs Nin." In DuBow, *Conversations with Anaïs Nin*, 235–50.
Berwick, Keith. "A Conversation with Anaïs Nin." In DuBow, *Conversations with Anaïs Nin*, 52–69.
DuBow, Wendy M., ed. *Conversations with Anaïs Nin*. Jackson: University Press of Mississippi, 1994.
Eckman, Fern Marja. "The Non-legend of Anaïs Nin." In DuBow, *Conversations with Anaïs Nin*, 172–77.
Edmiston, Susan. "Portrait of Anaïs Nin." In DuBow, *Conversations with Anaïs Nin*, 43–51.
Freeman, Barbara. "A Dialogue with Anaïs Nin." In DuBow, *Conversations with Anaïs Nin*, 186–94.
Getzoff, Carole. "A Spy in the House of Nin." *Village Voice*, 6 Jan. 1975, 17.
Hoffman, Milton. "An Interview with Anaïs Nin." In DuBow, *Conversations with Anaïs Nin*, 143–51.
Jay, Karla. "Two Interviews with Anaïs Nin." In DuBow, *Conversations with Anaïs Nin*, 133–42.

Loeb, Clare. "Anaïs Nin on Women's Liberation." In DuBow, *Conversations with Anaïs Nin,* 27–39.
McBrien, William. "Anaïs Nin: An Interview." In DuBow, *Conversations with Anaïs Nin,* 203–20.
Roberts, Frank. "Writers at Work: Anaïs Talks with Frank Roberts." In DuBow, *Conversations with Anaïs Nin,* 3–14.
Stern, Daniel, and Dominique Browning. "Anaïs Nin: An Interview." In DuBow, *Conversations with Anaïs Nin,* 221–34.
Stocking, Susan. "Personas Unmasked in Visit with Anaïs Nin." In DuBow, *Conversations with Anaïs Nin,* 98–103.
Terkel, Studs. "Interview with Anaïs Nin." In DuBow, *Conversations with Anaïs Nin,* 152–71.
Williamson, Nancy, Evelyn Clark, and Barbara Reyes. "A Conversation with Anaïs Nin." In DuBow, *Conversations with Anaïs Nin,* 75–91.

OTHER SOURCES

Allyn, David. *Make Love, Not War: The Sexual Revolution; An Unfettered History.* Boston: Little, Brown, 2000.
Anaïs Observed: A Portrait of Anaïs Nin. Directed by Robert Snyder. 1973. Mystic Fire Video, 1995. Videocassette.
Anshaw, Carol. "Anaïs Nin: Many Words, Many Lovers and a Host of Lies." Review of *Anaïs: The Erotic Life of Anaïs Nin,* by Noël Riley Fitch. *Chicago Tribune,* 24 Oct. 1993.
Arana-Ward, Marie. "Playgirl of the Western World." Review of *Anaïs Nin: A Biography,* by Deirdre Bair. *Washington Post,* 16 Apr. 1995.
Ariker, Shirley. "Shirley Ariker." In Franklin, *Recollections,* 75–76.
Bair, Deirdre. *Anaïs Nin: A Biography.* New York: G. P. Putnam's Sons, 1995.
———. "The Making of Anaïs Nin: A Biography." Interview by Paul Herron. *A Café in Space: The Anaïs Nin Literary Journal* 7 (2010): 27–34.
Balakian, Anna. Review of *Diary of Anaïs Nin, 1944–1947,* vol. 4. *New York Times Book Review,* 16 Jan. 1972.
Barillé, Elizabeth. *Anaïs Nin: Naked under the Mask.* Translated by E. Powell. London: Lime Tree, 1992.
Beasley, Chris. *Gender and Sexuality: Critical Theories, Critical Thinkers.* London: Sage, 2005.
Bemrose, John. "Lies and Whispers." Review of *Anaïs Nin: A Biography,* by Deirdre Bair. *Maclean's,* 6 Mar. 1995, 85.
Benstock, Shari. *Women of the Left Bank: Paris, 1900–1940.* Austin: University of Texas Press, 1986.

Bishop, Thomas. "Pick of the Paperbacks." Review of *Diary of Anaïs Nin, 1931–1934*, vol. 1. *Saturday Review*, 31 May 1969, 29.

Bloom, Lynn Z. "'I Write Myself for Strangers': Private Diaries as Public Documents." In *Inscribing the Daily: Critical Essays on Women's Diaries*, edited by Suzanne L. Bunkers and Cynthia A. Huff, 23–37. Amherst: University of Massachusetts Press, 1996.

Bloom, Lynn Z., and Orlee Holder. "Anaïs Nin's *Diary* in Context." *Mosaic* 11, no. 2 (1978): 191–202.

Bobbitt, Joan. "Truth and Artistry in the *Diary of Anaïs Nin*." In Jason, *Critical Response*, 190–98.

Bowie, Malcolm. "Freud and the Art of Biography." In *Mapping Lives: The Uses of Biography*, edited by Peter France and William St. Clair, 177–92. Oxford: Oxford University Press, 2002.

Braudy, Leo. *The Frenzy of Renown: Fame and Its History*. New York: Vintage Books, 1986.

Brooker, Peter. "Early Modernism." In *The Cambridge Companion to the Modernist Novel*, edited by Morag Shiach, 32–47. Cambridge: Cambridge University Press, 2007.

Broyard, Anatole. "Of Art, Ecstasy and Water." Review of *Diary of Anaïs Nin, 1944–1947*, vol. 4. *New York Times*, 26 Oct. 1971.

Buckmaster, Henrietta. "Incantations: For the Initiated Only." Review of *Diary of Anaïs Nin, 1944–1947*, vol. 4. *Christian Science Monitor*, 11 Nov. 1971.

———. "What Is the Sum of Her Words?" Review of *Diary of Anaïs Nin, 1931–1934*, vol. 1. *Christian Science Monitor*, 16 Jun. 1966.

Bunkers, Suzanne L., and Cynthia A. Huff. "Issues in Studying Women's Diaries: A Theoretical and Critical Introduction," in Bunkers and Huff, *Inscribing the Daily*, 1–20.

———, eds. *Inscribing the Daily: Critical Essays on Women's Diaries*. Amherst: University of Massachusetts Press, 1996.

Burke, David. *Writers in Paris: Literary Lives in the City of Lights*. Berkeley, CA: Counterpoint, 2008.

Butcher, Fanny. "A Long Awaited Literary Flight." Review of *Diary of Anaïs Nin, 1931–1934*, vol. 1. *Chicago Tribune*, 22 May 1966.

Casterton, Julia. Commentary on "Looking Again at Anaïs Nin," by Maxine Molyneux and Julia Casterton. In Jason, *Critical Response*, 215–32.

Centing, Richard, ed. "The Henry Miller Odyssey." *Under the Sign of Pisces: Anaïs Nin and Her Circle* 1, no. 1 (Winter 1970): 3–9.

———. "Spying on the Doors." *Under the Sign of Pisces: Anaïs Nin and Her Circle* 1, no. 2 (Spring 1970): 11.

———. "Teaching Anaïs Nin." *Under the Sign of Pisces: Anaïs Nin and Her Circle* 2, no. 3 (Summer 1971): 6–7.

Charnock, Ruth. "Shaming the Shameless: What Is Dangerous about Anaïs Nin?" *Dangerous Women Project,* 29 June 2016. http://dangerouswomenproject.org/2016/06/29/anais-nin.

Chicago, Judy. "Anaïs Nin: Writer or Perfume?" *Gadfly Online,* 30 July 2001, www.gadflyonline.com.

Culley, Margo. "Introduction to *A Day at a Time: Diary Literature of American Women, from 1764 to 1895.*" 1985. In Smith and Watson, *Women, Autobiography, Theory,* 217–21.

Cutting, Rose Marie. Introduction to *Anaïs Nin: A Reference Guide.* Boston: G. K. Hall, 1978.

Darwin, Charles. *The Descent of Man and Selection in Relation to Sex.* New York: D. Appleton, 1896.

Davidon, Ann Morrissett. "Anaïs Nin vs. Gore Vidal: Bon Mots and Billets Doux." *Village Voice,* 17 Jan. 1977, 80–82.

Davis, Flora. *Moving the Mountain: Women's Movement in America since 1960.* New York: Simon and Schuster, 1991.

Dearborn, Mary V. *The Happiest Man Alive: A Biography of Henry Miller.* New York: Simon and Schuster, 1991.

Dettmar, Kevin J. H. Introduction to *A Companion to Modernist Literature and Culture,* edited by David Bradshaw and Kevin J. H. Dettmar, 1–5. Malden, MA: Blackwell Publishing, 2006.

Dettmar, Kevin J. H., and Stephen Watt. Introduction to *Marketing Modernisms: Self-Promotion, Canonization, Rereading,* edited by Kevin J. H. Dettmar and Stephen Watt, 1–8. Ann Arbor: University of Michigan Press, 1996.

Diepeveen, Leonard. "'I Can Have More Than Enough Power to Satisfy Me': T. S. Eliot's Construction of His Audience." In *Marketing Modernisms: Self-Promotion, Canonization, Rereading,* edited by Kevin J. H. Dettmar and Stephen Watt, 37–60. Ann Arbor: University of Michigan Press, 1996.

DuBow, Wendy M., ed. *Conversations with Anaïs Nin.* Jackson: University Press of Mississippi, 1994.

———. Introduction to DuBow, *Conversations with Anaïs Nin,* ix–xx.

———. "Ninny or Not." In Herron, *Anaïs Nin,* 191–94.

Duxler, Margot Beth. *Seduction: A Portrait of Anaïs Nin.* Boulder, CO: EdgeWorks, 2002.

Dyer, Richard. *Heavenly Bodies: Film Stars and Society.* London: BFI Macmillan, 1986.

———. *Stars.* Rev. ed. London: British Film Institute, 1998.

Eakin, Paul J. *How Our Lives Become Stories: Making Selves.* Ithaca, NY: Cornell University Press, 1999.

Esquire. "The 75 Greatest Women of All Time." 19 Apr. 2010.

Ferrone, John. "The Making of *Delta of Venus.*" *A Café in Space: The Anaïs Nin Literary Journal* 7 (2010): 53–60.

———. "The Making of *Henry and June*, the Book: Correspondence, 1985–1986." *A Café in Space: The Anaïs Nin Literary Journal* 4 (2007): 8–21.
Fitch, Noël Riley. *Anaïs: The Erotic Life of Anaïs Nin*. London: Abacus, 1996.
Foote, Audrey C. "Her Own Best Work of Art." Review of *Diary of Anaïs Nin, 1955–1966*, vol. 6. *Washington Post*, 29 Aug. 1976.
France, Peter, and William St. Clair, eds. *Mapping Lives: The Uses of Biography*. Oxford: Oxford University Press, 2002.
Franklin, Benjamin, V, ed. *Recollections of Anaïs Nin by Her Contemporaries*. Athens: Ohio University Press, 1996.
———. "The Selling of *A Spy in the House of Love*." In Nalbantian, *Anaïs Nin*, 254–77.
Franklin, Benjamin, V, and Duane Schneider. *Anaïs Nin: An Introduction*. Athens: Ohio University Press, 1979.
Freud, Sigmund. "Some Psychological Consequences of the Anatomical Distinction between Sexes." In *The Masculinity Studies Reader*, edited by Rachel Adams and David Savran, 14–20. Malden, MA: Blackwell, 2002.
Fuller, Edmund. "A Feminist Writes without Hostility." Review of *A Woman Speaks*, by Anaïs Nin, edited by Evelyn Hinz. *Wall Street Journal*, 13 Apr. 1976.
Garrigue, Jean. Review of *Diary of Anaïs Nin, 1939–1944*, vol. 3. *New York Times Book Review*, 23 Nov. 1969.
———. "The Self behind the Selves." Review of *Diary of Anaïs Nin, 1931–1934*, vol. 1. *New York Times Book Review*, 24 Apr. 1966.
Getzoff, Carole. "A Spy in the House of Nin." *Village Voice*, 6 Jan. 1975.
Glass, Loren. *Authors Inc.: Literary Celebrity in the Modern United States, 1880–1980*. New York: New York University Press, 2004.
Gobatto, Nancy. "Anaïs Nin and Feminism: An Overview." *A Café in Space: The Anaïs Nin Literary Journal* 4 (2007): 45–62.
Goyen, William. "Portrait of the Artist as a Diarist: The Diary of Anaïs Nin." Review of *Diary of Anaïs Nin, 1947–1955*, vol. 5. *New York Times Book Review*, 14 Apr. 1974.
Gray, Richard. *A History of American Literature*. Malden, MA: Blackwell Publishing, 2004.
Hall, Calvin S. *A Primer of Freudian Psychology*. New York: Meridian, 1999.
Hamilton, Peter. "Representing the Social: France and Frenchness in Post-war Humanist Photography." In *Representation: Cultural Representation and Signifying Practices*, edited by Stuart Hall, 75–150. London: Sage, 1997.

Harris, Bertha. "Who Chose These Women, and Why?" *Village Voice*, 30 Sept. 1972, 71.

Hawkins, Anne Hunsaker. *Reconstructing Illness: Studies in Pathography*. 2nd ed. West Lafayette, IN: Purdue University Press, 1999.

Henke, Suzette. *Shattered Subjects: Trauma and Testimony in Women's Life Writing*. Basingstoke, UK: Macmillan, 2000.

———. "Suzette Henke." In Franklin, *Recollections*, 119–25.

Henry & June. Directed by Philip Kaufman. Universal Studios, 1990. DVD.

Herron, Paul, ed. *Anaïs Nin: A Book of Mirrors*. Huntington Woods, MI: Sky Blue Press, 1996.

———. Introduction to Herron, *Anaïs Nin*, xxxii–xlii.

Hinerman, Stephen. "(Don't) Leave Me Alone: Tabloid Narrative and the Michael Jackson Child-Abuse Scandal." 1999. In Marshall, *Celebrity Culture Reader*, 454–69.

Hinz, Evelyn J. Introduction to Hinz, *A Woman Speaks*, vii–xv.

———. Review of *Diary of Anaïs Nin, 1944–1947*, vol. 4. *Contemporary Literature* 13, no. 2 (Spring 1972): 255–57.

———, ed. *A Woman Speaks: The Lectures, Seminars, and Interviews of Anaïs Nin*. London: Penguin Books, 1992.

Hoffman, Nancy. "Serialized Life." Review of *Diary of Anaïs Nin, 1947–1955*, vol. 5. *New Republic*, 15 June 1974, 31–32.

Hollows, Joanne. *Feminism, Femininity, and Popular Culture*. Manchester: Manchester University Press, 2000.

hooks, bell. "Power to the Pussy: We Don't Wannabe Dicks in Drag." In *Madonnarama: Essays on Sex and Popular Culture*, edited by Lisa Frank and Paul Smith, 65–80. Pittsburgh: Cleis Press, 1993.

Huyssen, Andreas. *After the Great Divide: Modernism, Mass Culture, Postmodernism*. Bloomington: Indiana University Press, 1986.

Isserman, Maurice, and Michael Kazin. *America Divided: The Civil War of the 1960s*. Oxford: Oxford University Press, 2000.

Jaffe, Aaron. *Modernism and the Culture of Celebrity*. Cambridge: Cambridge University Press, 2005.

Jason, Philip K. *Anaïs Nin and Her Critics*. Columbia, SC: Camden House, 1993.

———, ed. *The Critical Response to Anaïs Nin*. Westport, CT: Greenwood Press, 1996.

———. "Dropping Another Veil: Anaïs Nin's *Henry and June*." In Jason, *Critical Response*, 199–204.

———. "The Gemor Press." *Anaïs: An International Journal* 2 (1984): 24–36.

———. Introduction to Jason, *Critical Response*, 1–7.
Jelinek, Estelle C. "Anaïs Nin: A Critical Evaluation." In Jason, *Critical Response*, 45–54. Originally published as "Anaïs Reconsidered" in *Off Our Backs: A Women's Newsjournal*, 31 Dec. 1974.
Jenkins, Henry. *Textual Poachers: Television Fans and Participatory Culture*. New York: Routledge, 1992.
John-Steiner, Vera. *Creative Collaboration*. Oxford: Oxford University Press, 2000.
Jones, Delilah. "Unfolding an Erotic Life." Review of *Anaïs: The Erotic Life of Anaïs Nin*, by Noël Riley Fitch. *St. Petersburg Times*, 23 Jan. 1994.
Jong, Erica. "A Story Never Told Before—Reading the New, Unexpurgated Diaries of Anaïs Nin." In Jason, *Critical Response*, 205–14.
Jurecic, Ann. *Illness as Narrative*. Pittsburgh: University of Pittsburgh Press, 2012.
Katz, Frances. "In Search of the Real Anaïs Nin." Review of *Anaïs: The Erotic Life of Anaïs Nin*, by Noël Riley Fitch. *Boston Herald*, 25 Nov. 1993.
Kennedy, Gerald. *Imagining Paris: Exile, Writing and American Identity*. New Haven, CT: Yale University Press, 1993.
Kirkus Reviews. Unsigned review of *Anaïs Nin: A Biography*, by Deirdre Bair. 15 Dec. 1994.
Kirsch, Robert. "Journal of a Troubled Journey." Review of *Diary of Anaïs Nin, 1931–1934*, vol. 1. *Los Angeles Times*, 17 Apr. 1966.
Knowles, Jocelyn. "Anaïs Nin Has Done It Again." Review of *Diary of Anaïs Nin, 1934–1939*, vol. 2. *Los Angeles Times*, 25 Jun. 1967.
Kraft, Barbara. *Anaïs Nin: The Last Days, a Memoir*. Huntington Woods, MI: Sky Blue Press, 2011.
———. "Barbara Kraft." In Franklin, *Recollections*, 141–52.
Krizan, Kim. "Gore Vidal's Life: How He Distorted His Relationship with Anaïs Nin." *A Café in Space: The Anaïs Nin Literary Journal* 10 (2013): 5–17.
Leber, Michelle M. Review of *Delta of Venus*, by Anaïs Nin. *Library Journal*, 1 May 1977, 1044.
Lee, Hermione. *Biography: A Very Short Introduction*. Oxford: Oxford University Press, 2009.
Lehman, Peter, and William Luhr. *Thinking about Movies: Watching, Questioning, Enjoying*. 2nd ed. Oxford: Blackwell, 2003.
Lewis, Pericles. *The Cambridge Introduction to Modernism*. Cambridge: Cambridge University Press, 2007.

Loftus, Elizabeth, and Katherine Ketcham. *The Myth of Repressed Memory: False Memories and Allegations of Sexual Abuse.* New York: St. Martin's Press, 1994.

Luckhurst, Roger. "Memory Recovered/Recovered Memory." In *Literature and the Contemporary: Fictions and Theories of the Present,* edited by Roger Luckhurst and Peter Marks, 80–93. Harlow, UK: Pearson Education, 1999.

———. *The Trauma Question.* London: Routledge, 2008.

Luria-Sukenick, Lynn. "The Diaries of Anaïs Nin." In Jason, *Critical Response,* 172–77.

Malcolm, Janet. *The Silent Woman: Sylvia Plath and Ted Hughes.* London: Papermac, 1994.

Maloff, Saul. "The Seven Veils." Review of *Diary of Anaïs Nin, 1934–1939,* vol. 2. *Newsweek,* 3 July 1967, 36.

Marcus, Laura. *Auto/biographical Discourses: Criticism, Theory, Practice.* Manchester: Manchester University Press, 1994.

Marshall, P. David, ed. *The Celebrity Culture Reader.* London: Routledge, 2006.

———. "Intimately Intertwined in the Most Public Way: Celebrity and Journalism." In Marshall, *Celebrity Culture Reader,* 315–23.

———. Introduction to Marshall, *Celebrity Culture Reader,* 1–15.

———. "New Media—New Self: The Changing Power of Celebrity." In Marshall, *Celebrity Culture Reader,* 634–44.

Martin, Jay. *Always Merry and Bright: The Life of Henry Miller.* Santa Barbara, CA: Capra Press, 1978.

Marwick, Arthur. *The Sixties: Cultural Revolution in Britain, France, Italy, and the United States, c. 1958–c. 1974.* Oxford: Oxford University Press, 1998.

Mazzocco, Robert. "To Tell You the Truth." Review of *The Paris Diary of Ned Rorem,* by Ned Rorem; *The Diary of Anaïs Nin, 1931–1934,* vol. 1, by Anaïs Nin; and *A Very Easy Death,* by Simone de Beauvoir. *New York Review of Books,* 8 Sept. 1966.

McDowell, Leslie. *Between the Sheets: Nine 20th Century Women Writers and Their Famous Literary Partnerships.* New York: Overlook Duckworth, 2012.

McGrath, Charles. "The Delts of Venus." *New Yorker,* 5 June 1978, 33–35.

McMillian, John. *Smoking Typewriters: The Sixties Underground Press and the Rise of Alternative Media in America.* Oxford: Oxford University Press, 2011.

McRobbie, Angela. *The Aftermath of Feminism: Gender, Culture and Social Change.* London: Sage, 2009.

Mesic, Penelope. "Flings and Eros: Anaïs Nin and the Trials of Making Avant-Garde Whoopee." Review of *Anaïs Nin: A Biography*, by Deirdre Bair. *Chicago Tribune*, 19 Mar. 1995.

Miller, Henry. "Un Etre Etoilique." In Jason, *Critical Response*, 147–54.

———. "Miller on Nin." *Village Voice*, 26 May 1966, 5–6.

Millett, Kate. "Anaïs—A Mother of Us All: The Birth of the Artist as Woman." *Anaïs: An International Journal* 9 (1991): 3–8.

Moi, Toril. *Simone de Beauvoir: The Making of an Intellectual Woman*. Oxford: Blackwell, 1994.

Moore, Harry T. "A Long-Awaited Diary." Review of *Diary of Anaïs Nin, 1931–1934*, vol. 1. *St. Louis Dispatch*, 1 May 1966, B4. Microfilm. Anaïs Nin Papers, Charles E. Young Research Library, University of California, Los Angeles.

Moran, Joe. *Star Authors: Literary Celebrity in America*. London: Pluto Press, 2000.

Morrisson, Mark S. "Nationalism and the Modern American Canon." In *The Cambridge Companion to American Modernism*, edited by Walter Kalaidjian, 12–35. Cambridge: Cambridge University Press, 2006.

———. "Publishing." In *A Companion to Modernist Literature and Culture*, edited by David Bradshaw and Kevin J. H. Dettmar, 133–43. Malden, MA: Blackwell, 2006.

Mulvey, Laura. "Visual Pleasure and Narrative Cinema." In *The Norton Anthology of Theory and Criticism*, edited by Vincent B. Leitch, William E. Cain, Laurie A. Finke, Barbara E. Johnson, John McGowan, T. Denean Sharpley-Whiting, and Jeffrey J. Williams, 218–92. London: W. W. Norton, 2001.

Nalbantian, Suzanne. *Aesthetic Autobiography: From Life to Art in Marcel Proust, James Joyce, Virginia Woolf and Anaïs Nin*. Basingstoke, UK: Macmillan, 1994.

———, ed. *Anaïs Nin: Literary Perspectives*. New York: St. Martin's Press, 1997.

New Yorker. Unsigned review of *Diary of Anaïs Nin, 1934–1939*, vol. 2. 5 Aug. 1967, 83.

———. Unsigned review of *Diary of Anaïs Nin, 1947–1955*, vol. 5. 13 May 1974, 159.

———. Unsigned review of *Diary of Anaïs Nin, 1955–1966*, vol. 6. 21 Jun. 1976, 120.

Nin-Culmell, Joaquín. "Anaïs, My Sister." In Nalbantian, *Anaïs Nin*, 23–26.

Nussbaum, Felicity A. "The Ideology of Genre." 1989. In Smith and Watson, *Women, Autobiography, Theory*, 165–67.

Ohmann, Richard. "The Shaping of a Canon: U.S. Fiction, 1960–1975." *Critical Inquiry* 10, no. 1 (Sept. 1983): 199–223.

Palm Beach Post. "Biography Explores Complex Life of Nin." Unsigned review of *Anaïs: The Erotic Life of Anaïs Nin*, by Noël Riley Fitch. 13 Mar. 1994.

Pawlik, Joanna. "Artaud in Performance: Dissident Surrealism and the Postwar American Literary Avant-garde." *Papers of Surrealism*, no. 8 (2010): 1–21. www.surrealismcentre.ac.uk/papersofsurrealism/journal8/acrobat%20files/Articles/Pawlik%20final%20version.pdf.

Pennington, Jody W. *The History of Sex in American Film.* London: Praeger, 2007.

Pierpont, Claudia Roth. *Passionate Minds: Women Rewriting the World.* New York: Vintage Books, 2000.

Pineau, Elyse Lamm. "A Mirror of Her Own: Anaïs Nin's Autobiographical Performances." In Jason, *Critical Response*, 233–52.

Podnieks, Elizabeth. *Daily Modernism: The Literary Diaries of Virginia Woolf, Antonia White, Elizabeth Smart, and Anaïs Nin.* Montreal: McGill-Queen's University Press, 2000.

Pollitt, Katha. "Apologia Ended." Review of *Diary of Anaïs Nin, 1966–1974*, vol. 7. *New York Times Book Review*, 13 July 1980.

———. Review of *Incest*, by Anaïs Nin. *New York Times Book Review*, 22 Nov. 1992.

Rado, Lisa, ed. *Modernism, Gender, and Culture: A Cultural Studies Approach.* New York: Garland, 1994.

Raphael, Maryanne. *Anaïs Nin: The Voyage Within.* Lincoln, NE: iUniverse, 2003.

Richard-Allerdyce, Diane. *Anaïs Nin and the Remaking of Self: Gender, Modernism, and Narrative Identity.* DeKalb: Northern Illinois University Press, 1998.

Rielly, Edward J. *American Popular Culture through History: The 1960s.* Westport, CT: Greenwood, 2003.

Rodden, John. *George Orwell: The Politics of Literary Reputation.* London: Transaction Publishers, 2003.

Romano, Carlin. "Anaïs Nin: The Diarist Who Would Be a Courtesan." Review of *Anaïs Nin: A Biography*, by Deirdre Bair. *Philadelphia Inquirer*, 23 Apr. 1995.

Rosenkrantz, Gayle Nin. "Gayle Nin Rosenkrantz." In Franklin, *Recollections*, 1–5.

Russ, Joanna. *How to Suppress Women's Writing.* Austin: University of Texas Press, 1983.

Salber, Linde. *Tysiąc i jedna kobieta: Anaïs Nin i jej życie* [Thousand and one woman: The story of Anaïs Nin]. Translated by M. Dutkiewicz. Gdynia, Poland: Uraeus, 1999.

Schneider, Duane. "Duane Schneider." In Franklin, *Recollections*, 54–59.

———. "Fusion of Two Worlds." Review of *Diary of Anaïs Nin, 1934–1939*, vol. 2. *Kenyon Review* 30, no. 1 (1968): 137–40.

Scholar, Nancy. *Anaïs Nin*. Boston: Twayne, 1984.

Schwartz, Lawrence H. *Creating Faulkner's Reputation: The Politics of Modern Literary Criticism*. Knoxville: University of Tennessee Press, 1990.

See, Carolyn. "Anaïs Nin Trapped in a Web of Love." Review of *Henry and June*, by Anaïs Nin. *Los Angeles Times Book Review*, 6 Oct. 1986.

Seymour, Miranda. "Shaping the Truth." In *Mapping Lives: The Uses of Biography*, edited by Peter France and William St. Clair, 253–66. Oxford: Oxford University Press, 2002.

———. "Truth Wasn't Sexy Enough: Anaïs Nin's Diaries Were a Fraud and Even Her Marriages Were Lies." Review of *Anaïs: The Erotic Life of Anaïs Nin*, by Noël Riley Fitch. *New York Times Book Review*, 17 Oct. 1993.

Shapiro, Karl. "The Charmed Circle of Anaïs Nin." In Jason, *Critical Response*, 154–57.

Showalter, Elaine. *The Female Malady: Women, Madness and English Culture, 1830–1980*. London: Virago Press, 1987.

———. *A Jury of Her Peers: American Women Writers from Anne Bradstreet to Annie Proulx*. London: Virago, 2009.

Sickles, Robert. *American Popular Culture through History: The 1940s*. Westport, CT: Greenwood Press, 2004.

Silver, Brenda R. *Virginia Woolf Icon*. Chicago: University of Chicago Press, 1999.

Smith, Sidonie. *A Poetics of Women's Autobiography: Marginality and the Fictions of Self-Representation*. Bloomington: Indiana University Press, 1987.

———. *Reading Autobiography: A Guide for Interpreting Life Narratives*. Minneapolis: University of Minnesota Press, 2001.

Smith, Sidonie, and Julia Watson. "Situating Subjectivity in Women's Autobiographical Practices." In Smith and Watson, *Women, Autobiography, Theory*, 3–52.

———, eds. *Women, Autobiography, Theory: A Reader*. Madison: University of Wisconsin Press, 1998.

Spencer, Sharon. *Collage of Dreams: The Writings of Anaïs Nin*. Chicago: Swallow Press, 1977.

———. "Sharon Spencer." In Franklin, *Recollections*, 77–85.

Stern, Daniel. "The Novel of Her Life." Review of *Diary of Anaïs Nin, 1944–1947*, vol. 4. *Nation*, 29 Nov. 1971, 570–71.

———. "Princess of the Underground." Review of *Diary of Anaïs Nin, 1934–1939,* vol. 2. *Nation,* 4 Mar. 1968, 311–13.

Stone, Laurie. "Anaïs Nin: Is the Bloom off the Pose?" Review of the *Diaries,* by Anaïs Nin. *Village Voice,* 26 July 1976, 43–44.

Storey, John. *Cultural Studies and the Study of Popular Culture.* 2nd ed. Athens: University of Georgia Press, 2003.

Stuhlmann, Gunther. Introduction to Stuhlmann, *Literate Passion,* v–xxi.

———, ed. *A Literate Passion: Letters of Anaïs Nin and Henry Miller, 1932–1953.* San Diego, CA: Harcourt Brace, 1987.

———. Introduction to *The Diary of Anaïs Nin, 1931–1934,* vol. 1, by Anaïs Nin, 1–8. New York: Harcourt Brace, 1966.

———. Preface to *The Diary of Anaïs Nin, 1966–1974,* vol. 7, v–x. New York: Harcourt Brace Jovanovich, 1980.

Templin, Charlotte. *Feminism and the Politics of Literary Reputation: The Example of Erica Jong.* Lawrence: University Press of Kansas, 1995.

Tong, Rosemarie. *Feminist Thought: A Comprehensive Introduction.* London: Routledge, 1995.

Tookey, Helen. *Anaïs Nin, Fictionality and Femininity: Playing a Thousand Roles.* Oxford: Clarendon Press, 2003.

Vidal, Gore. "Taking a Grand Tour of Anaïs Nin's High Bohemia via the Time Machine." Review of *Diary of Anaïs Nin, 1944–1947,* vol. 4. *Los Angeles Times,* 26 Sept. 1971.

Wagner-Martin, Linda. *Telling Women's Lives: The New Biography.* New Brunswick, NJ: Rutgers University Press, 1994.

Walker, Alice. "Anaïs Nin: 1903–1977." *Ms.,* Apr. 1977, 46.

Wallace, Kevin. "The Diarist Who Sold Out the House." *San Francisco Chronicle,* 8 Apr. 1974, 2. Microfilm. Anaïs Nin Papers, Charles E. Young Research Library, University of California, Los Angeles.

Whitman, Aldan. "Books of the Time." Review of *Diary of Anaïs Nin, 1934–1939,* vol. 2. *New York Times,* 22 July 1967.

Williams, Jeffrey J. "Academostars: Name Recognition." 2001. In Marshall, *Celebrity Culture Reader,* 371–88.

Wilson, Edmund. Review of *Under a Glass Bell,* by Anaïs Nin. Excerpt from "Doubts and Dreams: *Dangling Man* and *Under a Glass Bell.*" In Jason, *Critical Response,* 75–76.

Wilson, Elizabeth. *Bohemians: The Glamorous Outcasts.* London: I. B. Tauris Publishers, 2000.

Wolcott, James. "Life among the Ninnies." *New York Review of Books,* 26 June 1980.

Wood, Susan. "Nin's 'Erotica'—Writings to Please a Wealthy Patron." Review of *Delta of Venus,* by Anaïs Nin. *San Francisco*

Chronicle magazine *This World,* 24 July 1977, p. 42. Microfilm. Anaïs Nin Papers, Charles E. Young Research Library, University of California, Los Angeles.

Zinnes, Harriet. "Collector's Item." Review of *Delta of Venus,* by Anaïs Nin. *New York Times Book Review,* 10 July 1977.

———. "Harriet Zinnes." In Franklin, *Recollections,* 23–30.

Index

abortion, 129, 147, 183, 185. *See also* Nin, Anaïs: abortions of
adaptation: film, 141, 156, 170 (see also *Henry & June*); theater, 149
Allendy, René, 6, 39, 44, 54, 60, 74, 81, 82, 86, 153, 157, 165, 167, 191, 192
American Academy and Institute of Arts and Letters: Nin as a member of, 89
American culture: in the 1940s, 19, 37, 41, 208; in the 1960s and 1970s, 4, 46, 57, 65, 73, 79–81, 91, 98, 103, 185
Anaïs: An International Journal, 132, 150, 231n5
Anaïs: The Erotic Life of Anaïs Nin, 142, 162–64, 188. *See also* Fitch, Noël Riley
Anaïs Anaïs (perfume), 172–74, 179
Anaïs Nin: A Biography, 142, 197. *See also* Bair, Deirdre
Anaïs Nin Trust, 150, 173
Artaud, Antonin, 39, 60, 67–68, 71, 75, 76, 77; popular in the 1960s, 68; Theatre of Cruelty, 68
authorship, 13, 152
autobiography criticism, 4, 23–30, 48, 95–96, 144

Bair, Deirdre, 7, 109, 144, 174, 175; and biography of Nin, 142–43, 197–200, 205, 217n34, 231n4; on Nin's abortion, 185; on Nin's earnings, 42, 89, 117; on Nin's publishing attempts, 7, 33, 37, 42–43; on Nin's rewriting the diary, 10–11, 38; on Nin's self-promotion, 41, 110, 115

Balakian, Anna, 93, 104, 110
Balakian, Nona, 45, 110
Barillé, Elizabeth, 143, 161–62, 166
Barthes, Roland, 13
Beach, Sylvia, 69, 142; *Shakespeare and Company*, 69
beatniks, 79
Beat Poets, 72
Beauvoir, Simone de, 17, 43, 44, 131, 142, 170
Benstock, Shari, 69, 85, 203, 223n37
biography: genre of, 189–90, 196, 209; of Nin, 5–9. *See also* Bair, Deirdre; Barillé, Elizabeth; Fitch, Noël Riley
Black Sun Press, 63, 69
Bogner, Inge, 7
bohemian artist, 59, 76–77
bohemian myth, 74, 76, 79
Bradley, William Aspenwall, 33–34, 46
Buckmaster, Henrietta, 94, 100

Café in Space: The Anaïs Nin Literary Journal, A, 3, 12, 150, 156, 201
celebrity, 121, 135; creation of, 15–16, 56, 90–91, 114, 118, 125; female celebrities, 16–17; literary celebrity (celebrity authors), 12, 13–16; and modernism, 22–23; Nin as (*see under* Nin, Anaïs); production and reception of, 56, 90–91, 99, 102, 118, 133; promotion of, 16, 19, 115; representation of, 165
celebrity culture, 4, 16, 22, 90
Chicago, Judy, 110, 113, 114, 173–74, 205; *The Dinner Party*, 113, 205

Index

Chicago Review, 119, 120, 121, 134, 137
Chicago Tribune, 92, 100, 101, 149, 197
Christian Science Monitor, 94, 100
Civil Rights movement, 98
Cold War, 41, 68, 80
communism, 41, 80
consciousness-rising, 99, 125, 130
counterculture, 57, 65, 68, 79–81, 89
creativity, 2, 59, 181, 222n7
Criterion, 65, 99, 105
Crosby, Caresse, 40, 63, 64, 69–70; *The Passionate Years*, 69, 70
Culley, Margo, 23, 25, 48–49, 50
Culmell-Nin, Rosa (Anaïs Nin's mother), 5–6, 10, 86, 137, 161–62, 194, 214n14
Cutting, Rose Marie, 91–92, 105, 116

Dearborn, Mary V., 67, 174, 175
Delta of Venus, 7, 144–150, 154, 164, 180; as best seller, 141, 145; content analysis of, 145; editing of, 146; publication of, 144–45; reviews of, 147–48
Deren, Maya, 7, 72, 107
Dettmar, Kevin, 18, 22, 23
diary (in general): as disregarded genre, 23–26; as genre, 22, 25, 46, 94; and readers' expectations, 26; as truthful, 26
diary, Nin's: advertisements for, 130; as art, 33, 34, 35, 46, 61, 93; attempts to publish, 7, 30, 33–46; as bargaining card, 29, 31, 42; beginning of, 6, 10, 57; double construction of, 50–51; functions of, 6, 25–29; as hybrid form, 11, 26, 27; vs. journal, 2, 214n13; as "liary," 198; marketing of, 30–46; as marketing tool, 29; Miller's comments on, 33, 45, 46, 53, 54, 99, 107; Nin critics on, 26–30; Nin's revisions/rewritings of, 10–11, 32–45, 52–54, 60, 217n34; original diary, 10–11, 12, 26, 27, 29, 38, 42, 50, 51, 87, 99, 107, 108, 140, 151–52, 157; persona in, 3, 9, 12, 16, 29, 47–56, 114, 117, 134, 135; publication of, 45, 88; and readers' disappointment in Nin, 2, 142, 155; and relation between text and life, 28; reviews of, 91–109, 136, 178; and self, 28–30, 31, 56, 59, 60, 82, 87, 117; self-portraits in, 9, 15, 30, 47, 57–87, 90, 114, 135, 180; selling of the original, 10, 42, 140; as topic of interviews, 119, 121, 123–26, 134; as truthful, 152; unexpurgated diaries, 1, 2, 11–12, 140, 144, 151, 155, 163, 164, 167, 172, 182, 196, 197, 199, 203, 205, 209, 212 (see also *Henry and June*; *Incest*)
Diary of Anaïs Nin, The, 2, 10–12, 57, 59, 64, 65, 176
Diary 1, 9, 30, 52, 54, 57, 58, 59, 60–62, 66–68, 71, 73, 76, 77–78, 81, 83, 85–86, 88, 89, 91, 92, 93, 94, 99, 100–102, 104, 107, 123, 130, 141, 142, 151, 152, 153, 165, 176, 182, 183, 184, 207
Diary 2, 36, 54, 58, 59, 63, 71, 75, 80, 91, 93, 94, 97, 104
Diary 3, 58, 59, 71–72, 80, 81, 91, 94, 97, 145, 146
Diary 4, 59, 72, 73, 92, 93, 104, 107, 108, 130, 136
Diary 5, 59, 72, 78, 92, 109
Diary 6, 59, 72, 109
Diary 7, 11, 88, 109, 110, 115, 176–78, 179, 198, 199
reviews of, 91–109, 136, 178
DuBow, Wendy, 116, 200, 202
Durrell, Lawrence, 63, 71, 97, 172, 201
Dutton (publisher), 8, 41, 108
Duxler, Margot, 143, 164, 167, 180–81, 194–95
Dworkin, Andrea, 149
Dyer, Richard, 15, 16, 90, 136

Eakin, Paul John, 30, 122
Early Diary of Anaïs Nin, The, 11, 150
Egoist Press, 63
Eliot, T. S., 19, 69, 71, 105, 113

erotica: Nin as a forerunner of female, 147; Nin's doubts about publishing, 145; and pornography, 149, 180; reviews of Nin's, 147–48. See also *Delta of Venus;* Nin, Anaïs, works of: *Little Birds*
Evans, Oliver, 110–11, 112

Faber and Faber (publishing house), 36
False Memory Syndrome (FMS), 187–88
fame, 14, 91, 115, 136, 215n6. See also Nin, Anaïs: fame of
fans: acafans, 201; disappointed in Nin, 155 (*see also* diary, Nin's: and readers' expectations); Henry Jenkins on, 201; Nin's small circle of, 9, 100; ridiculing of Nin's, 178
femininity: Nin as embodiment/essence of, 17, 96, 97, 131, 133, 172, 173; Nin on, 82, 85, 86; rejected by feminism, 87, 98
feminism: appropriated by Nin, 127; and approval of Nin, 132, 168, 182; divisions within, 149, 179, 182; liberal, 98; Nin on, 129–30, 176; and objections to Nin, 2, 98, 131, 177, 182–83, 185; radical, 98; second-wave, 98
Ferrone, John, 144–46, 150–51, 152, 154, 168
Fitch, Noël Riley, 115, 142, 143, 162–164, 166, 170, 172, 173, 188, 189–90, 191–92, 193, 194, 196, 197, 198, 199, 231n3, 231n4
Foucault, Michel, 13
Freud, Sigmund, 21, 22, 75, 82, 83, 84, 189, 190, 191; influence on culture of, 83; on women, 83

Garrigue, Jean, 94, 97, 104, 130
Gay Liberation, 98
gaze, 160
Gemor Press, 7–8, 39, 63–64, 65, 213n10
gender: bias, 19; and celebrity, 16; roles, 86; and women writers, 16–18, 23

Ginsberg, Allen, 68, 72
Glass, Loren, 13, 14, 115
Guiler, Hugh (Hugo), 6, 7, 8, 9, 42, 43, 45, 54, 61, 64, 117, 152, 153, 155, 159; engravings by, 63–64

Harcourt Brace, 1, 9, 12, 45, 90, 219n70
Hawkins, Anne, 207–8
Haydn, Hiram, 45, 54
H.D. (Hilda Doolittle), 21, 170
Hemingway, Ernest, 70, 71, 214n2; *A Movable Feast,* 70
Henke, Suzette, 88, 144, 175, 181, 186, 192–93, 194, 201
Henry and June (the diary), 11, 51, 58, 66, 141, 150–55, 161, 164, 168, 169, 176, 180, 184; editing of, 150–52
Henry & June (the movie), 155–61, 169, 205, 206, 214n2; cast of, 155; director of, 155; and movie ratings, 155–56; reviews of, 157, 169–70
Herlihy, James Leo, 8, 11, 59, 72
Herron, Paul, 12, 142, 143, 156, 200, 212
Hinz, Evelyn, 110, 111, 115, 117, 228n56
hippies, the, 57, 79
Hogarth Press, 63
Hollows, Joanne, 98
Houghton Mifflin (publishing house), 37, 219n70
Hours Press, 63
Hugo, Ian. *See* Guiler, Hugh
Huyssen, Andreas, 22

identity, 31, 57, 63, 75, 133, 138, 196, 211; American, 41; and feminism, 98; and narrative, 5, 30, 49, 123; and Nin's diary, 9, 28, 49, 56; postmodern view of, 48; of women's representative, 113, 122, 126, 127, 130–31, 138, 176
illness narratives. *See* pathography
image making/production, 5, 16, 118
incest, 2, 38, 53, 144, 145, 184, 188–89, 191, 195
Incest, 1, 11, 58, 142, 144, 155, 184, 185, 186, 188, 196; reviews of, 196

Index

incest recovery movement, 186
institutional readers, 91, 211
interviews with Nin, 2, 15, 89, 91, 109, 116, 118–38; as celebrity formation, 16, 56, 115, 118, 122; content analysis of, 119–20; and Nin as a women's representative, 122–29; and reality-effect, 133

Jaffe, Aaron, 19, 112
Jason, Philip, 6, 39, 41, 57, 64, 149, 152, 201, 213n10
Jelinek, Estelle, 116, 130, 131–32, 228n53
Jong, Erica: on Nin, 134, 172, 182; reputation of, 17, 105, 106, 182
Joyce, James, 71, 168, 214n2
Jurecic, Ann, 207, 208

Kaufman, Philip, 155, 156–60, 169, 205, 206, 233n30
Kirsch, Robert, 92, 93, 96, 101, 110, 130
Knapp, Bettina, 110, 201
Knowles, Jocelyn, 94, 97, 98
Kraft, Barbara, 112, 114, 143, 181–82, 206–7, 208, 209, 231n3

Lawrence, D. H., 20, 21, 35, 58, 69, 114, 151, 153, 158, 168, 199
Leary, Timothy, 79
Lee, Hermione, 190
Library Journal, 92, 147
life narratives, 24, 25, 28, 29, 94–95, 96, 113
literary collaboration, 51, 170, 171. *See also* Miller, Henry: collaboration with Nin
literary marketplace, 67, 105, 115. *See also* marketplace
literary reputation, 19, 112. *See also* reputation
little magazine, 7, 64–65, 105
Los Angeles, 8, 10, 113
Los Angeles Times, 1, 9, 14, 89, 92, 94, 96, 97, 110, 112, 130, 131, 136, 139, 154, 169
Louveciennes, 60, 70, 73, 120, 122, 153, 174
LSD, 78–79, 80

Luckhurst, Roger, 187, 188, 236n69
lying: to Hugh Guiler, 9; Nin criticized for, 2, 136, 182, 197

Madonna, 1, 3, 163, 215n6
Mailer, Norman, 117
Marcus, Laura, 23, 27, 95
marketable personality, 14, 87
marketing strategies, 15, 16, 23
marketplace, 15; and gender, 16; and modernism, 18–19, 22, 23. *See also* literary marketplace
Marshall, P. David, 15, 16, 55–56, 90, 133, 210, 211
Martin, Jay, 174, 175
Marwick, Arthur, 57, 65, 79, 221n16
Memory War, 187, 188, 192
Miller, Alice, 189, 190, 193
Miller, Henry, 26; biographies of, 174–75; collaboration with Nin, 6, 32, 36, 40, 51, 59, 61, 66–67, 71, 105, 107, 141, 155; comments on Nin's diary, 33, 45, 46, 53, 54, 99, 107; criticized by feminists, 132–33, 168; letters to Nin, 43, 59, 106, 123; and Nin as popular dyad, 58, 167–72; Nin capitalizing on reputation of, 67, 71, 106–7; Nin meeting, 6, 32; Nin's descriptions of, 34, 51–53, 58, 66–67, 74, 75, 76, 77, 151; popular in the 1960s, 67, 105, 106; portrayed in *Henry & June* (see *Henry & June*); and relationship with Nin, 32, 51, 66–67, 152, 153, 156, 206; *Tropic of Cancer,* 32, 61, 67, 69, 105, 156, 160, 168
Miller, June, 6, 58, 60, 76, 77–78, 102, 152, 155, 157, 168, 170, 206
Millett, Kate, 95, 131, 132–33, 168
modernism, 59, 62, 64; and celebrity culture, 22–23; Nin influenced by, 19–20; Nin's place in, 18–22, 203; and Paris, 71; and women writers, 19
Moi, Toril, 17
Moore, Harry T., 96, 101, 130, 199
Moran, Joe, 13, 14, 15, 16, 103, 115, 198

Moré, Gonzalo, 7–8, 39
Morrow, William, 44
Motion Picture Association of America (MPAA), 155, 169
Ms. magazine, 129, 180, 185
Mulvey, Laura, 160

Nalbantian, Suzanne, 20
narrative recovery, 192
Nation, 92, 93
Neuilly, 5
New Critics, 19, 96
New Republic, 92, 103, 104, 109
Newsweek, 92, 95, 97, 130
New York, 6, 7, 8, 31, 35, 37, 59, 62, 65, 66, 72, 78, 120, 122, 137, 146, 206
New Yorker, 8, 30, 92, 95, 103, 104, 109, 148, 185
New York Review of Books, 95, 101, 103, 104, 178
New York Times, 9, 44–45, 92, 104, 112, 129, 139, 149, 168, 178, 196, 197
New York Times Book Review, 92, 93, 94, 97, 103, 104, 110, 147
Nin, Anaïs
  abortions of, 7, 17, 142, 182, 183, 184, 185, 186
  acting as advertisement, 116
  as artist's model, 6
  bigamy of, 8
  and cancer, 9, 143, 207
  career of, 8, 10, 19, 39, 57, 58, 87, 90, 105, 106, 108, 110, 117, 129, 139, 167, 178
  as celebrity, 2, 4, 9, 14, 15, 87, 91, 102, 117, 199
  criticized by feminists (*see* feminism: and objections to Nin)
  depression of, 40
  as diarist (*see* diary, Nin's)
  diary persona of (*see* diary, Nin's: persona in)
  diary persona vs. public persona, 12, 15, 47, 55–56, 87, 134, 135
  as embodiment/essence of femininity, 17, 96, 97, 131, 133, 172, 173
  and erotica (see *Delta of Venus; erotica; Little Birds*)
  eroticization of, 102, 103, 139, 141, 144, 150, 155, 160, 161, 198, 204
  and expurgated diaries (*see* diary, Nin's: unexpurgated diaries)
  fame of, 13, 89, 111, 115, 116, 199 (*see also* fame)
  on femininity, 82, 85, 86
  on feminism, 129–30, 176
  and homosexuality, 78, 223n37
  as icon, 1, 4, 87, 89, 102, 176, 204
  and incest (*see* incest; Nin, Joaquín (Nin's father): Nin's incestuous relationship with)
  income of, 42, 89, 116–17
  interviews with (*see* interviews with Nin)
  languages of, 6, 11
  lectures of, 2, 15, 56, 88, 90, 115, 116–18, 129, 177, 199
  as legend, 30, 87, 90, 100, 101, 102, 117, 137, 138, 174, 177, 207
  lies of (*see* lying)
  lovers of, 6, 7, 8, 32, 39, 152, 154, 164, 171
  marriages of, 6, 8, 9
  obituaries on, 9, 129, 139, 180
  pathologization of, 186, 198
  portraits of (*see* diary, Nin's: self-portraits in)
  praised by feminists (*see* feminism: and approval of Nin)
  and psychoanalysis (*see* psychoanalysis)
  public persona of, 3, 4, 5, 15, 90, 91, 112, 114, 117, 122, 126, 133, 138, 140, 213n3
  "real" Anaïs Nin, 48, 49, 50, 81, 141, 142, 143
  representations of, 5, 12, 47, 50, 55, 58 (*see also* diary, Nin's: self-portraits in)
  as reviewer, 111–14
  as seductress (*see* seduction)
  self-absorption of, 18, 46, 95, 102, 204
  self-construction/self-creation of, 3, 5, 28, 29, 30, 39, 49, 55, 56, 60, 62, 65, 71, 76, 82, 87, 90, 112, 114, 117, 122
  self-marketing/self-promotion of, 2, 12, 15, 40, 90, 116, 127, 178

Nin, Anaïs (cont.)
  sexual affairs of, 6–7, 9, 37, 51, 53, 66, 171, 184
  and sexuality, 2, 31, 102–103, 119, 145, 147, 148, 159, 182
  status of, 9, 30, 66, 89, 99, 100, 119, 120, 128, 198, 203
  and stillbirth (see Nin, Anaïs: abortions of)
  as trauma survivor, 29, 142, 144, 186–95
  as women's representative, 113, 122–33, 142, 176, 178, 180
Nin, Anaïs, works of:
  Children of the Albatross, 41
  Cities of the Interior, 9, 42, 89
  Delta of Venus: Erotica (see *Delta of Venus*)
  D. H. Lawrence: An Unprofessional Study, 6, 61
  The Diary of Anaïs Nin (see *Diary of Anaïs Nin, The*)
  Fire, 11, 155
  Henry and June (see *Henry and June*)
  House of Incest, 6, 35, 61, 89
  Incest (see *Incest*)
  Ladders to Fire, 8, 41
  Little Birds, 7, 145, 146, 147, 149, 180
  Mirages, 12, 205
  Novel of the Future, 110
  Seduction of the Minotaur, 42, 89
  A Spy in the House of Love, 8, 89
  This Hunger, 8, 39, 40, 64, 222n20
  Trapeze, 12, 205
  Under a Glass Bell, 8, 30, 39, 40, 41, 89
  (The) Winter of Artifice, 6, 7, 8, 39, 40, 42, 61, 89, 213n10
  A Woman Speaks, 117–18, 129, 131, 168
Nin, Joaquín (Nin's father), 5, 6, 35, 44, 60, 74, 75, 137; Nin abandoned by, 10, 167, 183, 186, 193, 194; Nin's incestuous relationship with, 1, 2, 6–7, 36, 38, 53, 144, 165, 166, 184, 186, 188–89, 191, 192, 195
Nin, Thorvald (Nin's brother), 5, 38, 54

Nin-Culmell, Joaquín (Nin's brother), 5, 45, 193, 214n14
NOW (National Organization for Women), 98, 124

Oates, Joyce Carol, 208–9
Obelisk Press, 6
off our backs (magazine), 129, 130, 131, 228n53
Ohmann, Richard, 103–104
Orwell, George, 101, 102, 105

Paris, 5, 6, 7, 12, 19, 31, 32, 35, 57, 58, 60, 63, 66, 68, 69, 70, 71, 76, 85, 113, 120, 121, 122, 137, 142, 157, 163, 168, 169, 206
pathography, 207, 208
patriarchy, 98, 182, 183
Perlès, Alfred, 54, 67, 71, 73
Pierpont, Claudia Roth, 185
Plath, Sylvia, 96, 154, 170, 186, 214n2
Podnieks, Elizabeth, 10, 11, 22, 28, 30, 49, 191, 200, 203, 214n13
Pole, Rupert, 8, 9, 11, 12, 145, 146, 150, 151, 152, 172, 176, 196, 209
Pollitt, Katha, 109, 178, 185, 196
press reviews of Nin's works. See reviews
production/consumption dialectic, 15, 18. See also celebrity: production and reception of
Proust, Marcel, 20, 22, 99, 105, 168
psychoanalysis, 35, 58, 73, 81, 82, 83, 86, 98, 113, 130, 144, 157, 189, 190, 191, 192, 200
publicity, 16, 44, 45, 103, 156
Putnam (publishing house), 43

Random House, 42
Rank, Otto, 6, 35, 36, 39, 54, 60, 78, 81, 82, 120; in relationship to Freud, 75, 82, 83; on women, 83, 84
reputation: vs. evaluation, 101; of Jong, 105; of Nin, 105, 107, 139, 142, 155, 178, 179, 180; of Orwell, 105
reviewing business, 16, 103–4, 109
reviews: of *Henry & June* (the movie), 157, 169–70; of *Incest*,

196; by institutional readers, 91, 211; of Nin's biographies, 196–97, 204; of Nin's *Diary,* 91–109, 136, 178; of Nin's erotica, 147–48; of Nin's fiction, 8, 30, 40, 41; by ordinary readers, 211; of women authors, 17, 18
Richard-Allerdyce, Diane, 21, 57, 144, 192, 193, 194
Rodden, John, 101, 102, 105
Roth, Philip, 96

Salber, Linde, 116, 193, 224n2
Saturday Review, 100, 103, 104
Schneider, Duane, 27, 29, 93, 110, 175, 201
Scholar, Nancy, 27, 28, 29, 110, 166, 179
scopophilia, 160
scriptotherapy, 192
Second Wave (magazine), 128, 129
seduction, 165–67; as defensive mechanism, 167; diary as, 165–66
self-publication, 6, 8. See also Gemor Press
sexual abuse, 187, 188, 189, 192, 193
sexual revolution, 103, 147
Seymour, Miranda, 189, 197
Shakespeare and Company, 70. See also Crosby, Caresse
Shapiro, Karl, 30, 93, 130
Showalter, Elaine, 26, 179, 195, 224n4
Siana Editions, 6
Silberman, James (of Random House), 42–43, 44
Silver, Brenda, 18, 118, 213n3, 215n11, 233n28
sixties, the, 59, 60, 63, 65, 141, 147, 221n16
Sky Blue Press, 12
small presses, 23, 64
Smith, Sidonie, 24, 96, 144
Spencer, Sharon, 26, 28, 110, 149, 182, 201

star. See celebrity
stardom, 14, 165
Stein, Gertrude, 69, 70
Stern, Daniel, 93, 110
St. Louis Dispatch, 95, 96, 101
Stuhlmann, Gunther, 8, 11, 12, 27, 42, 43, 73, 99, 100, 106, 168, 231n5
Swallow, Alan, 9, 42, 44, 106
Swallow Press, 9

Templin, Charlotte, 17, 91, 94, 105, 106, 114
Tong, Rosemarie, 148, 179
Tookey, Helen, 18, 21, 22, 28, 30, 49, 57, 150, 203, 212, 213n3
transition, 20, 21, 65
Twain, Mark, 115

unexpurgated diaries. See diary, Nin's: unexpurgated diaries

Vidal, Gore, 7, 41, 72, 105, 109, 201; critical of Nin, 107–8, 136, 178
Vietnam War, 80
Village Voice, 94, 107, 109, 110, 131, 134

Walker, Alice, 129, 180
Washington Post, 92, 97, 139, 170
Wilson, Edmund, 8, 30, 40, 72, 100
Wilson, Elizabeth, 57, 74, 75, 76–77, 80, 85, 138
women's movement, 18, 57, 89, 97, 98, 116, 117, 118, 120, 123, 124, 125, 126, 127, 128, 129, 130, 131, 132, 133, 138, 176, 177, 181, 183
Woolf, Virginia, 18, 21, 63, 84, 118, 200; "A Room of One's Own," 84; Shakespeare's sister, 84
World War II, 6, 37, 41, 59, 80, 81, 172

Young, Marguerite, 112, 130

www.ingramcontent.com/pod-product-compliance
Lightning Source LLC
Chambersburg PA
CBHW031411290426
44110CB00011B/342